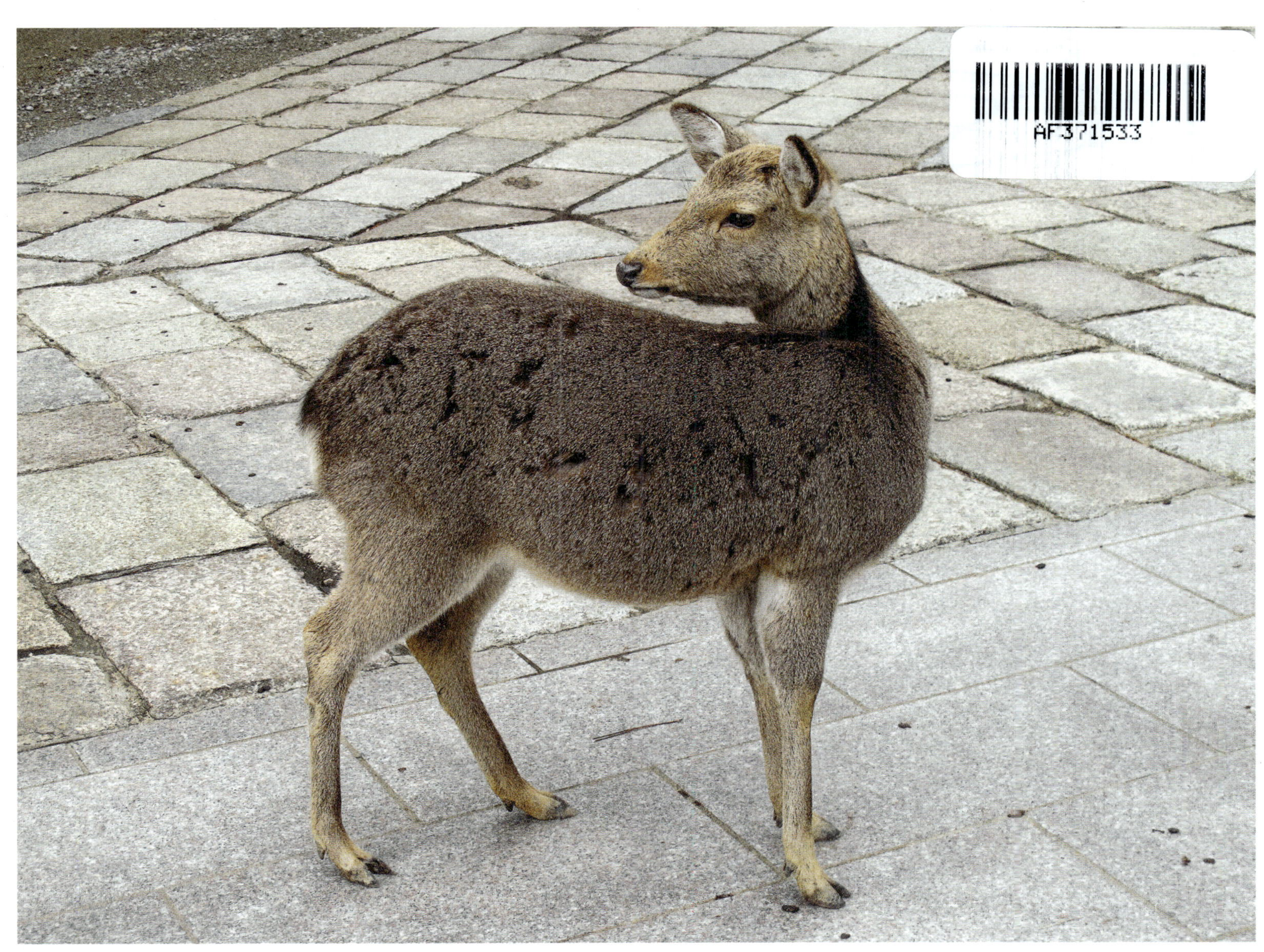

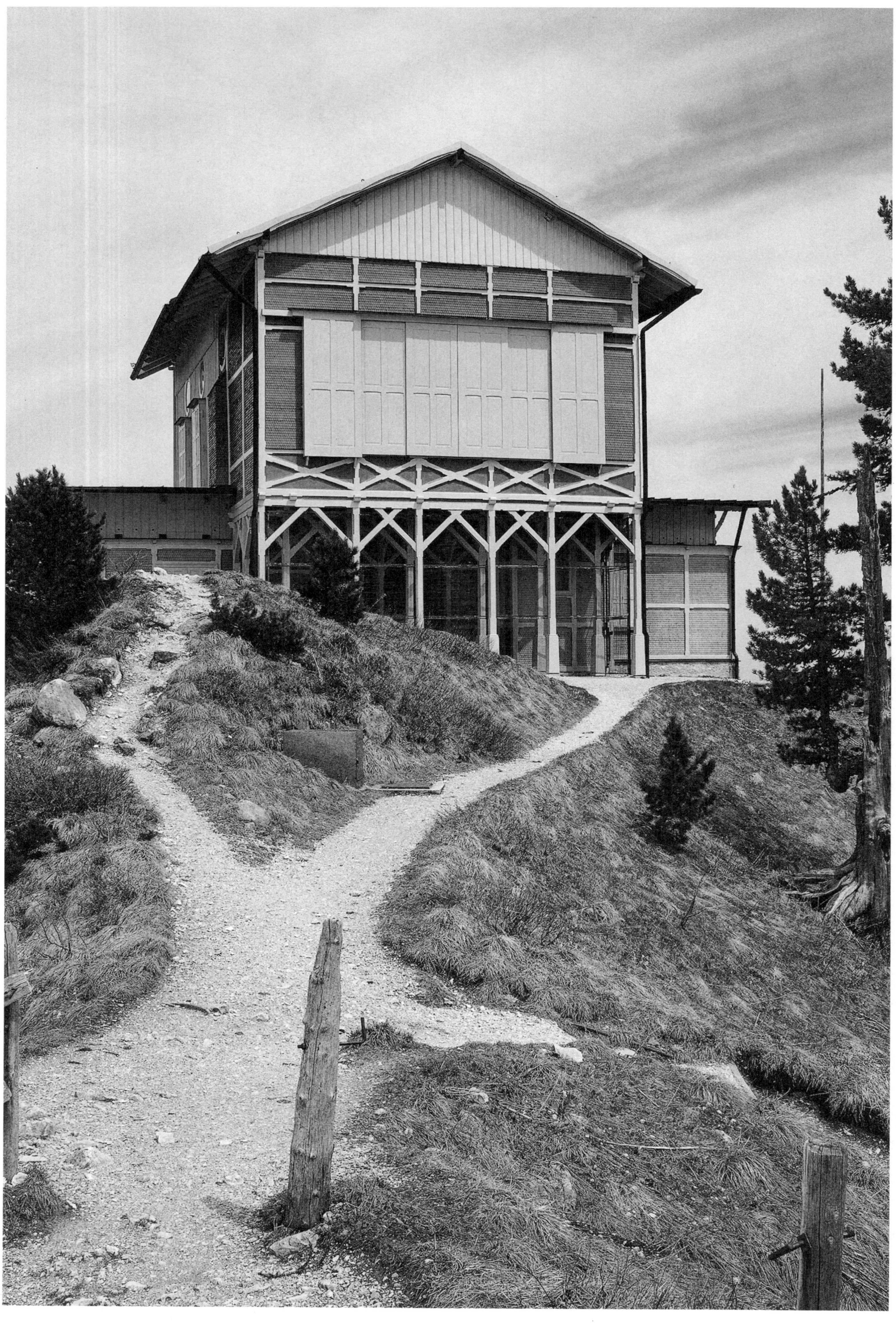

1.

The book is the carrier for my
(photographic) series.

The printed page is the perfect form
for the reproducibility
of the photographic image.

3.

The spread contextualizes the
single images.

4.

The sequence of pages may provide
yet another context.

5.

The collections of images are mirrored in
the collectability of the actual book.

The ratio between the quality of the printing
and the quality of the image
is more complex than to be read 1:1.

The relation between form and content is as equally important as both parts separately, but all parts may represent different values.

The fetishistic character of the printed matter
may provide the extra layers
to strengthen the iconic value of its images.

The book, as an object, gains strength
as it gets re-contextualized by its
viewer, owner, or bookcase in which it stands.

The connections between different
publications may be
invisible but are always present.

The steps made in the publishing
process are solely
based on artistic principles.

The financial risks involved in publishing
should elevate the
project instead of holding it back.

If the book is like a building, then
the publisher's catalogue
needs proper urban planning.

Each published title must add value
to the existing ones.

All books that are not made are,
at least, just as important.

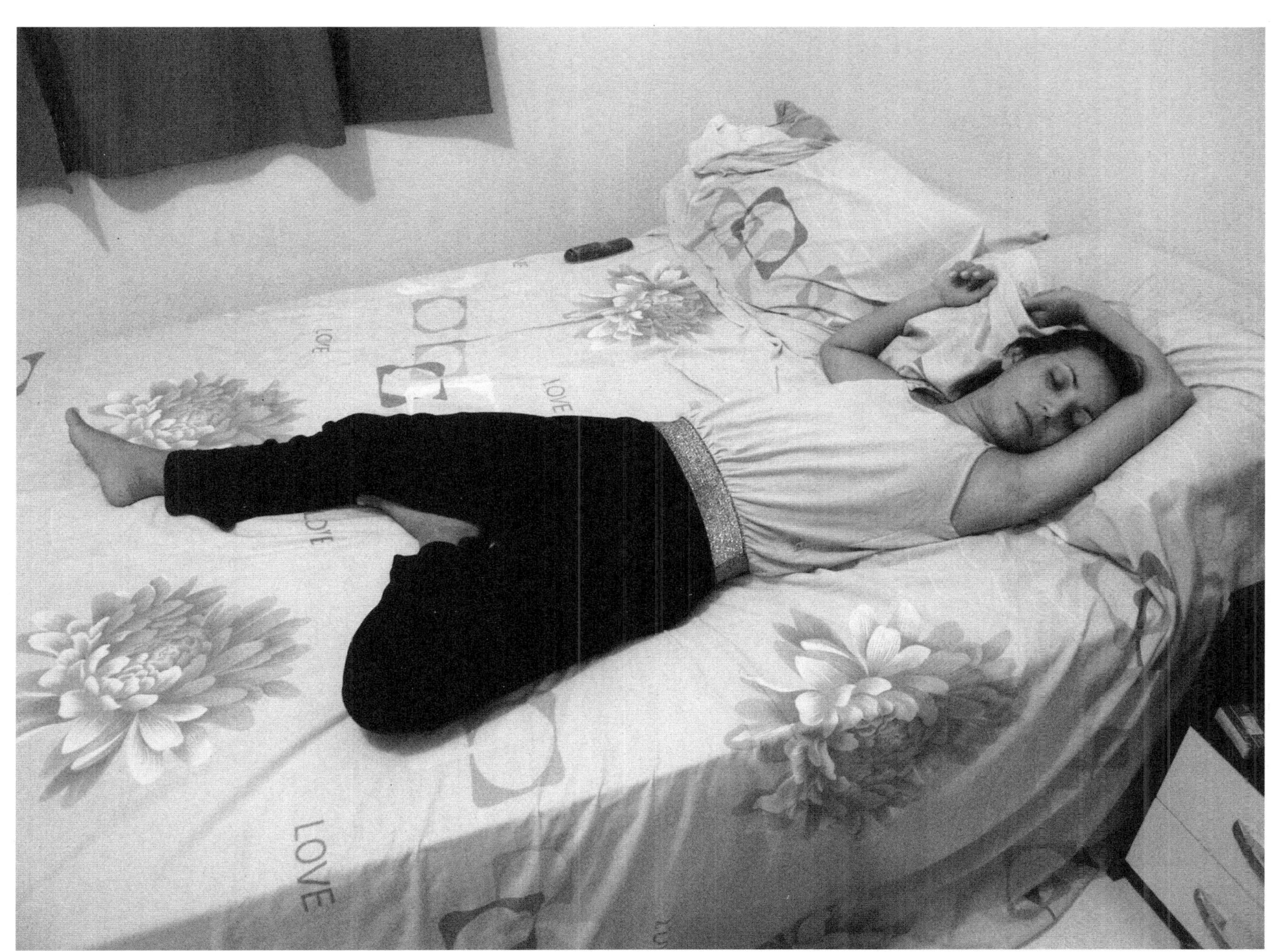

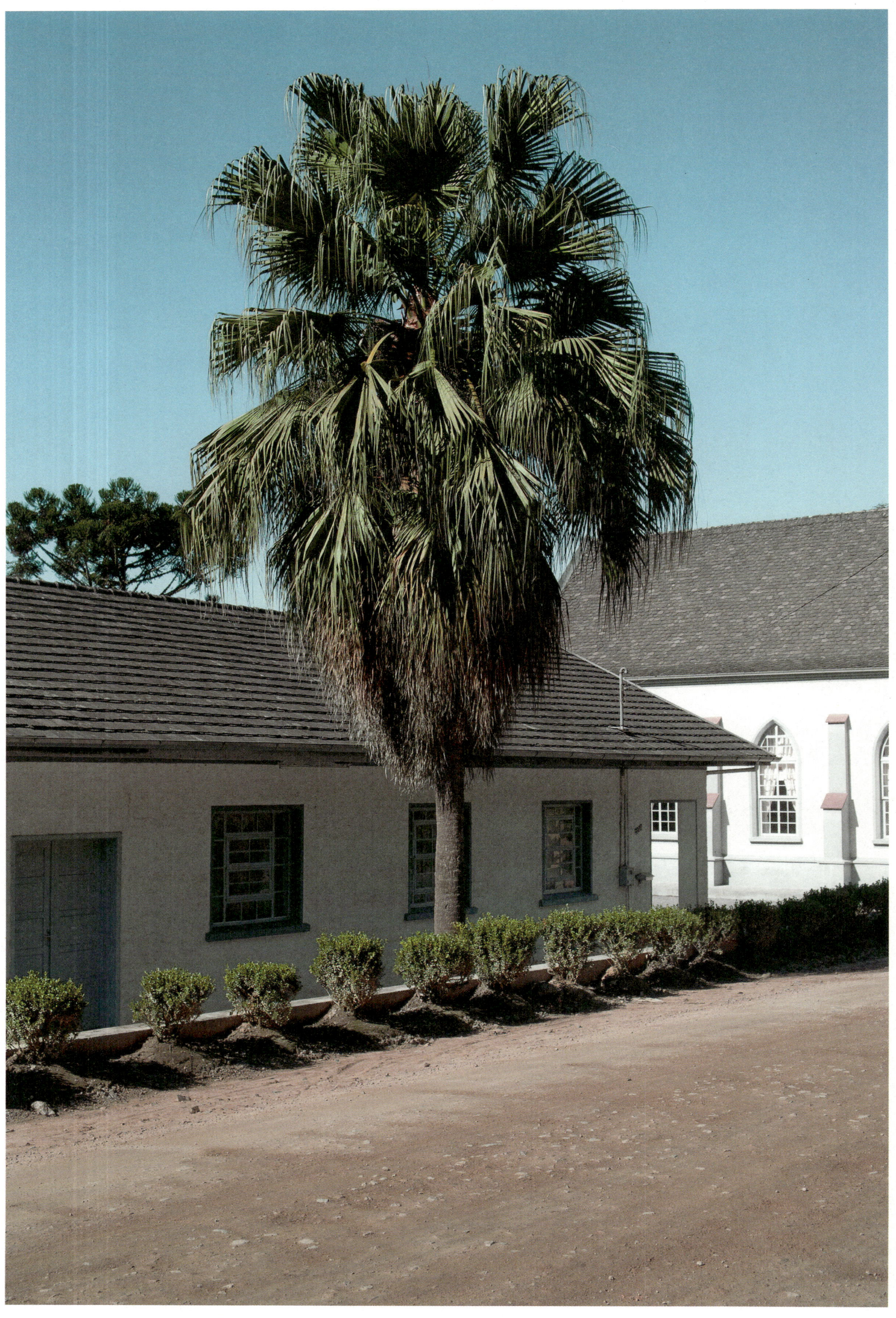

Erik van der Weijde

THIS IS NOT MY BOOK

Spector Books

4478zine's Publishing Manifesto

1–15

Prostitution, Art Books and Marketing

25–28

Costs and Profits

31–37

Everyday Life, the Sequence, the Book, or Five Stacks of Books for Erik van der Weijde

41–46

Landscapes of Books

47–101

One plus One

103–108

From the Page to the Sequence, from the Sequence to the Book

111–114

Back and Forth

115–123

Reading Ed Ruscha and Talking with Erik

125–128

The Unfinished Projects

131–133

Prostitution, Art Books and Marketing

by Erik van der Weijde

The other night I was walking my dog when we passed by a prostitute who offered me her services. I declined—it would have been a hassle with the dog—, but it made me think about the similarities between her job and mine (making artist books). Today I wrote down some tips for people who want to get into either of those businesses.

Every man that walks by is a possible client. Look him directly in the eye to see if he will take the bait. Look at a hundred guys and maybe one or two will go for it. Look at none and nobody will go for it. Get your book seen. In stores, on blogs, at fairs, on social media: If a hundred people see it, maybe one or two will buy it.

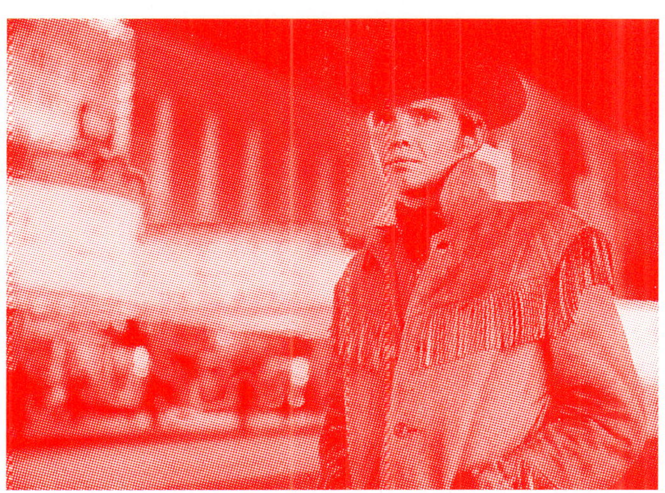

You don't need to be the prettiest Jenny on the block. Just present well what you're offering. A nice short skirt, some make-up and clean hair may already do the trick and will favor your odds. Your clients will choose the packaging, most of the time, even instead of the real product, or service. So if you don't have the best photographs or other graphic content, a strong design and added value through production will favor your odds. Opinions on the actual work or fuck will be formed later.

Never think there isn't any market for your product. Never think nobody will buy your book. Remember those girls with the bad skin, missing teeth and meth addiction: Even they make a few bucks every day.

The excitement and foreplay are important factors in the client's experience. Making preparations like choosing the type of girl or hotel and how to approach her are all part of an experience. Whether you're a blond or a brunette doesn't matter, because eventually you will fit into a client's experience. Do you remember that time when you went to a bookstore and found that really great book? Then you took it home and read it on your couch, with a cup of coffee or a beer? Wasn't that a nice afternoon?

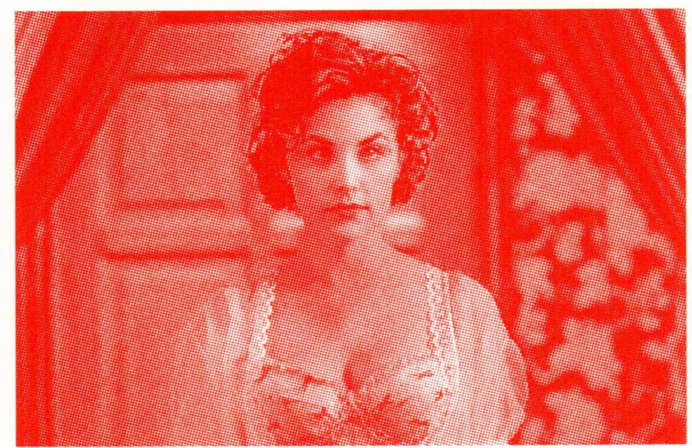

Keep in mind that your clients want to take part in the illusion you created. They want to play along in this fantasy where you are the experienced, coveted, 19-year-old photo model they can possess for a while. Someone who buys your book can own that experience and feel this reality you created. Your customer may want to be entertained, inspired or be part of it in another way, part of this world-on-a-page.

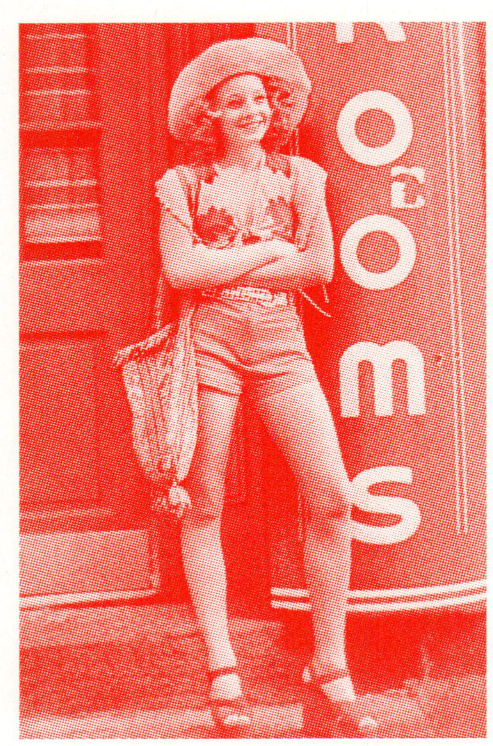

In a bookstore many publishers fight for the attention of the public. Some buyers will always come back to the same familiar faces and experience while others look for something new and fresh. In the brothel the Madam can help the client to find what he looks for and in the bookstore the owner or seller can make or break your sales. Stay on good terms with the store owners and Madams.

If you are afraid of any risks in the business, you may want to start with a massage, phone-sex or webcam streaming. There are plenty of—digital— alternatives to make a book, such as Blurb or Lulu.

Be sure to get paid first. And don't spend all your hard-earned money on drugs.

Don't let negative feedback get to you. Most of the time it's your client's frustration with his own performance that makes him say bad things about your services—or book.

Besides the fixed price for the standard package you offer, you can consider special treatments for a higher price. Editions including prints and clamshell boxes can increase revenue. Signatures and numbers will make your customer feel special for which he will pay extra.

Nudity sells. The more you are willing to show, the more traffic you will drive to your business.

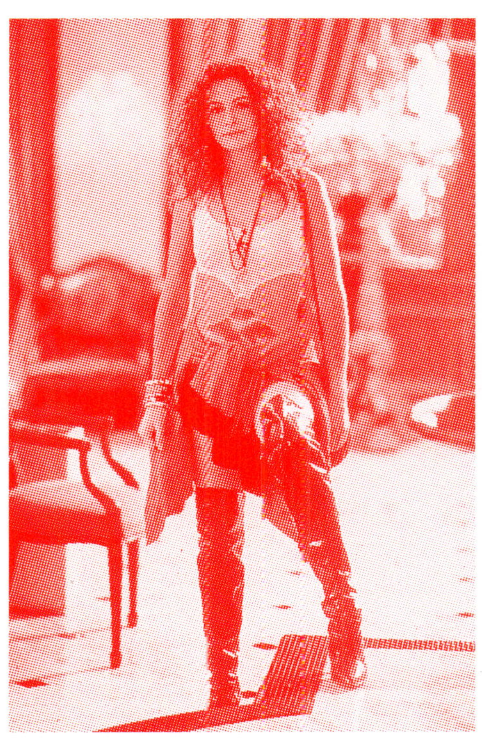

Some rich clients may pay for long-term contracts. Although there are not that many book collectors, the ones out there may provide you with some sort of steady income, as long as you keep the quality standards high enough.

A hype may be created around a newbie in the business. Hypes can drive up prices to extraordinary heights or lead to more sales. There are even girls who have auctioned their virginity. Entering competitions for book dummies also can be a helpful way to place yourself in the market.

Some clients prefer to save their money and spend it all at once during a two week trip to Thailand or Brazil. As a publisher you should attend a few book fairs every year to tap into the segment of clients that prefer to save their money and spend it all at once during a two day fair in Paris or New York.

As an alternative for self-publishing and doing all the work yourself, you can also approach a professional publisher who, for a fee, will manage the business part of the art. A pimp may offer protection, advertising services and transport for a part of your earnings.

Safety comes first. People will propose all sorts of things to you, but be careful not to do anything you're not comfortable with. Always use protection.

Do you remember the movie *Pretty Woman*? Well, that is a typical example of Hollywood illusion. Publishing books will not get you married to Richard Gere.

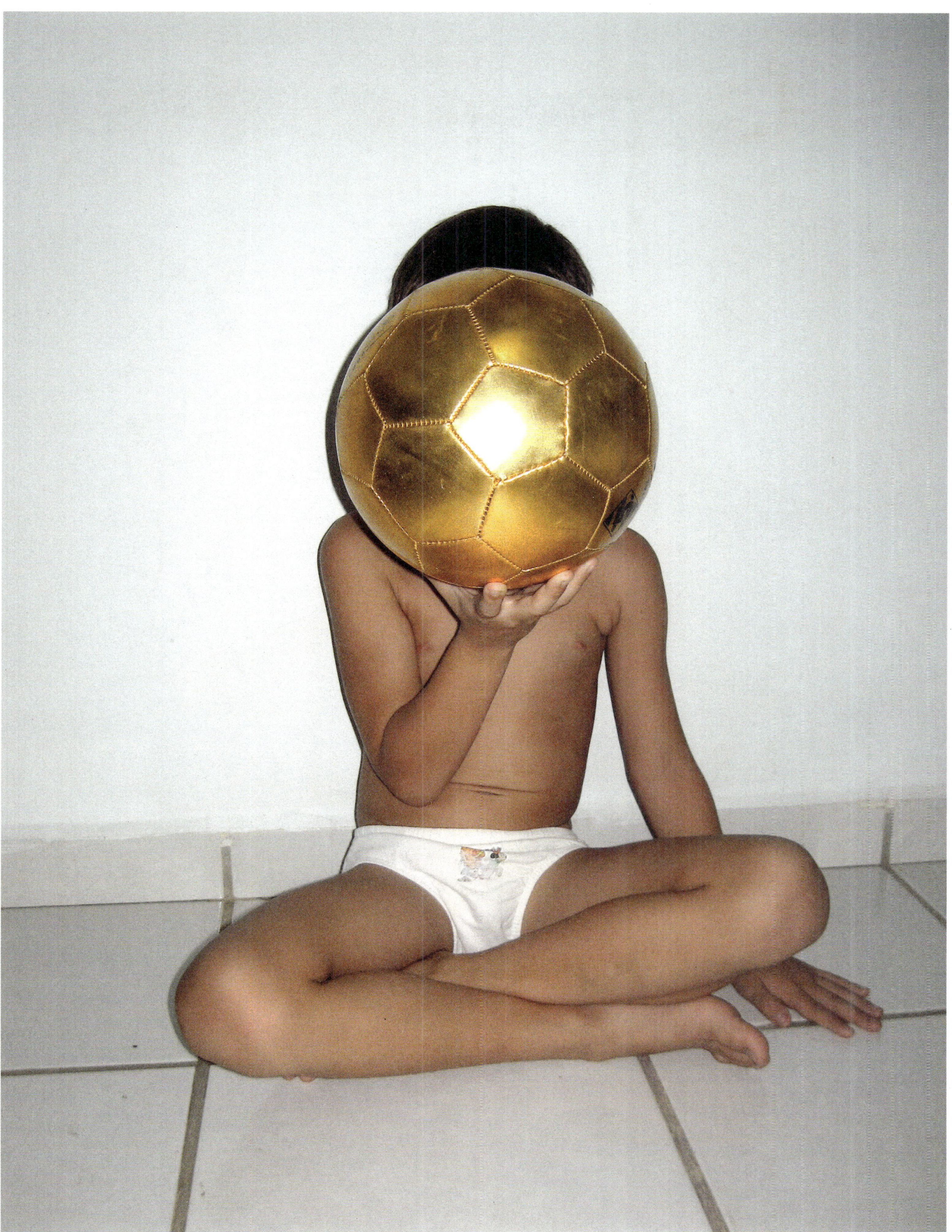

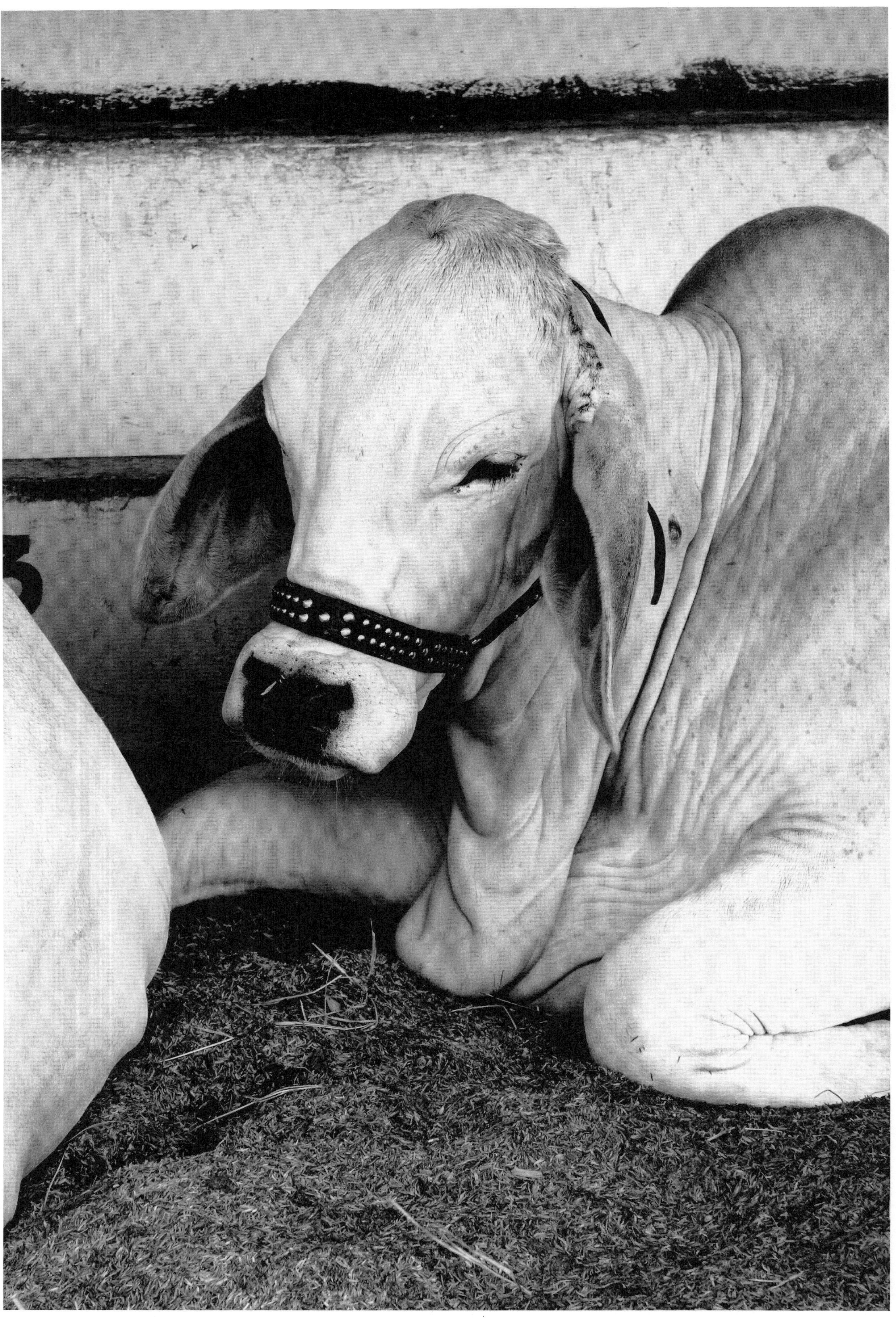

Costs and Profits

by Erik van der Weijde

The following entries give some behind-the-scenes information on a few of my titles. Costs, revenues and profits are specified for each title. Costs are (offset) production costs only (offset printing and binding), all in euros. Profits are based on sales minus production costs and do not take any other costs, such as transport, fees or overhead into consideration.

Die Wolken, 2012
Costs: −745 euros / Revenues: 2242 euros / Profits: 1497 euros

Just as *Der Baum* (2010), this title was inspired by a booklet from the German pre–World War II series *Der Eiserne Hammer*. The original booklet showed photographs of German skies and clouds, as this series was supposed to show the beauty and cultural history of the country. My edition of 200 copies contains heavily rasterized reproductions of fighter planes, taken from a 1982 yearbook. The colors I chose for the printing are based on US fighter plane insignias and instead of printing the different colors in one zine, I decided to copy the same zine three times, each one in a different color, so there is a red, a blue and a black version. The three versions have identical covers and come as a set. Thin newspaper stock contrasts with the violent imagery, but at the same time, it reminds us of printed media war stories.
　　These booklets were printed, again, in the local offset print shop. I thought they would charge me considerably for cleaning the plates and changing the ink between the three print runs, but the production assistant offered it to me for free.
　　The (financial) success of this title—a 300% return on my investment! —made me want to repeat an experimental use of color in 2013, which completely crashed and turned out to be a financial failure:

Havaianas, 2013
Costs: −605 euros / Revenues: 525 euros / Profits: −80 euros

Oh man, I really thought that *Havaianas* was a great idea and would be a sure hit: So I rolled some silkscreen ink on the sole of my flip-flop (size 43) and stamped it onto paper. I then scanned the image and had it reproduced, in offset, using the CMYK colors and their respective screen angles. The positions of the "feet" even resembled some weird Samba version and the whole publication became a sort of cultural comment / homage by using only printing techniques. A winner, right?

Now, two and a half years after I published *Havaianas*, I am still short 80 euros. OK, I did sell a few of the editions—unique stamped compositions on paper, whose revenues are not included here, but still I am very disappointed that not more people saw the geniality in this little gem.

foto.zine nr. 5, 2013
Costs: –1993 euros / Revenues: 3657 euros / Profits: 1664 euros

This set, once more, contains five different publications of the same size, but printed on different paper. Each collection of images was photographed in Brazil and contains a subject that is not—or not anymore—common in Europe.

Lixo shows a collection of dumpsters that you can find in front of every house. People put their trash in these dumpsters so it won't get flushed away by rain or opened easily by donkeys and rats. An interesting detail is that there is no store selling these dumpsters, so they're all custom made.

Fusca is the Portuguese word for the Volkswagen Beetle. There used to be so many more in the streets, but when the government relaxed conditions on payment plans for new cars, they rapidly disappeared from sight. I photographed this set in 2003, when I was still using film. Unfortunately humidity in Brazil worked hard on the not-so-well rinsed negatives which caused them to fade.

Motel shows the entrances of some motels in town. This phenomenon of the pay-by-the-hour motel is only more present in Japan. In Brazil most adultery and sex-before-marriage happens in these colorful settings. You enter by car and get a key handed through a small hole in the wall. When you're ready for your bill, it will also be delivered through a hole in the wall. You'll never see or interact with anyone else but your partner in a motel.

Buzios is the name of a small village just outside Natal. This village is more like a ghost town during eleven months of the year and inhabited only during summer vacation. Of course no Brazilian will spend a whole summer without their TV, hence the huge parabolic antennas on the roofs.

Jardins is the name of a posh neighborhood in São Paulo where everybody lives in gated apartment buildings. The little guard houses, equipped with bullet proof glass, are usually built in the same style as the residential building, so the owners don't notice them or feel as if they're living inside a prison.

The *foto.zine nr. 5* set was printed in Brazil, at three different local printers, in an edition of 400. This way I could use the quotes between them in order to get each of them to offer me their best prices. The papers used range from 55g newsprint to 90g Polen, so each edition has a specific touch to it. To emphasize their collectible and collective character I chose to only sell them as a set. I am sure that $1 + 1 + 1 + 1 + 1 =$ more than 5.

Contemporary Brazilian Politics, 2011
Costs: −243 euros / Revenues: 856 euros (donated) / Profits: −243 euros

One of the things that strikes me most as a European in Brazil is not the daily report on corruption, with politicians stealing from public funds, but the fact that the population doesn't seem to rise up against this. (There seems to be a general apathy towards larger societal issues, but their deeply rooted causes are not part of this text.)
For a while I had been collecting excerpts from international newspapers, online, about corruption in Brazil. For *Contemporary Brazilian Politics* I decided to publish parts of phrases from these clippings, not mentioning any name or specific case. I printed the text in white on a black background and used 100% ink printing on thin newspaper stock. This paper is not able to absorb all the ink, so there's a little bit left behind on the paper, which will rub off on the reader's fingers.
When I set the sales price for *Contemporary Brazilian Politics* I realized I didn't want to earn any money on this subject, so decided to donate all revenues to a social project in our town that works with children in a favela. A tiny percentage of the money stolen by politicians from these kids' futures finally reaches the children through this printed detour. When the dance group in this project needed fabrics for their Christmas presentation outfits, I decided to donate the printing costs I had invested in *Contemporary Brazilian Politics* as well.
I don't believe that artist's books can change the world, but I do believe that tiny gestures can add up and make a difference.

Parking Lot, 2011
Costs: −255 euros / Revenues: 1302 euros / Profits: 1047 euros

Jet lag in Japan can be really hard. I arrived in Ota-ku, a commuter ward in Tokyo, in January 2011 and had trouble sleeping. The Internet in my house wasn't working yet, so the nights were pretty long. I started taking night walks in the neighborhood, snapping some pictures on the way. After a few nights I had almost a hundred photos of parked cars with impeccable interiors, fit tightly into their tiny prefab garages.

The series that grew in my mind and on my memory card was in a way related to Ed Ruscha but was also the fruit of a personal experience in a strange place far from home. I reached out to some friends in a graphic design company in Tokyo to help me produce a small publication of this series and they got me in touch with a printing company in Osaka, that still did (image) letter press printing. Together with the designers, whom I had asked to also design the cover, we decided on a paper commonly used in Japan for Manga comics. After sending some samples back and forth we chose the raster, ink and paper for the cover and set the edition size of 200 copies at 1 euro production costs per copy. (After the great earthquake hit and I had to leave Japan, it cost me another 55 euros to ship the copies to Europe.)

This little publication is still one of my favorites, because of its simplicity, cultural references and the personal memories I have of its production. Maybe also a little bit because of the 500% return on my investment. I wish I'd invested more.

Nelore, 2012
Costs: −620 euros / Revenues: 1386 euros / Profits: 766 euros

Every year in October there is a ten-day cattle fair and exhibition in our town. I usually go there twice, first with my wife and son and we dream out loud of owning some of the beautiful horses and cows. The second visit I take only my camera and photograph many of the animals.

Nelore beef cattle were originally brought to Brazil from India. The Nelore has a distinct large hump over the top of the shoulder and neck. They have long legs which help them to walk in water and when grazing. The Nelore can adapt to everything except very cold climates. Brazil is the largest breeder of Nelore. The ladies in this zine are the contestants for the 2010 beauty contest, so they are well groomed and perfumed. Their pedigree and beauty will send their genes to many Brazilian tables during lunch hour, but for the moment they just have to look pretty.

At my local printer's I had found paper that was so roughly recycled that there were still particles of plastic and sometimes even metal in it, with a very coarse feeling to it. This yellow paper is usually used as a cover for waiter notebooks in cheaper restaurants and is called Capa (= cover) AG.

Nelore was printed on this paper in an edition of 400 of which I managed to distribute 300 copies quickly, and I kept the last box in my studio for future re-stocking. By the end of 2013, when I needed the last copies and opened the box, humidity had glued them all together and made them unrecognizable. The fire they went in that evening became pretty smoky and we were freed of mosquitoes for almost a week. Still, the profits of *Nelore* have bought our family roughly 135 kg of rump steak. Bon appetit.

foto.zine nr. 4, 2011
Costs: –4365 euros / Revenues: 6462 euros / Profits: 2097 euros

I had successfully contacted all five artists on my list for the *foto.zine nr. 4* series, but it took a while to get Takashi Homma's material due to his busy schedule. So when I finally had everything together, I went to the printing house the same week. In my rush I had not chosen the right paper for the covers and inside, which I only noticed when I received all 2000 copies of the five zines. The overall printing quality from this Brazilian printer wasn't great either. I didn't sleep well that night, because I had screwed up and fucked up the work of other artists.

The next day I decided to take my losses and print everything again at a higher quality (and way more expensive) printer's in the Netherlands. Even with the total 4 euros, that a recycling company gave me for the 2000 copies of that first print run, I had a hard time breaking even on this project.

In the end the quality of this publication contributed to this set becoming a steady seller at art book fairs, where it even got praised for the paper and reached a final "profit" of 2000 euros. Or, 1 euro per thrown-away copy from the first print run.

Bonsai, 2011
Costs: –2826 euros / Revenues: 3284 euros / Profits: 458 euros

During a residency in Tokyo, *Der Baum* was still going strong in sales. Inspired by Japan I decided to make a book that was related to *Der Baum* but was also the complete opposite. Where *Der Baum* dealt with subject matter, history and (hidden) stories, *Bonsai* had to deal with the image and the book as objects. Both titles are of exactly the same size and similar design and in some ways complement each other. For *Bonsai* I re-photographed the pictures in a book I had bought at a Korean (!) flea market, many years before. I digitally transformed the images into black and white negatives to emphasize their constructed, object-like quality.

I invested all the profits *Der Baum* had generated until then in the production of *Bonsai*, especially the Japanese thread binding and semi-matte varnish over the images. I had really thought this publication could cross over from the artist's book audience and infiltrate the coffee table books.

The truth is, *Bonsai* took almost four years to break even and never really got noticed. Similar to a very, very small tree.

Souvenir III, 2013
Costs: –1035 euros / Revenues: 1880 euros / Profits: 845 euros

When I photographed the 22 prostitutes for *Praia*, back in 2003, I used a Contax T2 with color film. But I also had an Olympus mju on hand, loaded with b/w film, which I used for the in-between scenes. Overexcited as I was with the results from the T2, I didn't even look at the b/w contacts until recently, when I found them hidden in a moving box in my storage unit. Of course the pictures were much less composed than the colored ones, but there were quite a few of them interesting enough to enlarge. Going through the work, so many years later, I had a lot of "oh yeah!" moments, like going through one's childhood album.

I ended up choosing 35 images which were printed in offset on card stock to resemble postcards, and had 100 pink binders produced and silk-screened in the Netherlands. It took me three full days to put all the cards in transparent sleeves and finish each binder.

If I divide the income of this title by the three days—or 24 hours—assembling, I made 35 euros an hour for those three days, which is similar to what a nuclear power reactor operator makes.

Privacy Settings, 2013
Costs: –1912 euros / Revenues: 1500 euros / Profits: –412 euros

It took me almost eight years to prepare myself emotionally to publish this title. I had photographed my son, while he was sleeping, over the course of one month. I imagine many parents look into their children's bedroom to check on them—or just to smell them—before going to bed. I don't think many parents decide to photograph their sleeping children and then print the images in a book and publish that as a work. So, as I said, it took me until 2013 to decide to actually publish a work I had finished many years earlier. On the day I had to upload the files to the printer I decided I wanted the images to rotate a few degrees, so that in the end the images on the pages, throughout the book, had made one complete turn. One child, one month, 360 degrees. Could have been any child, could have been any month, could continue endlessly. I was and still am aware of the high Why-would-I-care-about-your-kid's-pictures factor in this book, but I think I covered that in the title, *Privacy Settings*.

On social media both adults and teens can go very far in exposing their private lives, especially through pictures. What used to be confined to a family album, shown on special occasions to special visitors, has become a common daily practice in the 2000s. I am very pleased when artists and curators praise and buy the book and understand it for what it means and for what it could mean.

Unfortunately *Privacy Settings* is the worst-selling title from my catalogue. It hasn't made one step outside of the small artist / curator / collector community and so far has only cost me money, the equivalent of a bit under 14 euros per picture of my sleeping son.

O. Niemeyer, 2012
Costs: −6337 euros / Revenues: 10638 euros / Profits: 4301 euros

The book *O. Niemeyer* was ready to go to press. It had been in project-stage for almost a year and I had set a soft deadline for its release. Still, something was missing, I felt. I had photographed many of Oscar Niemeyer's buildings over the past six years, most of them in Brazil, but also all of his mainland European projects. Then, three days before uploading the files to the printer in Tallinn, I realized: I hadn't included the Pampulha project. A group of buildings around an artificial lake on the outskirts of Belo Horizonte, commissioned by Mayor Juscelino Kubitschek in the 1940s, who would later, as president, commission the new capital Brasilia. I vaguely remembered the first time I visited Lake Pampulha in 1995, during my first stay in Brazil. My best friend Tatiana had invited me to come visit Belo Horizonte and stay on her family's estate in the Pampulha neighborhood. One morning we went for a walk along the lakeside and got as far as Niemeyer's Saint Francis Church after a breakfast of pão de queijo and screwdrivers.

Years later I realized that morning had been my first encounter with (tropical) modernism and also had been a turning point in my personal life. In retrospect, that first encounter with Niemeyer's work was the basis for my decision to become an artist. So, of course, I had to include Pampulha in my Niemeyer book.

I bought a plane ticket for two days later and spent that day photographing as many buildings by Niemeyer in Belo Horizonte as I could. I flew back home in the evening after a tiring but satisfying 18 hours. I notified the printer the next day that I would need an extra 16 pages and now, three years after the first edition of *O. Niemeyer* was released, I still believe that going that extra mile in any book project pays off exponentially. Also, that extra shooting day, including the flights, cost me 8% of the project's profit until now.

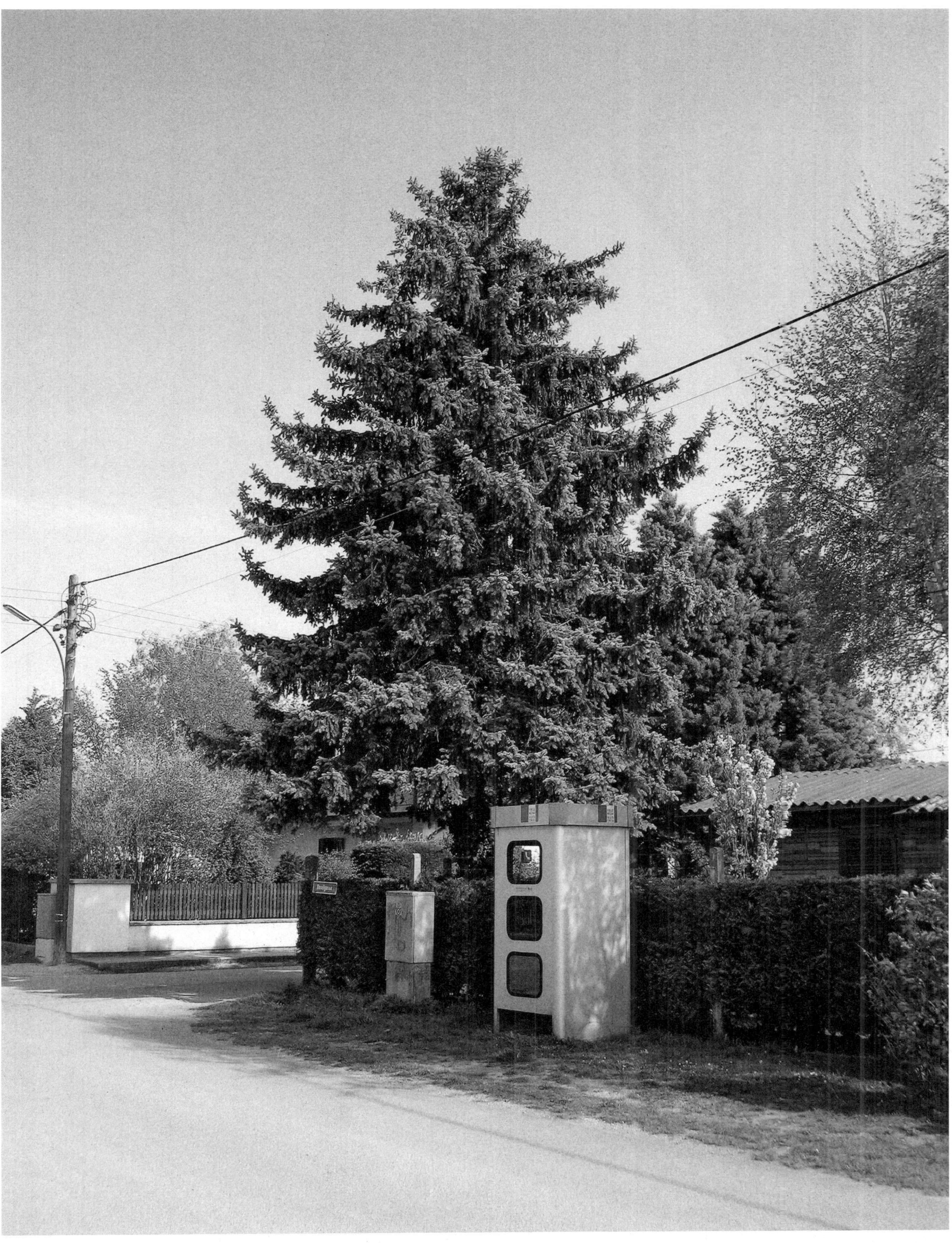

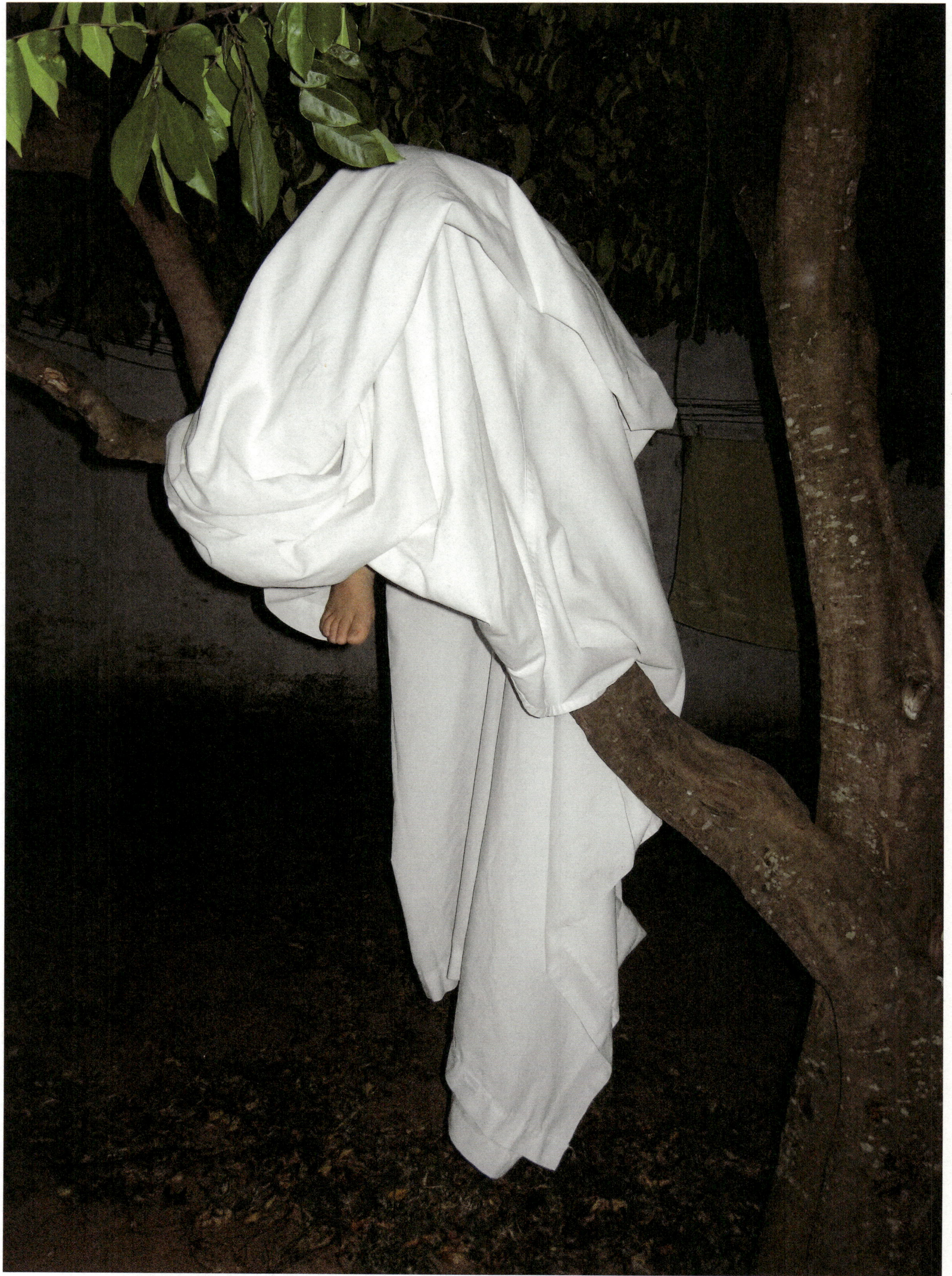

Everyday Life, the Sequence, the Book, or Five Stacks of Books for Erik van der Weijde

by Jan Wenzel

"That's the tree out there. It was my counterpart for many years, each year dying a bit more, sawed off a bit more, propped up a bit more, an iron hoop, yet another, one branch gone, the next, the next the last winter and the winter before, and before that. Today it has been knocked down. It stood cracked open for two months. Now, nothing more is left, only a big gap of sky," wrote the dramatist Einar Schleef about the chestnut tree in front of his window. If it had not been sawn off, cut up into discs, and now only "a big gap of sky" this chestnut tree would have fit outstandingly in the series of photographs that Erik van der Weijde presents in the book *Der Baum* (The Tree, 2010). "House in which Einar Schleef lived, Berlin," the image caption in the index might read. In the index in which each of the forty-eight trees depicted is attributed to a precise location at the beginning of the book. The photo on the cover of *Der Baum* shows a tree on the street where the kidnapping victim Natascha Kampusch was held; another picture shows a tree in the cemetery where Hitler's parents are buried; on one double page, on the left one can see a tree on Karl-Marx-Allee in Berlin, and on the right, a tree in the Hansa Quarter of Berlin. The photo of a tree on a street in São Paulo and one of a tree in an inner courtyard in Istanbul follow. There are no pictures of forests or parks in *Der Baum*. All of the trees photographed are part of an urban environment. In this series, Erik van der Weijde succeeds in showing the tree as an ideal everyday object—as something *that is simply also there*. Here, the tree does not stand for an idea of sublime nature, and it is also not a witness to history, as perhaps might be suggested the first moment by some of the locations selected. The tree is a thing in our everyday life, something that generally escapes our attention. Significant and insignificant at the same time. Banal, but also simply irreplaceable, which one realizes at the latest when, in place of one's own tree, only "a big gap of sky" remains.

"I believe that in a way, in everyday life, everything is present, if you look carefully," Erik van der Weijde once said in an interview. A sentence that might also have been formulated by the poet Rolf Dieter Brinkmann, who was sure it was not necessary to invent anything in literature, because looking closely at everything that is there in the now is more than sufficient and already a gigantic challenge. Perhaps Erik van der Weijde has a similarly sensitive alertness for the everyday as the author of *Rom, Blicke* (Rome, Views, 1979). In any case, he has the visual cautiousness to record his objects in such a way that they remain everyday. Unspectacular, relaxed. Significant and insignificant at the same time. This equanimity when taking photographs, which is also expressed in the fact that Erik van der Weijde tends to avoid the perfect single image because a surfeit of ambition, of a will to originality, already again obstructs the view of the everyday *as everyday* and distinguishes his work. In it, the conceptual structure is also characterized by reserve: No more than is specifically necessary, is what Erik van der Weijde's approach seems to be. And to be able to capture the everyday, "the sum of insignificant things," visually, what is necessary first and foremost is an understanding of an aesthetic process of repetition and variation; of processes that give rise to a unity in diversity: an understanding of the photographic sequence.

But what characterizes a photographic sequence? In the case of film, it is straightforward: The individual picture here is always embedded in a sequence of pictures. To look at it as an individual image, as a still, requires an analytical interest as well as the technical possibilities to interrupt the flow of images. Firstly, the individual image is laid open. In photography,

First stack

- Henri Lefebvre, *Critique of Everyday Life*, London / New York: Verso, 2002
- Eckhard Schumacher, *Gerade Eben Jetzt. Schreibweisen der Gegenwart*, Frankfurt am Main: Suhrkamp, 2003
- Agnes Heller, *Everyday Life*, London: Routledge, 1984
- Andy Warhol, *A. A Novel*, New York: Grove Press, 1968
- Hans-Peter Feldmann, *Die Toten. 1967–1993. Studentenbewegung, APO, Baader-Meinhof, Bewegung 2. Juni, Revolutionäre Zellen, RAF, ...*, Düsseldorf: Feldmann Verlag, 1998
- Mass-Observation, *First Year's Work, 1937–1938*, London: Lindsay Drummond, 1938
- Siegfried Kracauer, *Die Angestellten. Kulturkritischer Essay*, Leipzig / Weimar: Gustav Kiepenheuer Verlag, 1981
- Ilya Kabakov / Boris Groys, *Die Kunst des Fliehens. Dialoge über Angst, das heilige Weiß und den sowjetischen Müll*, Munich: Carl Hanser Verlag, 1991

the situation is different: Here, there are only individual images, and it is first the eye of the beholder that connects them, brings them together in one context. How the individual images ultimately enter into a dialogue with one another, whether gradually modified in their sequence of visual motifs and themes or related to each other contrapuntally; whether the sequence of images is characterized by clear cuts and jumps or by retarding moments and repetitions determines whether the individual image comes to the fore or whether we perceive the sequence of images as a sequence, as a flow of images. This syntactic level, the linking of images, and the meaning that arises from the context, from montage, rhythm and flow, takes up much less room in the analysis of photographs than in film analysis or the description of lyrics. Where is the formal school of photography? Where is there a language for how individual images enter into dialogue with one another? The understanding of which elements within a sequence of images gives rise to the interrelationship?

In his sequences of images, Erik van der Weijde generally works with the principle of repetition. Each one of his sequences has an easily definable topical and visual center. If his interest as an artist focuses on phenomena in his personal everyday life—which within his oeuvre are always taken up

Second stack

- Erik van der Weijde, *Der Baum*, Amsterdam: 4478zine, 2010
- *Der Baum im Bilde der Landschaft. Erlesene Naturaufnahmen*, Königstein im Taunus / Leipzig: Verlag Der Eiserne Hammer, 1931
- Annette von Droste-Hülshoff, *Die Judenbuche. Ein Sittengemälde aus dem gebirgichten Westfalen*, Stuttgart: Reclam, 2014
- Michael Schmidt, *Natur*, London: Mack, 2014
- Erik van der Weijde, *Palm Trees*, Amsterdam: 4478zine, 2009
- Edward Ruscha, *A Few Palm Trees*, Hollywood, CA: Heavy Industry Publications, 1971
- Edward Ruscha, *Colored People*, Los Angeles: self-published, 1972
- Albert Renger-Patzsch, *Bäume, Photografien schöner und merkwürdiger Beispiele aus deutschen Landen*, with an essay by Ernst Jünger, Ingelheim am Rhein: C.H. Boehringer Sohn, 1962
- Erik van der Weijde, *Bonsai*, Amsterdam: 4478zine, 2011
- Einar Schleef, *Kontaktbögen. Fotografie, 1965–2001*, Berlin: Akademie der Künste / Theater der Zeit, 2006
- Rolf Dieter Brinkmann, *Westwärts 1 & 2. Gedichte*, Reinbek bei Hamburg: Rowohlt-Taschenbuch-Verlag, 1975

anew and carried forward, are therefore anything but random—then the photo sequence is the proper form for appropriately articulating the everyday, which "in its triviality, is made up of repetitions," as the French philosopher Henri Lefebvre writes.

And the book is the proper medium for this articulation. Since, in a book, a sequence can be fixed. The sequence of images becomes a sequence of pages. Erik van der Weijde almost always works with one image per page and two images on the double page. The layout is reserved, the material page of the publication—the quality of the paper, the binding and workmanship, the image processing and print quality—simple, but precisely selected. Ultimately, the book objects are also supposed to retain an everyday character. Sometimes, the creative idea comments on the image sequence—for instance in *Privacy Settings* (2013), where the turning of the sleeping boy is doubled as a turning of the images on the page, or in *Die Wolken* (The Clouds, 2012), where the same image sequence is printed in three different colors—all in all, Erik van der Weijde conspicuously refrains from creative interventions in his publications, which form the center of his work. He concentrates on the image sequences, from which nothing should distract. It is based specifically on this simplicity that his photo books obtain their

Third stack

- Erik van der Weijde, *This Is Not My Wife*, Zurich / Amsterdam: Rollo Press / 4478zine, 2012
- Seiichi Furuya, *Portraits, Christine Furuya-Gößler, 1978 – 1985*, Salzburg: Fotohof, 2000
- Nigel Shafran, *Ruth on the Phone*, Amsterdam: ROMA Publications, 2012
- Seiichi Furuya, *Mémoires, 1978 – 1988*, Graz: Edition Camera Austria / Neue Galerie am Landesmuseum Joanneum, Graz, 1989
- *Hester. Depressed* (= *Re-Magazine 12, A magazine about one person*), Winter 2004 – 2005, Amsterdam: Re-Magazine, 2004
- Roswitha Hecke, *Irene*, Zurich: Edition Patrick Frey, 2011
- Wilfried F. Schoeller, *Hubert Fichte und Leonore Mau. Der Schriftsteller und die Fotografin, Eine Lebensreise*, Frankfurt am Main: S. Fischer Verlag, 2005
- Nobuyoshi Araki, *Diary Sentimental Journey* (Japanese edition), Tokyo: Shincho-sha, 1991
- Petra Elena Köhle / Nicolas Vermot Petit-Outhenin, *Dort, wo ich gestern hätte sein sollen. Ich bin heute hier*, Zurich: edition fink, 2010
- Seiichi Furuya, *Mémoires, 1978 – 1987*, Shizuoka / Graz: Izu Photo Museum / Camera Austria, 2010
- Brigitte Maria Mayer / Heiner Müller, *Der Tod ist ein Irrtum, Bilder, Texte, Autographen*, Frankfurt am Main: Suhrkamp, 2005

power and consistency. Nonetheless, the question of the media-specific dialectic between individual image and sequence emerges distinctly in them. Therefore, the question of the arrangement of images; images which seem banal and absolutely without meaning as individual images, but which take on a meaning in a specific arrangement. If the simplest way to create something complex consists of combining the simple, then the book, the page of the book, is an aggregate for this "reaction of images," a framework, a space. The photo books of Erik van der Weijde raise the question of whether one should not speak in future of the "book image" with the same legitimacy with which the term film image has been used in theory for some years. Since the pages of a book, and the book as object, are not only the material bearers of images. They structure the order of the images and change their semantic meaning by doing so. It is first upon leafing through the pages that the tree becomes the ideal everyday object.

"The connections between different publications may be invisible, but are always present," states Point 10 of van der Weijde's "4478zine's Publishing Manifesto" in which he outlines his artistic and publishing work with the medium in concise sentences. In this manifesto, van der Weijde describes the different medial operations involved in making an everyday image when

Fourth stack

- Friedl Kubelka, *Porträt Louise Anna Kubelka*, Salzburg: Edition Fotohof, 1998
- Erik van der Weijde, *This Is Not My Son*, Zurich / Amsterdam: Rollo Press / 4478zine, 2009
- Wiebke Loeper, *Moll 31*, Tübingen / Berlin: Edition J. J. Heckenhauer, 2005
- *Friedl Kubelka-Bondy*, Linz: Edition Neue Texte, 1984
- Einar Schleef, *Kontaktbögen. Fotografie, 1965 – 2001*, Berlin: Akademie der Künste / Theater der Zeit, 2006
- Knut Wolf Maron, *Ein Leben*, Bielefeld: Kerber, 2012
- Christian Lange, *Lange Liste 79 – 97*, Leipzig: Spector Books, 2012
- Jürgen Teller, *The Throne, the Robe, the Haircut* (Insert *Art Review*, issue 46) London: Art Review, 2010
- Frank Mädler, *Kopal*, Edition Fotohof, 2013
- Annelies Štrba, *Shades of Time*, Baden: Lars Müller Publishers, 1995
- Erik van der Weijde, *Privacy Settings*, Amsterdam: 4478zine, 2013

considered separately part of a semantic context that is ultimately able to lend this individual image, as banal as it might seem, an iconographic power. In this, the book functions as a contextualization machine that cross-links the individual image, establishes it within an arrangement. In the book as part of a sequence, but also in that the book establishes loose associations with other books that deal with similar visual phenomena. Thus, each of Erik van der Weijde's photographic series, since they exist in books, can become a building block for more complex structures: Within his oeuvre it is possible to connect the books thematically and visually, but also with other books. They form sequences in the bookshelf, a stack on a desk, and organize themselves virtually on their own into more complex visual systems, into another visual everyday culture. I was already lying in bed and still reading when Einar Schleef's photo series came to my mind, five pages in an extensive catalogue that the Akademie der Künste in Berlin published some years ago. I got up again, took the book from the bookshelf, leafed through it and read for a while, also found the shape of the tree on other contact sheets of Schleef again, wondered whether it was really a chestnut tree—in his texts Schleef always only called it "the tree," and then put the book onto the stack where *Der Baum* and some other books already lay.

Fifth stack

- Erik van der Weijde, *O. Niemeyer*, Zurich / Amsterdam: Rollo Press / 4478zine, 2012
- Erik van der Weijde, *Superquadra*, Amsterdam: ROMA Publications, 2010
- Olaf Nicolai, *Hotel Nacional Rio*, Zurich: Rollo Press, 2014
- Erik van der Weijde, *Wassertürme*, Amsterdam: 4478zine, 2008
- Arne Schmidt, *Wenn Gesinnung Form wird*, Leipzig: Spector Books, 2012
- Erik van der Weijde, *Souvenir I & II*, Amsterdam: 4478zine, 2012
- Erik van der Weijde, *Third Reich*, Amsterdam: 4478zine, 2014
- Susanne Kriemann, *12 650 000 (November 1941)*, Berlin, 2008
- Erik van der Weijde, *Siedlung*, Amsterdam: ROMA Publications, 2008
- Johanna Diel, *Borgo Romanità Alleanza*, Ostfildern: Hatje Cantz, 2014
- Erik van der Weijde, *foto.zine nr. 2*, series of five booklets, Amsterdam: 4478zine, 2007
- Eiko Grimberg, *Future History*, Baden: Kodoji Press, 2013

Germany

Brazil

Prostitution

Cars

Wife

Son

Relatives

Pets

Anonymity

Trees

Animals

Weapons

Violence

Landscapes of Books

"The connections between different publications may be invisible, but are always present," wrote Erik van der Weijde in his Publishing Manifesto. The relationships between different books exist at various levels, in content, in form, but also in a material sense. The entirety of these relationships remains "invisible," since it can never be made completely accessible. The landscapes of books on the following pages represent the attempt to display the abundance of connections as a spatial constellation—as a "side-by-side" of material artifacts.

To that effect, Erik van der Weijde's publications have been sorted into thirteen categories—Germany, Brazil, Prostitution, Cars, Wife, Son, Relatives, Pets, Anonymity, Trees, Animals, Weapons, Violence. They are classifications that encompass all the essential aspects of the book. Publications that belong to a specific category have been placed on one page. Publications that are assigned to a different category are placed on the opposite page which is set apart by its background color. In this way, a close-knit network of similarities and contrasts is established between the individual books on the one hand, but also between the juxtaposed classifications on the double-page spread (e.g. Germany–Brazil, Wife–Son, Trees–Animals). The individual categories are developed over a sequence of pages: We "leaf" through the pages of individual books, others are added or taken away. In a few spots, the right and left pages have been highlighted with the same color—the differences blur, the topics blend, the artist book is once again transformed into a continuum.

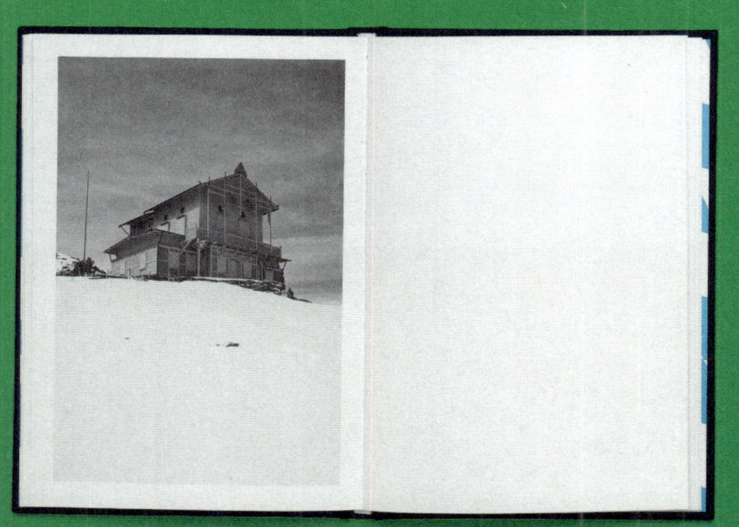

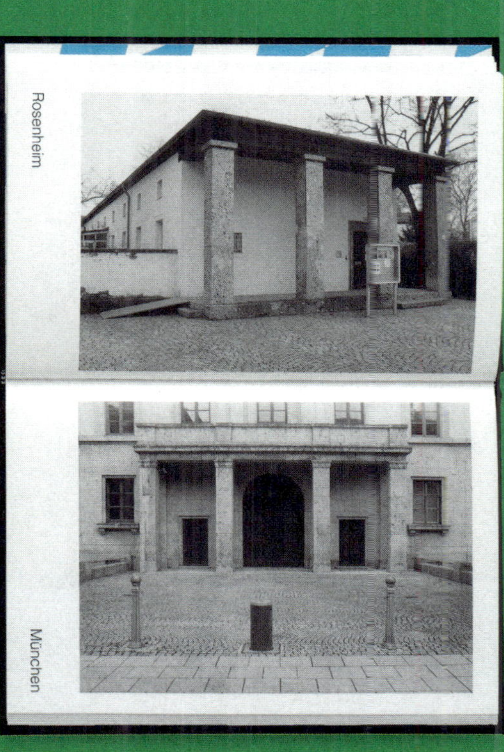

Rosenheim
München

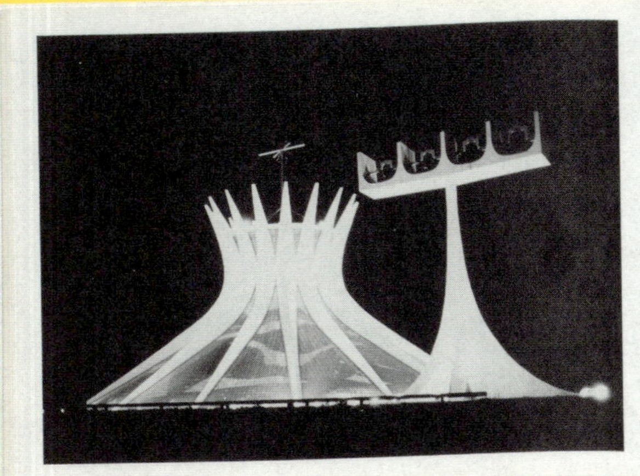

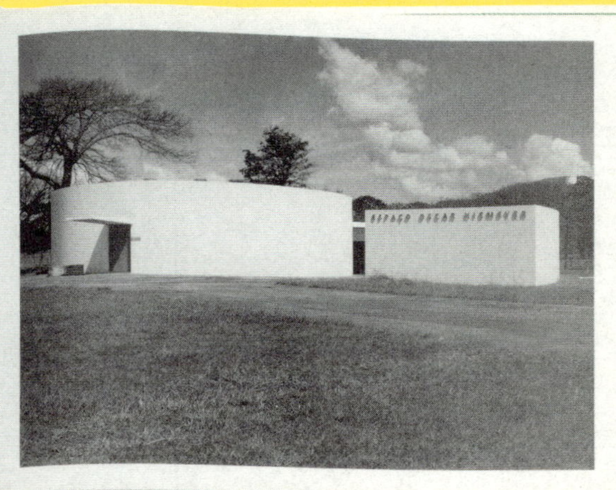

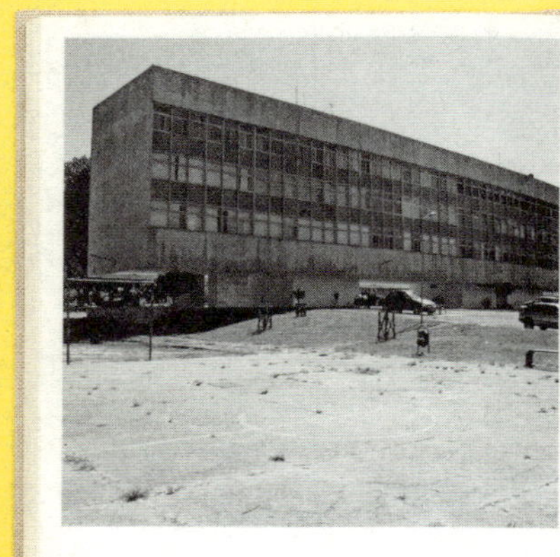

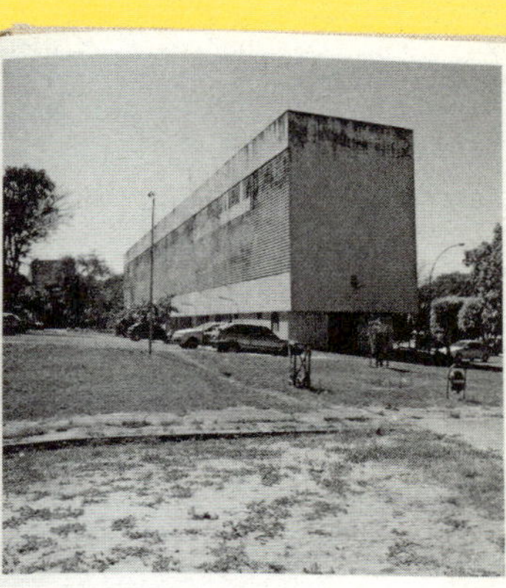

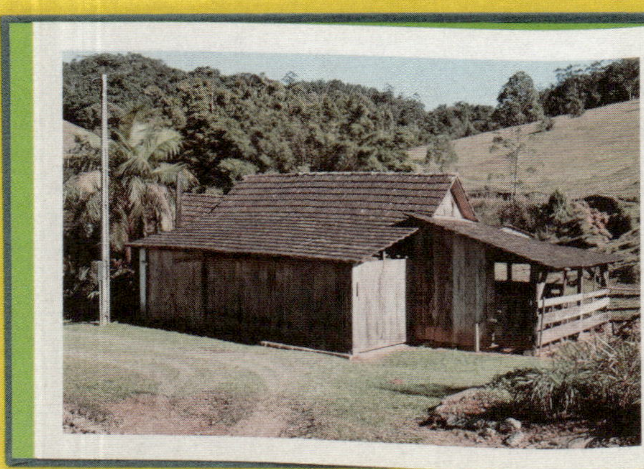

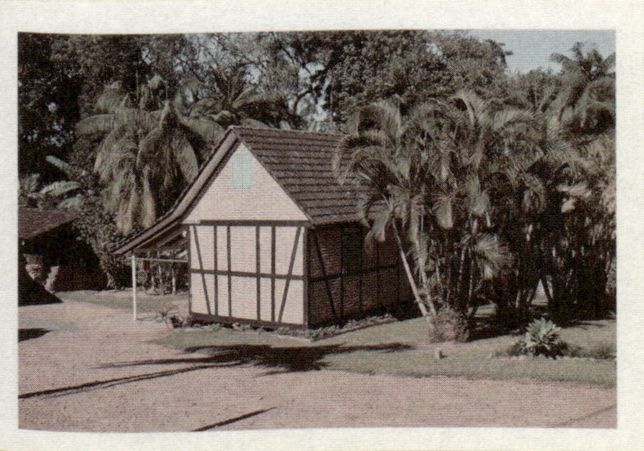

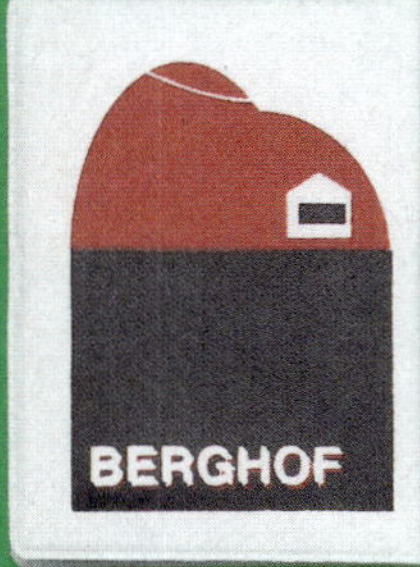
BERGHOF

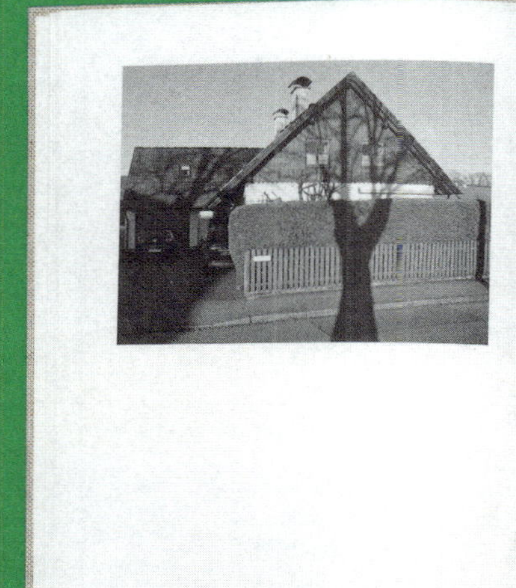

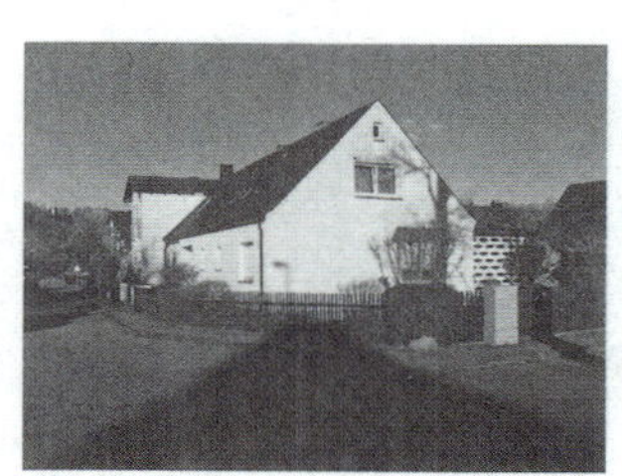

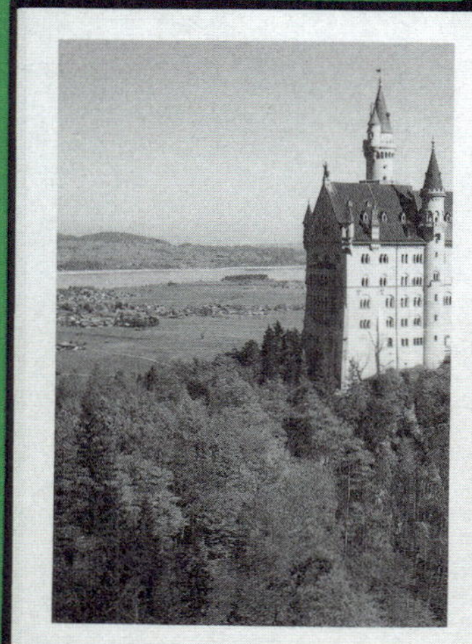

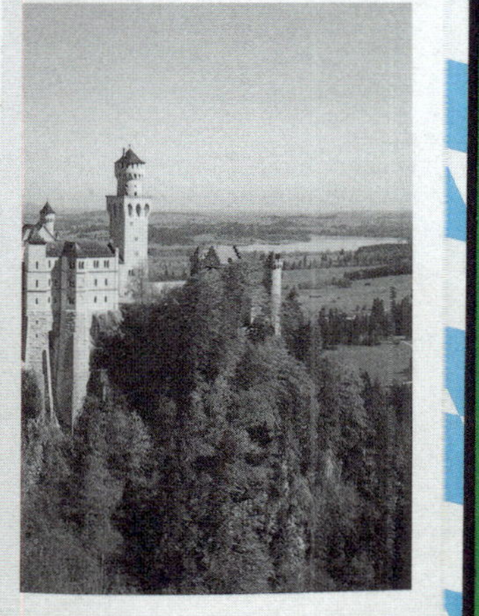

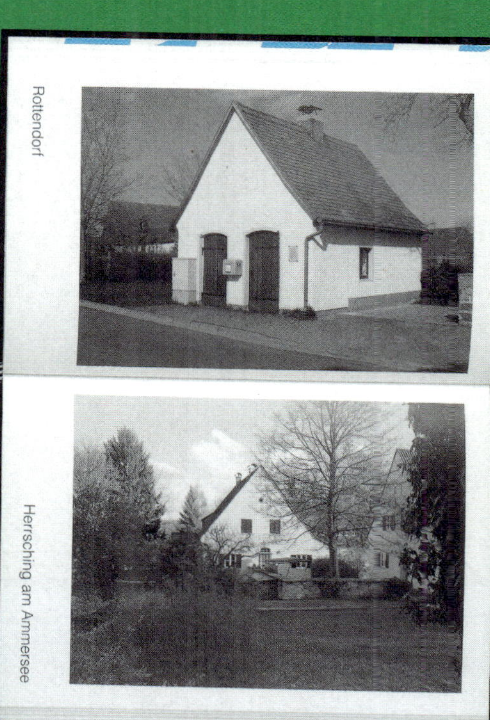
Rottendorf
Herrsching am Ammersee

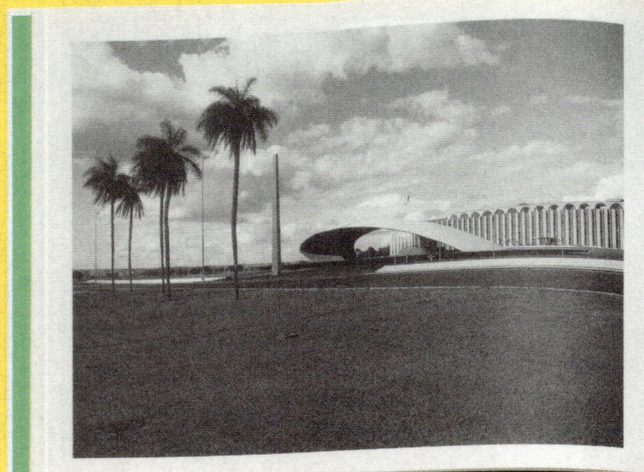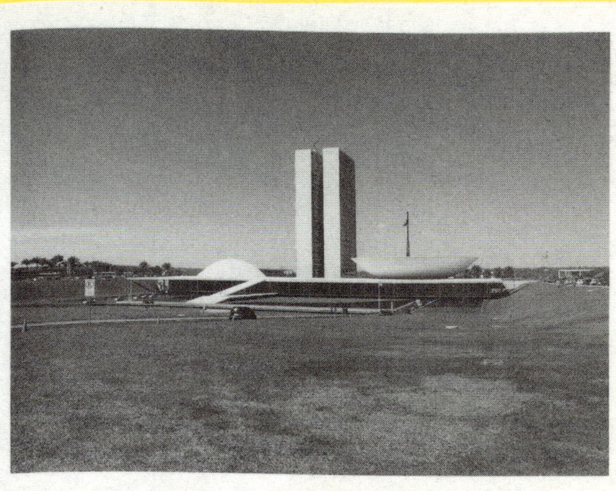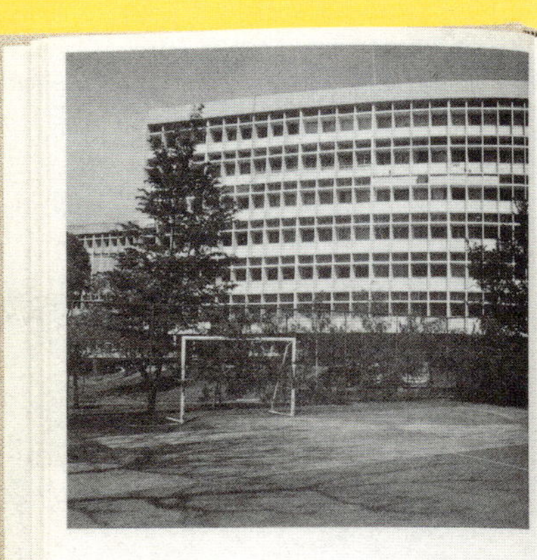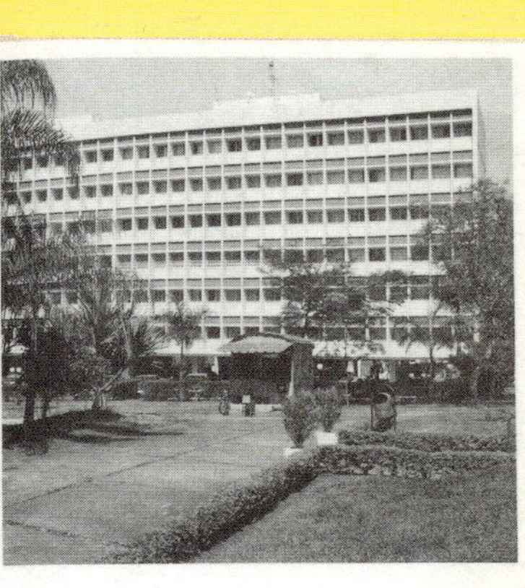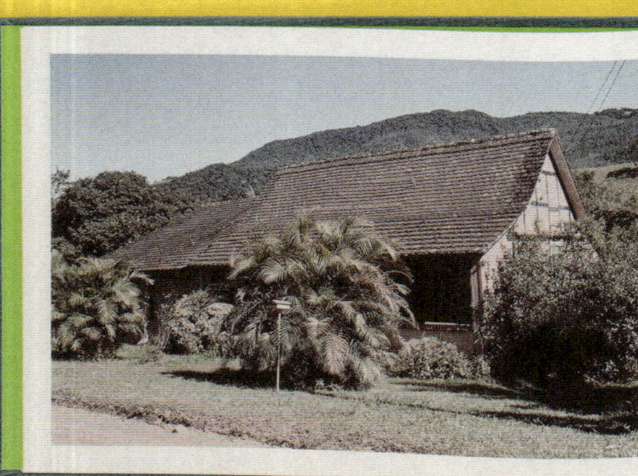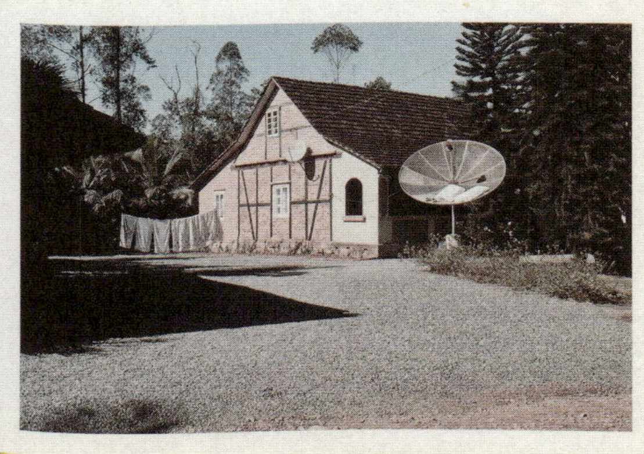

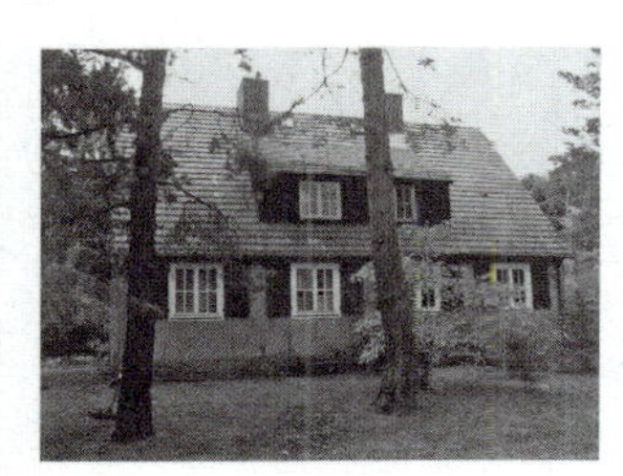

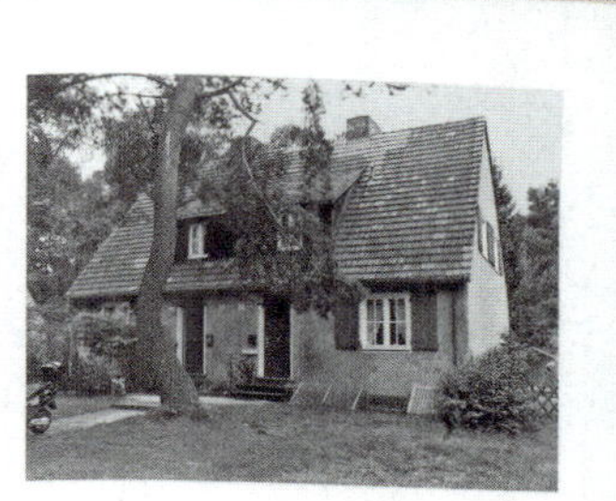

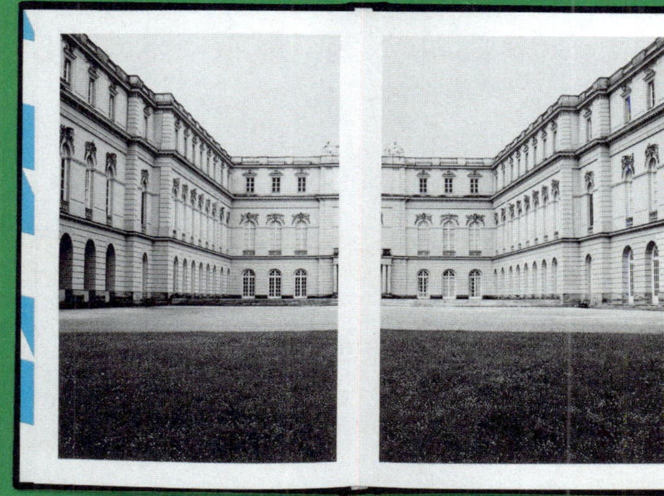

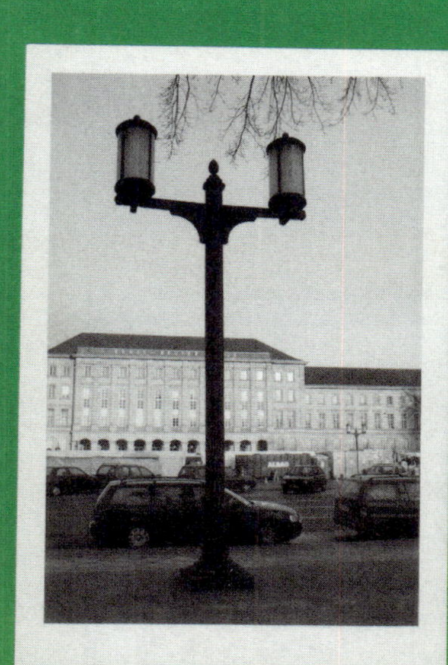

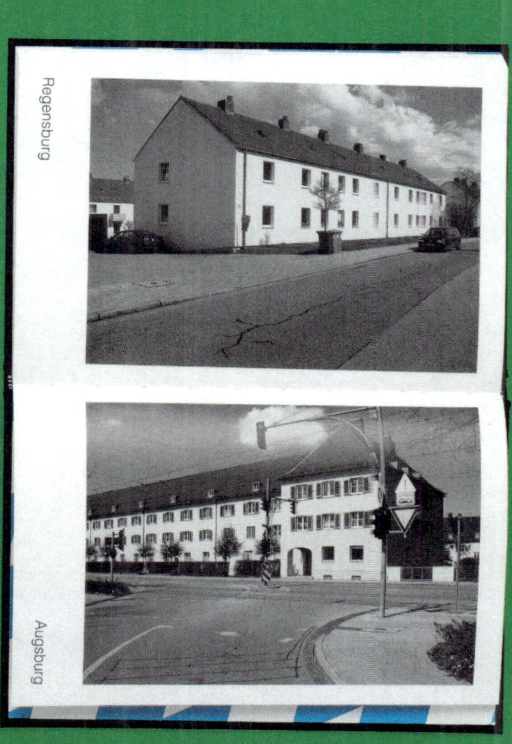
Regensburg
Augsburg

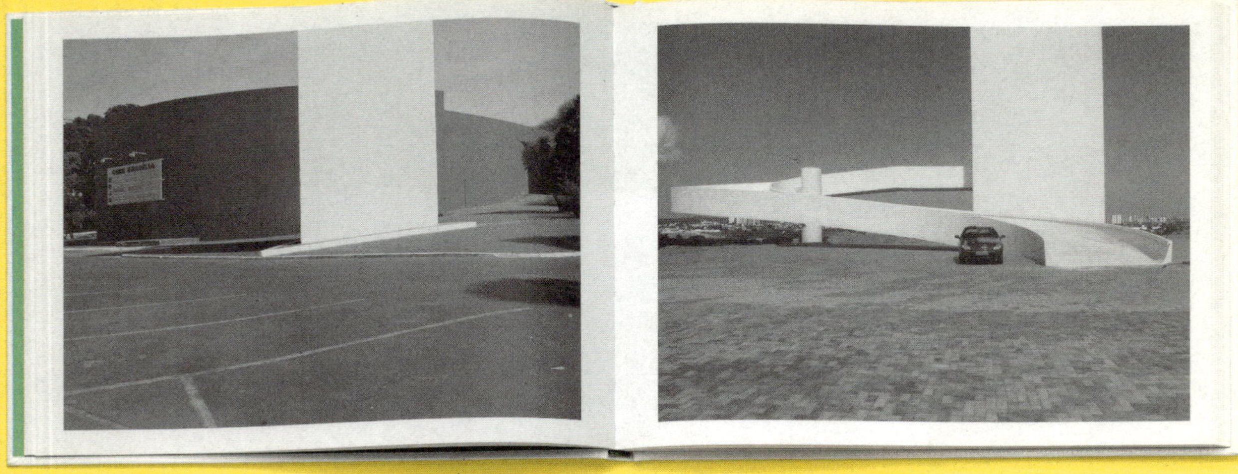

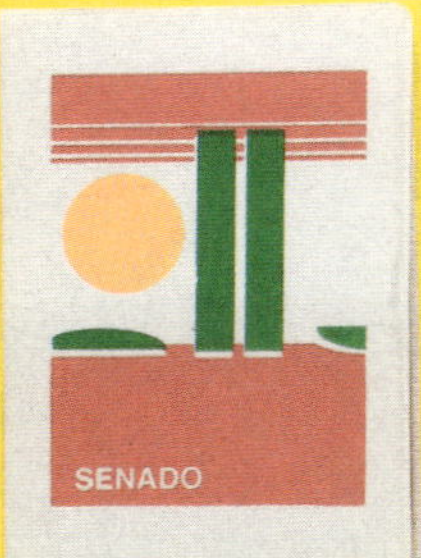
SENADO

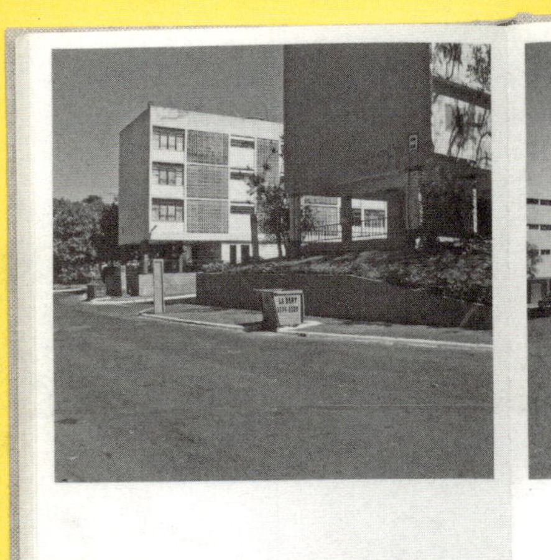

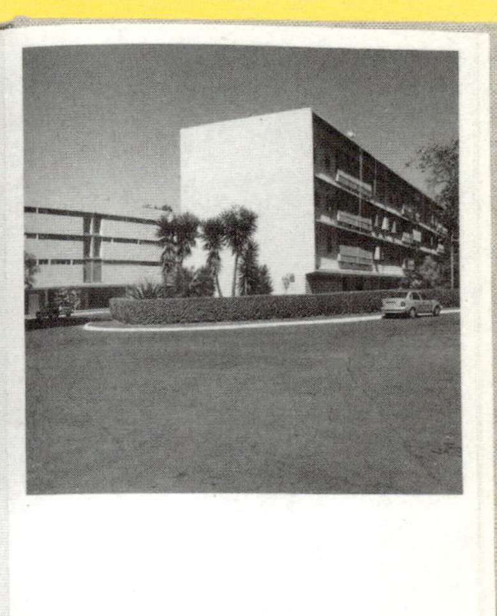

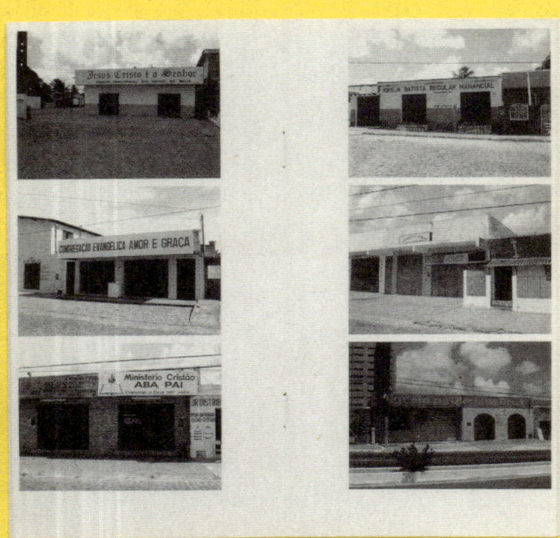
Jesus Cristo é o Senhor
IGREJA BATISTA REGULAR MARANGIAL
CONGREGAÇÃO EVANGÉLICA AMOR E GRAÇA
Ministério Cristão
ABA PAI

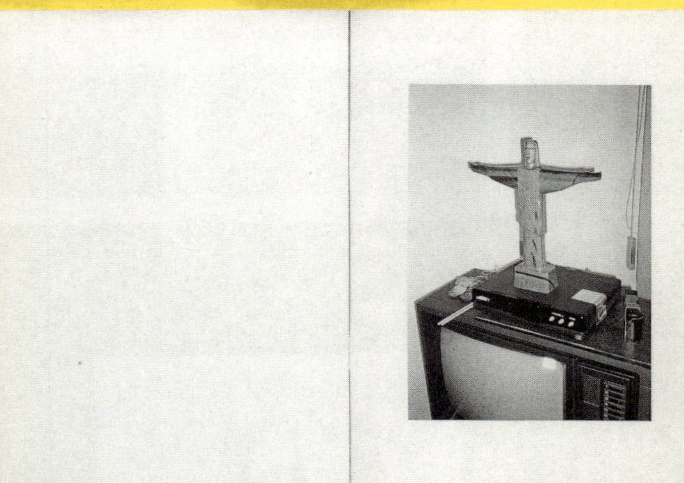

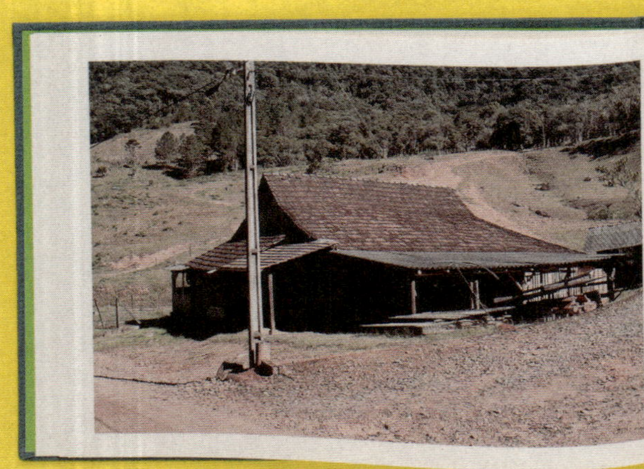

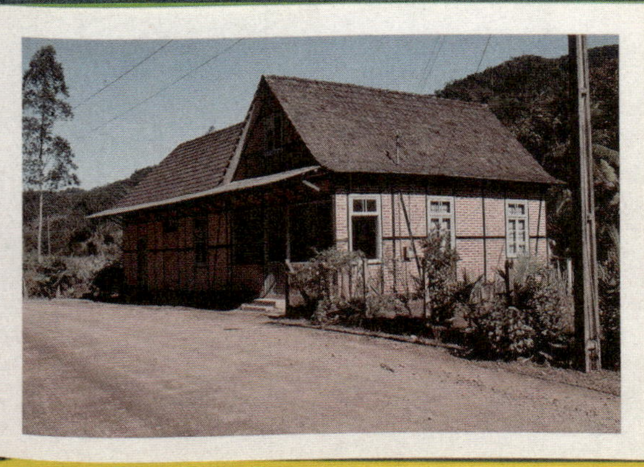

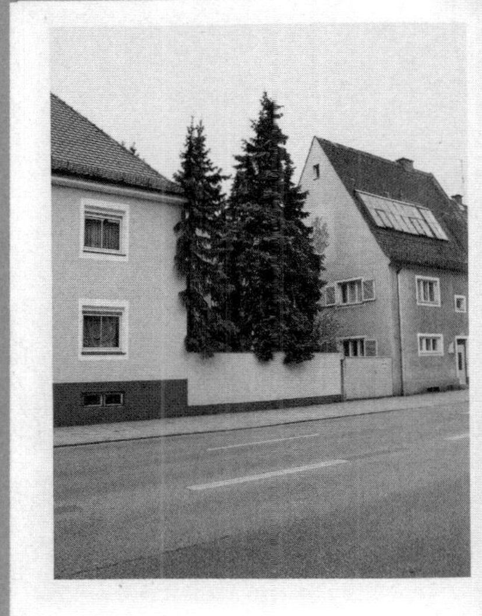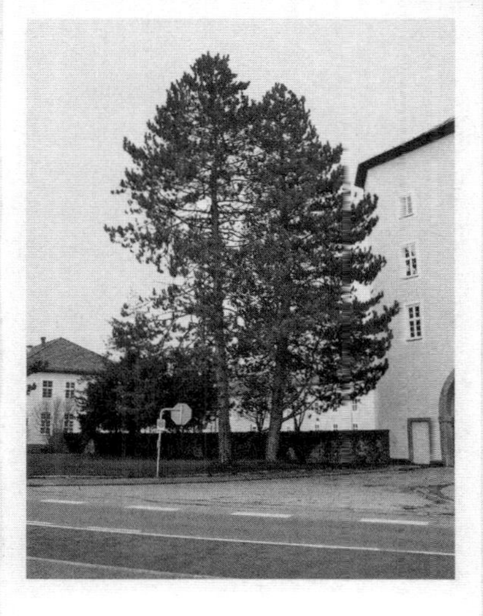

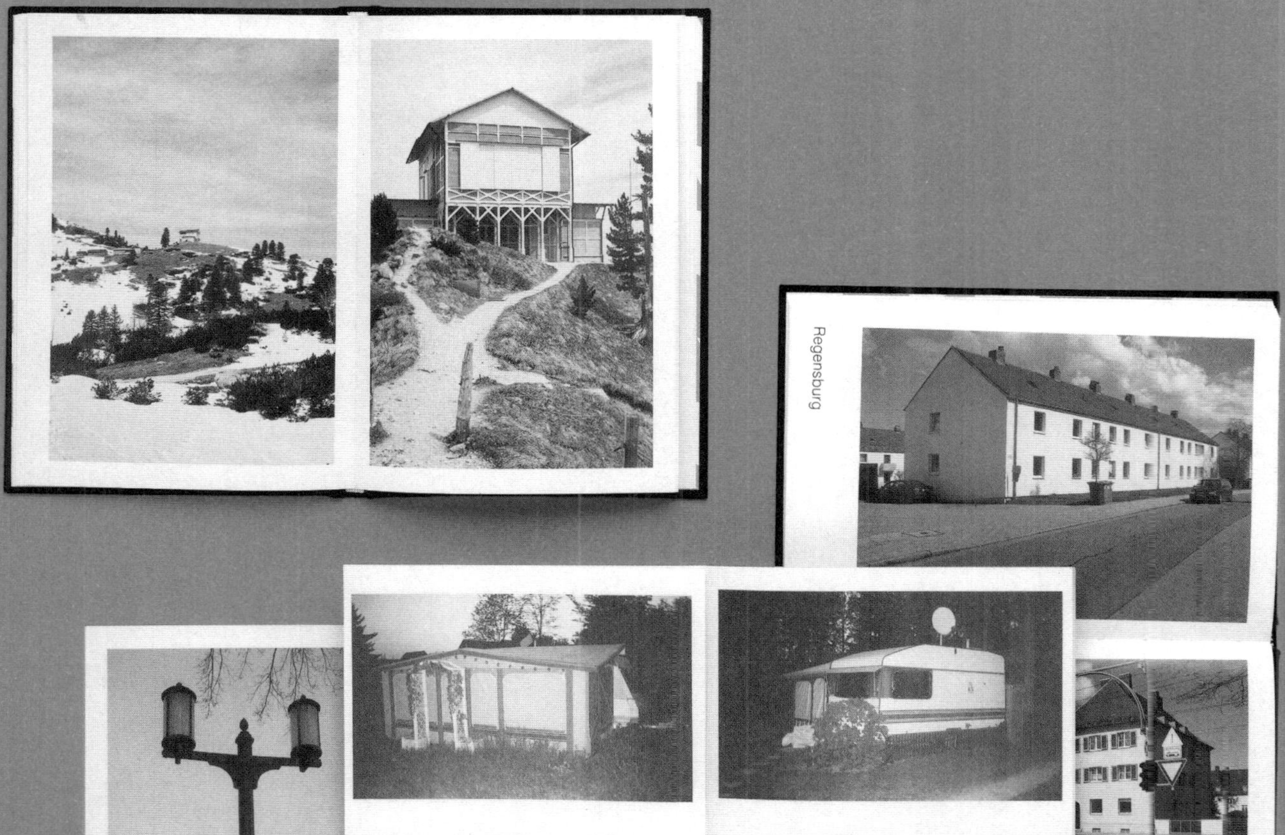

Regensburg

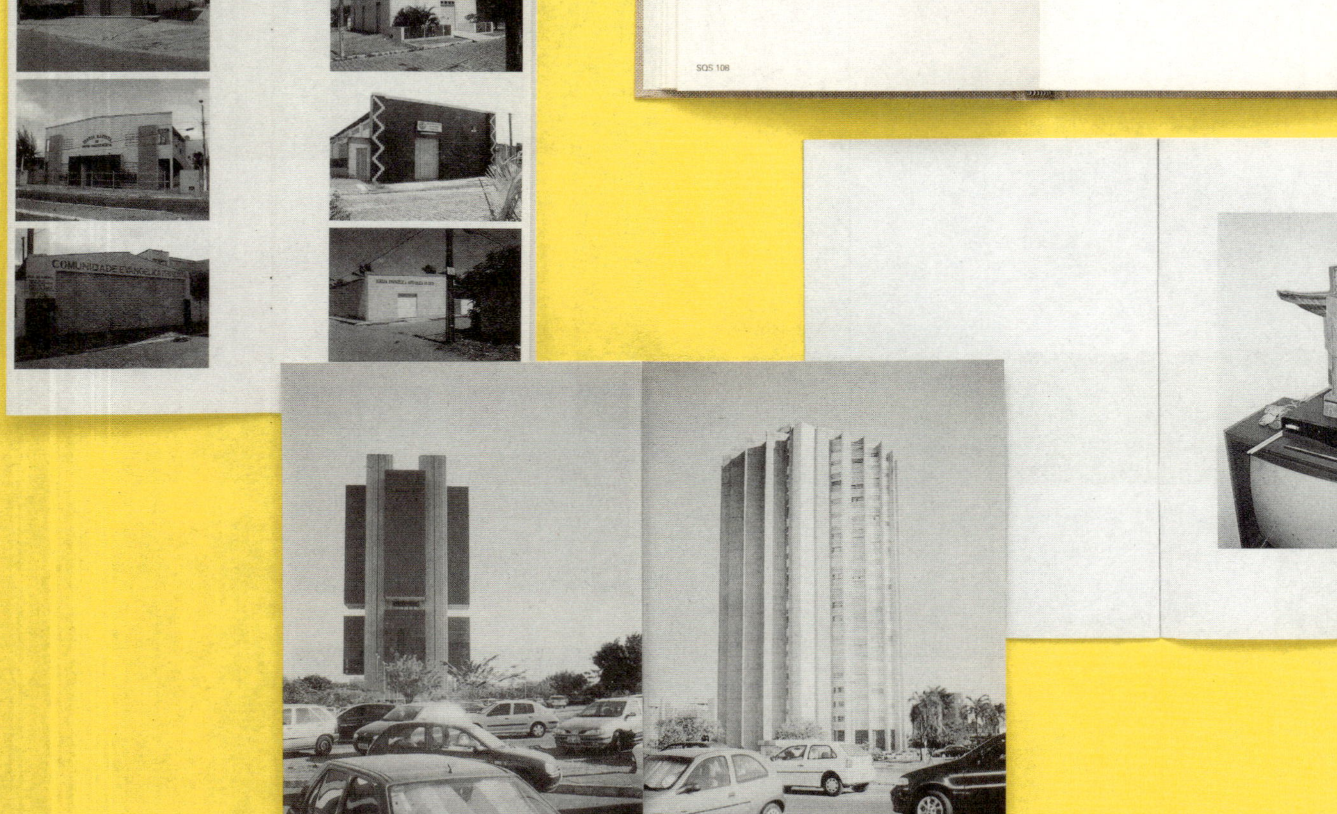
SQS 108

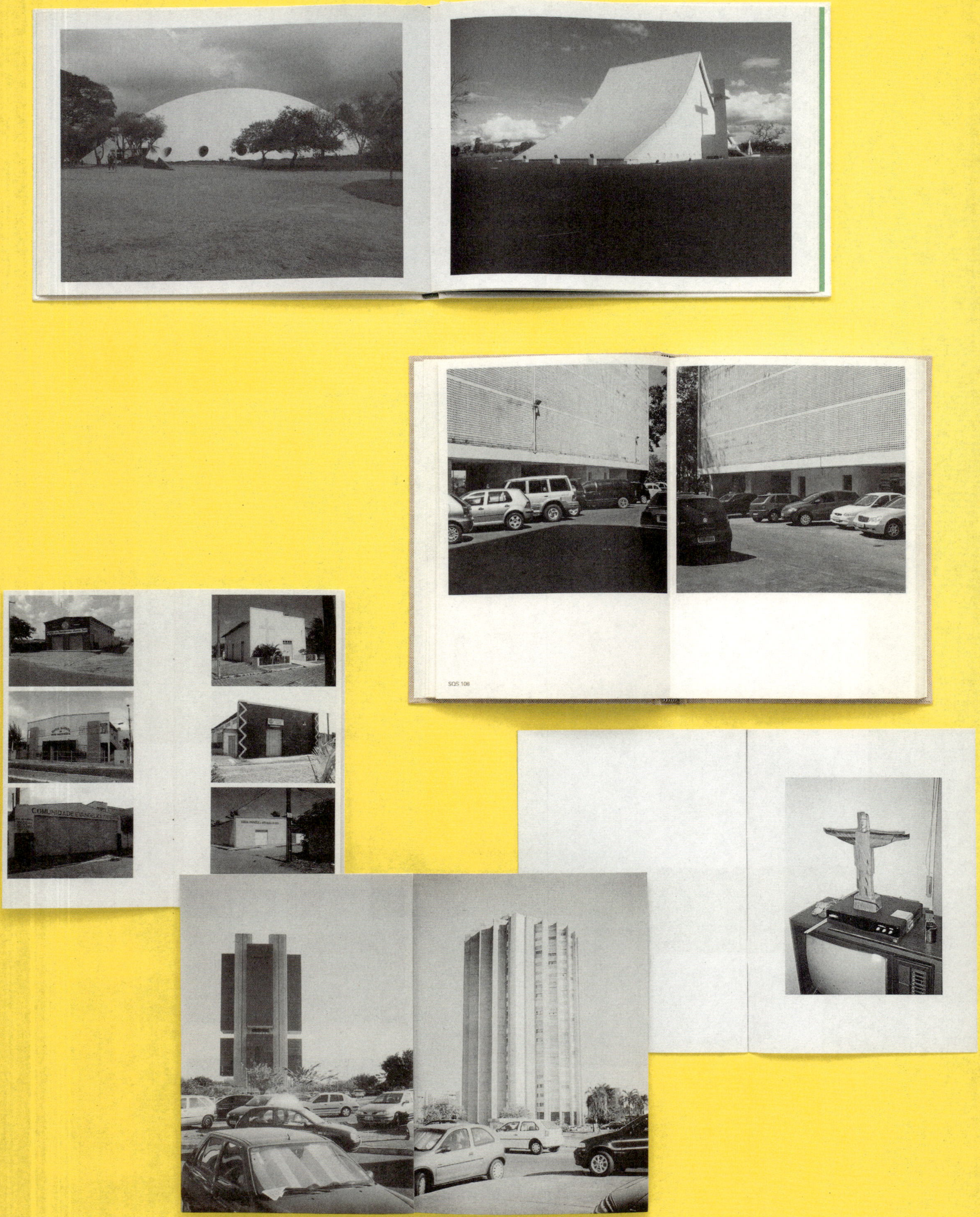

TABLE OF PLATES

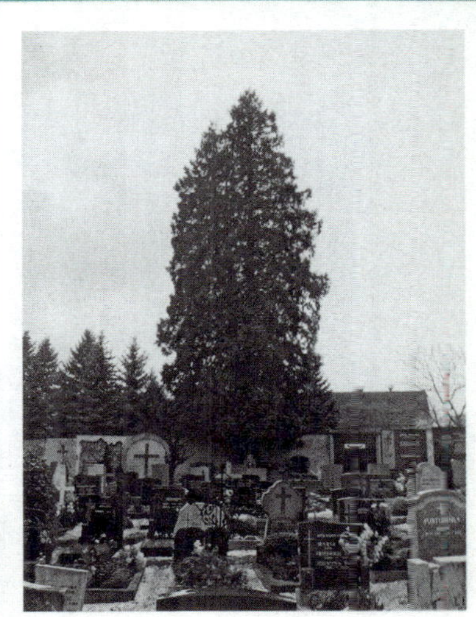

3 — Grave of Adolf Hitler's parents, Leonding
4 — Cemetery, Brasília
5 — Biennial building, São Paulo
6 — Parking lot, São Paulo
7 — Residential building, Brasília
8 — Museum, Berlin
9 — Museum, Kassel
10 — General Konrad barracks, Bad Reichenall
11 — Museum, Brasília
12 — Ordensburg, Sonthofen
13 — Ganghofersiedlung (former Siedlung Göringheim), Regensburg
14 — Road, München
15 — Jägerkaserne, Sonthofen
16 — Road, Kassel
17 — Residential street, Natal
18 — Alfama, Lissabon
19 — Printer, Natal
20 — Residential block, Le Havre
21 — Road, Natal
22 — Car, Natal
23 — Street where kidnap victim Natasha Kampusch was held, Strasshof a.d. Nordbahn
24 — Karl-Marx-Allee, Berlin
25 — Hansaviertel, Berlin
26 — Parking lot, München
27 — Burger King, Nürnberg
28 — Heidi Haus, Maienfeld
29 — Residential street, Porto
30 — Residential street, München
31 — Residential street, Regensburg
32 — Weissenhof siedlung, Stuttgart
33 — Ganghofersiedlung (former Siedlung Göringheim), Regensburg
34 — School, Kassel
35 — Residential block, Brasília
36 — Copan building, São Paulo
37 — Avenida Paulista, São Paulo
38 — Street, São Paulo
39 — Street, São Paulo
40 — Street, Milano
41 — former SS barracks, Nürnberg
42 — Residential building, Rio de Janeiro
43 — Palace, Istanbul
44 — Museum, Varese
45 — Park, Kassel
46 — Elementary school Adolf Hitler attended, Fischlham

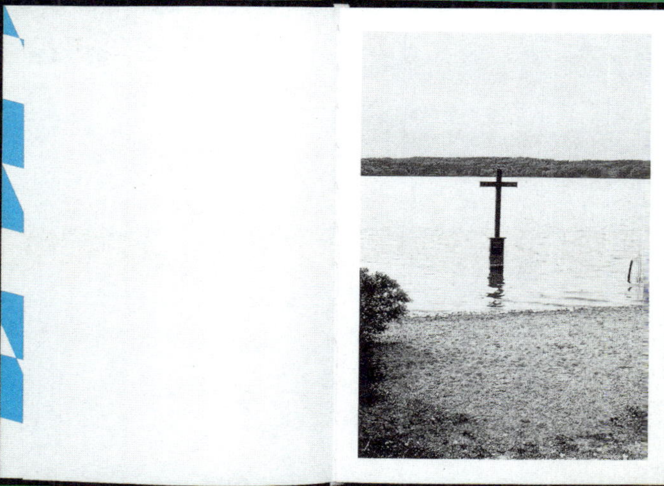

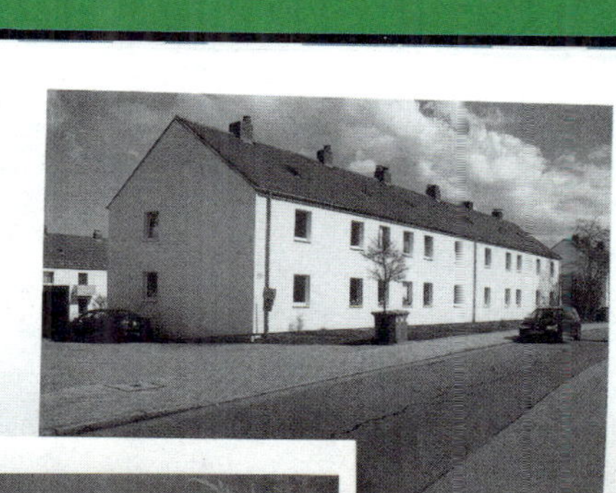

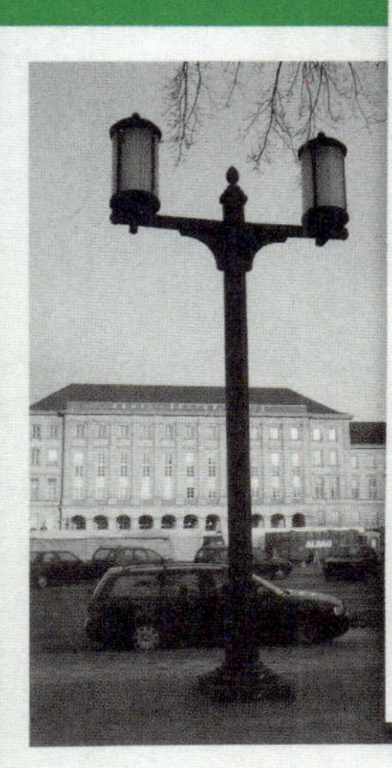

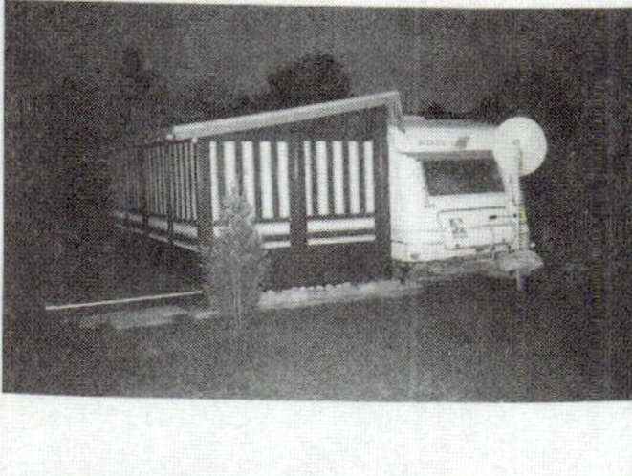

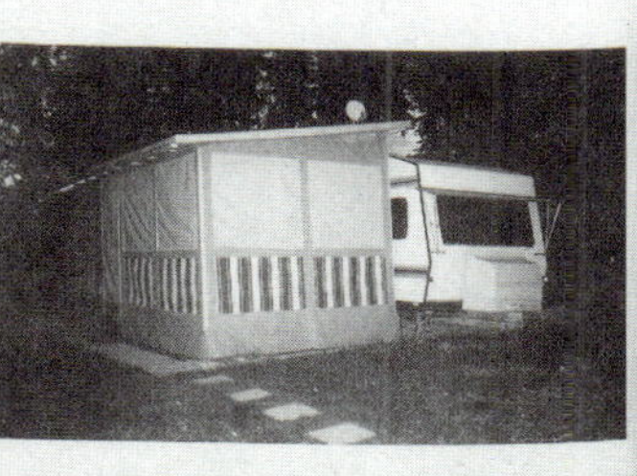

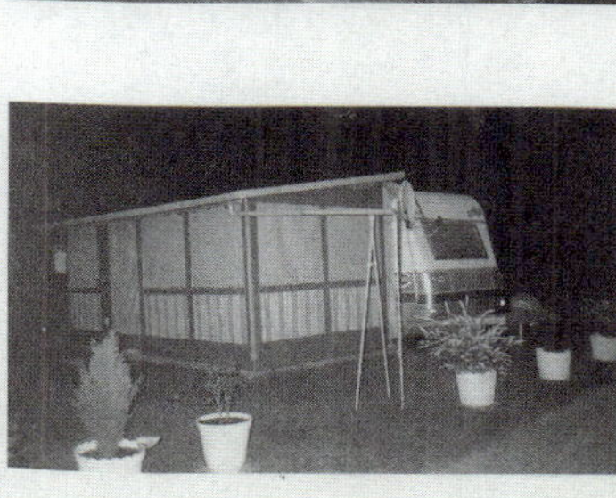

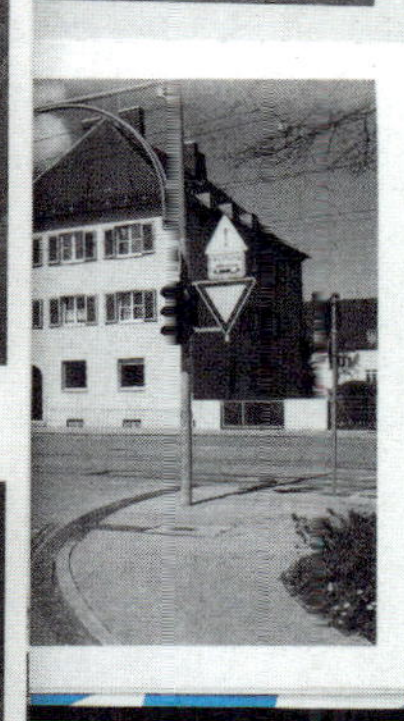

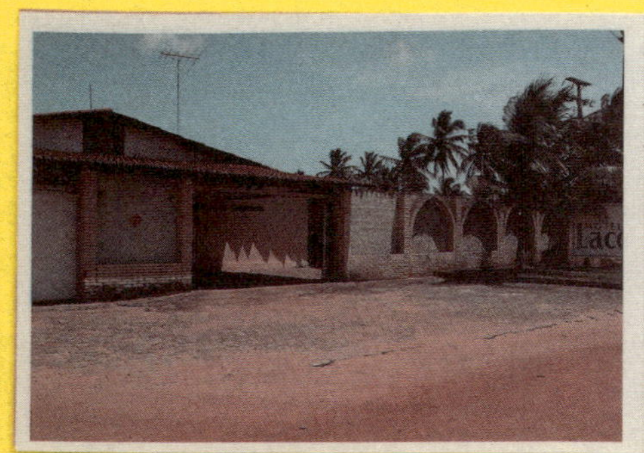
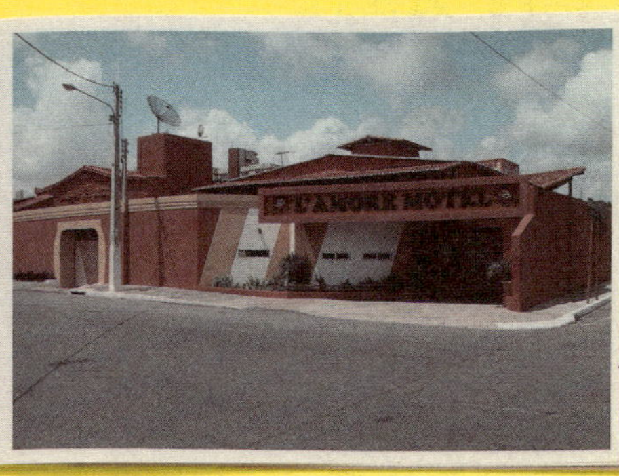
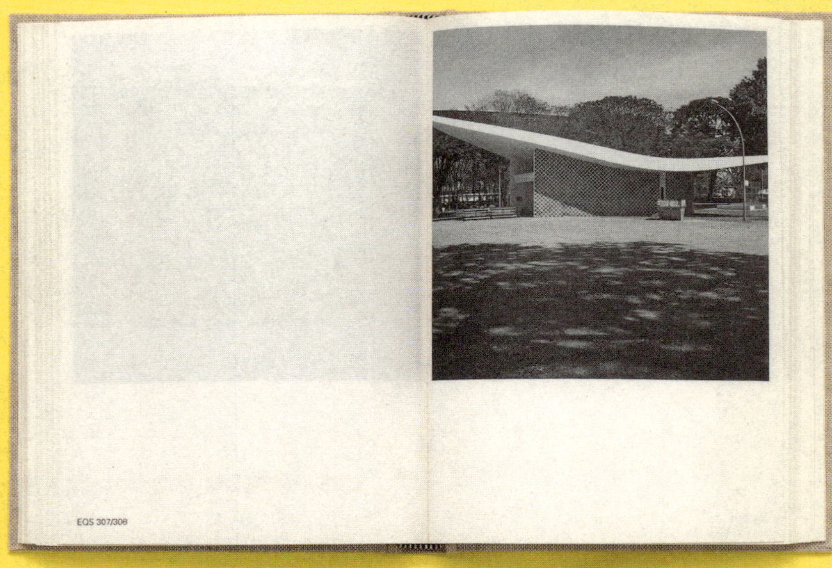
EQS 307/308
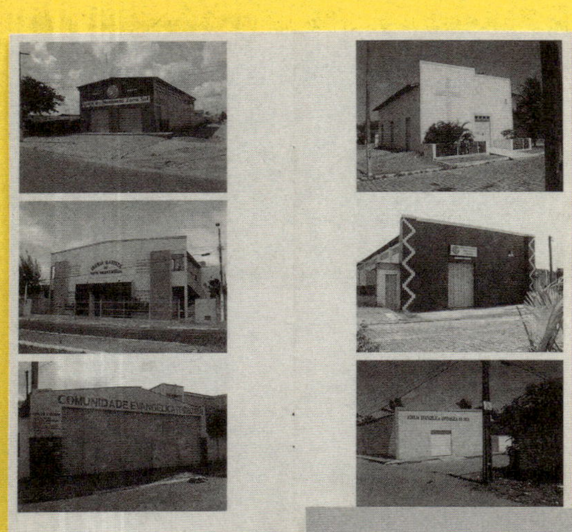
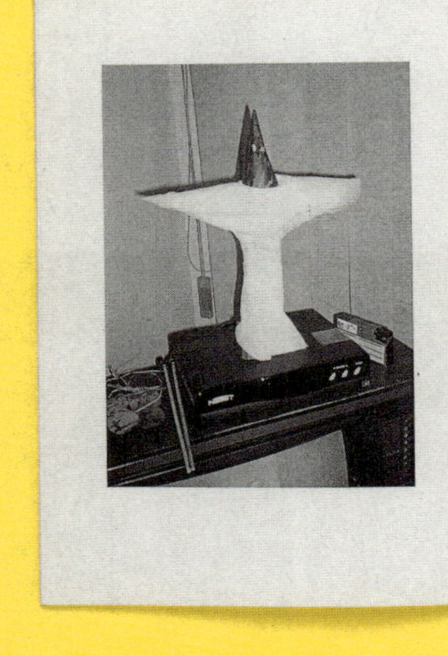

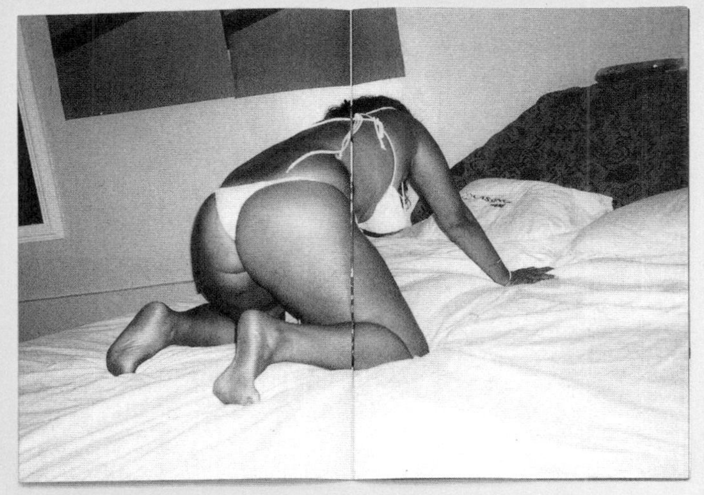

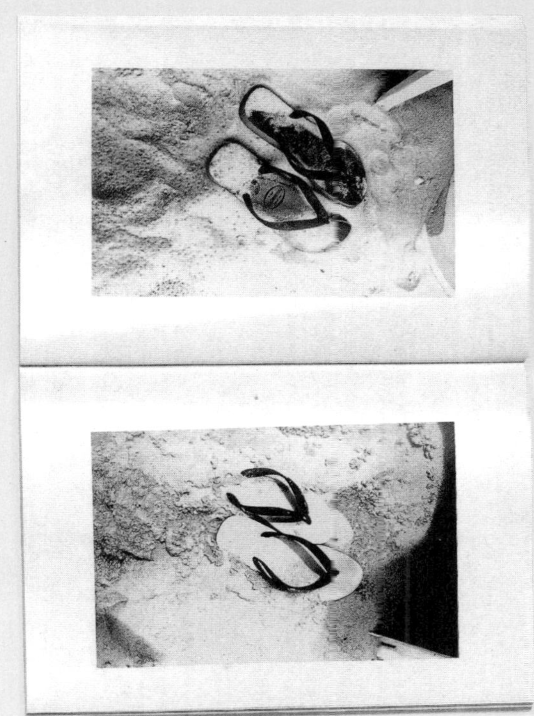

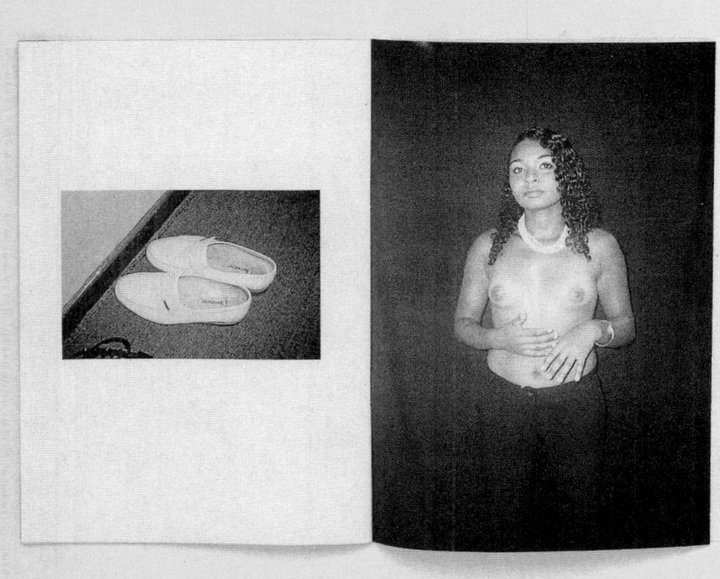

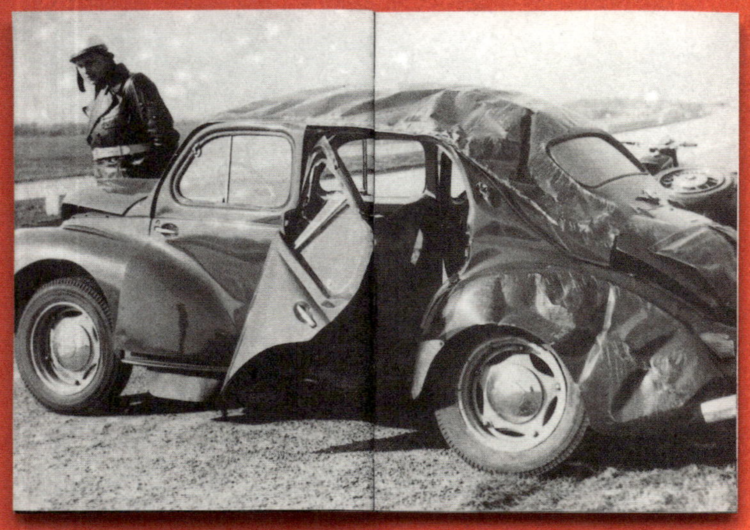

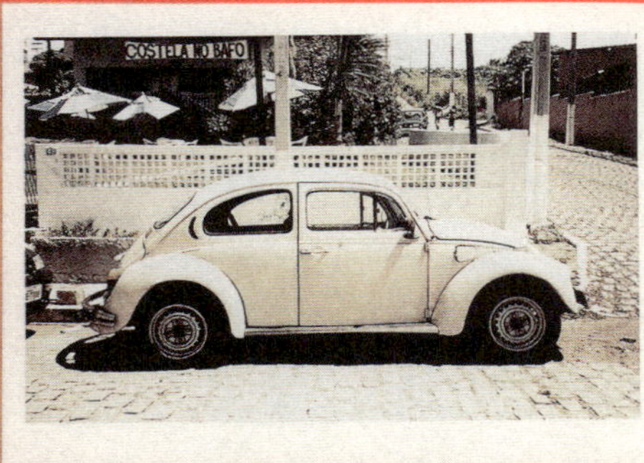

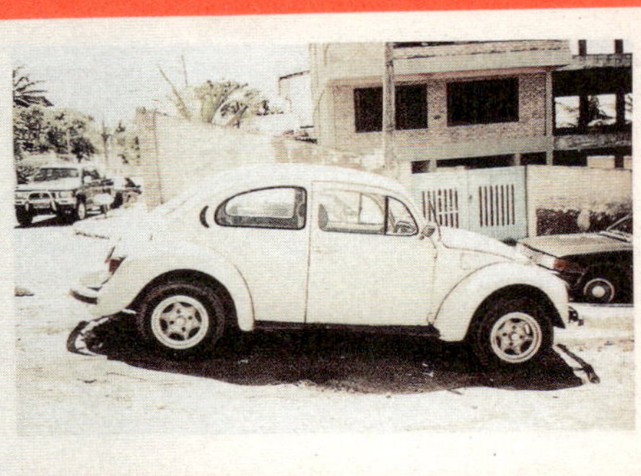

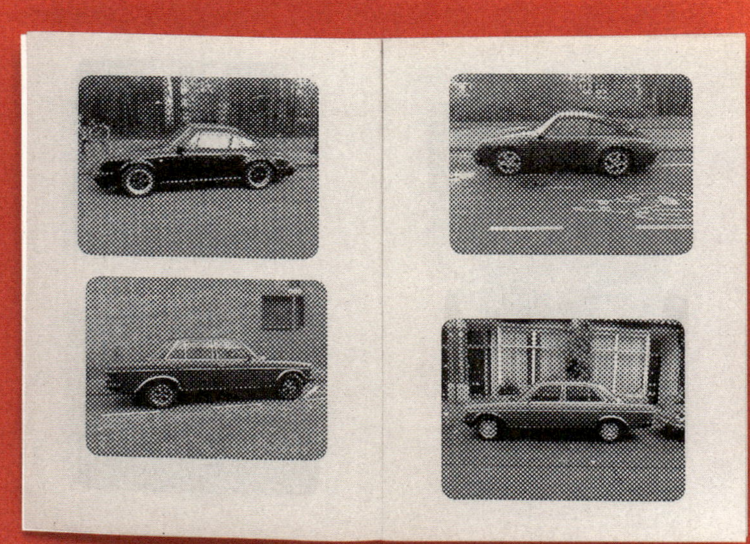

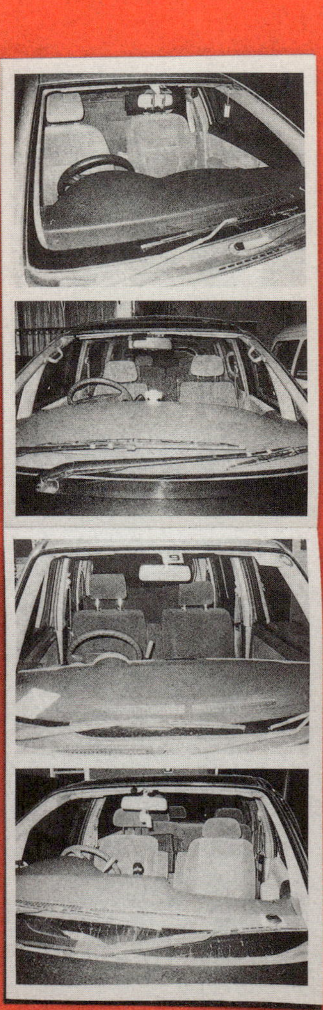

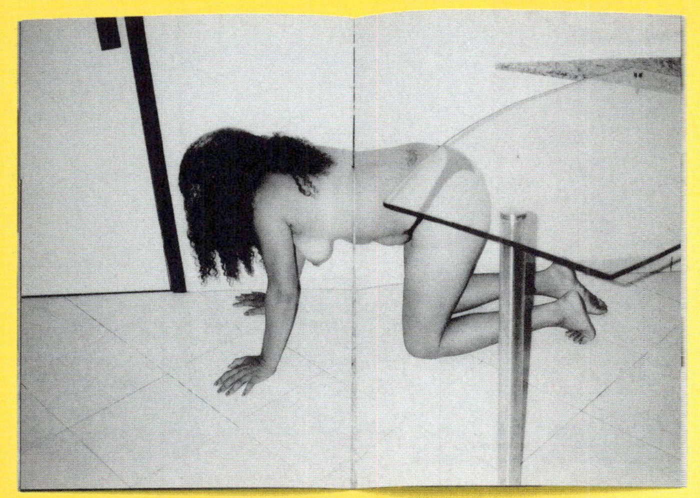
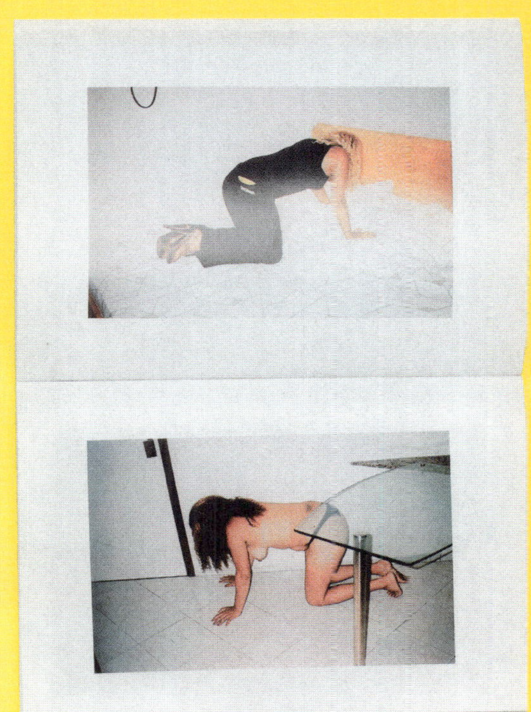
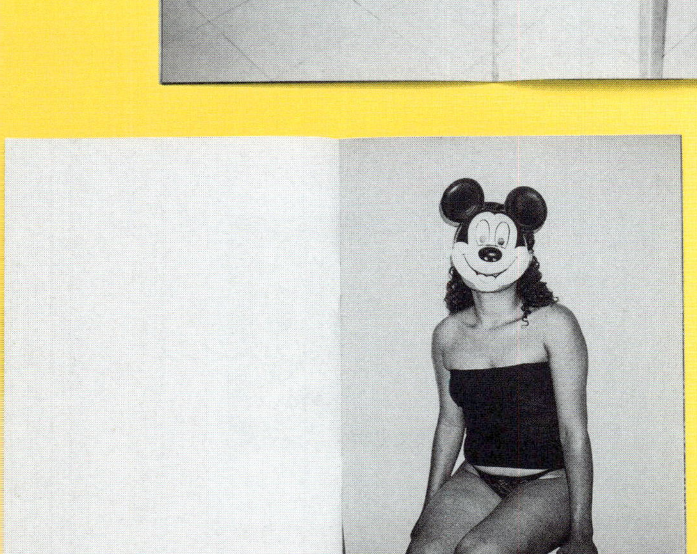
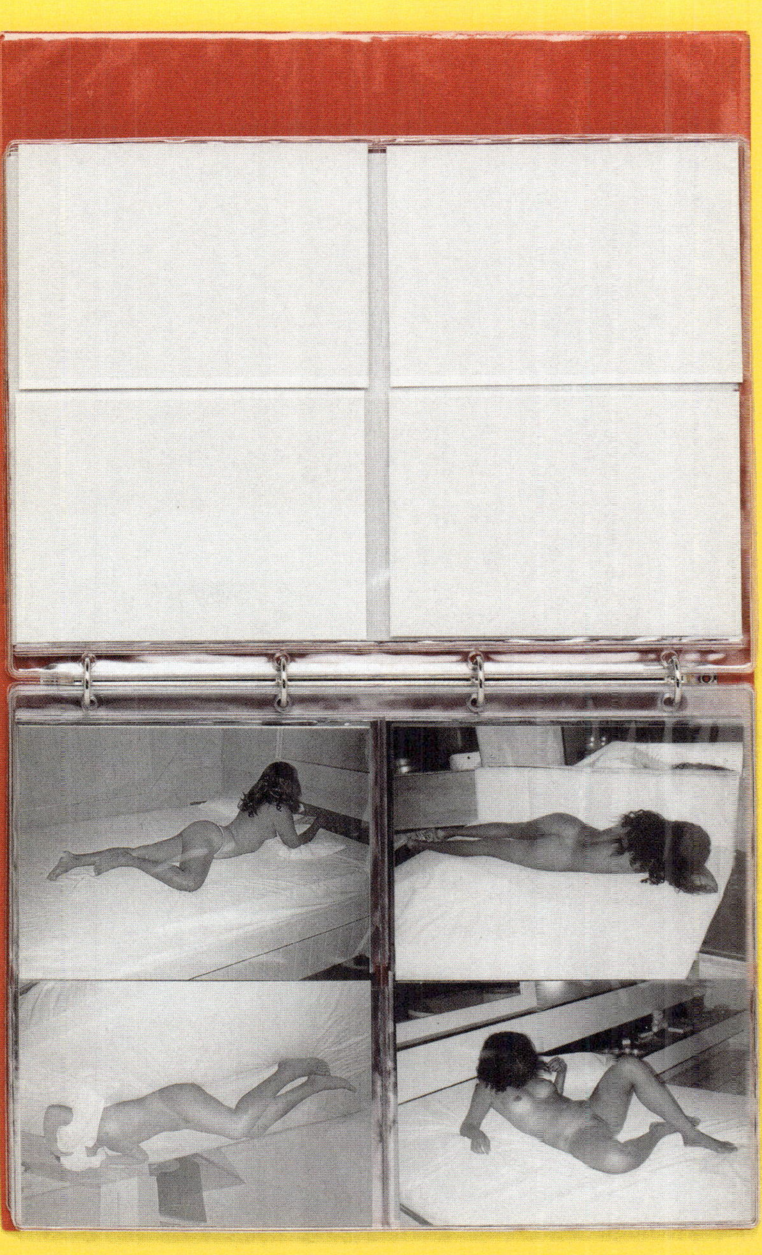
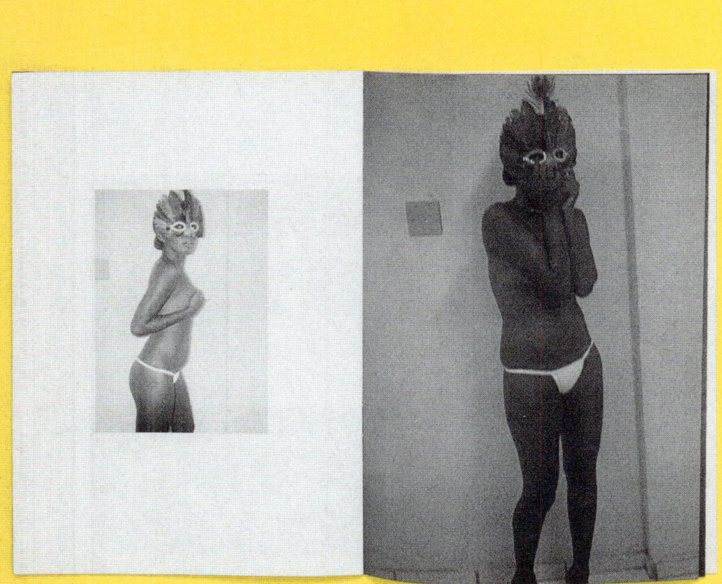

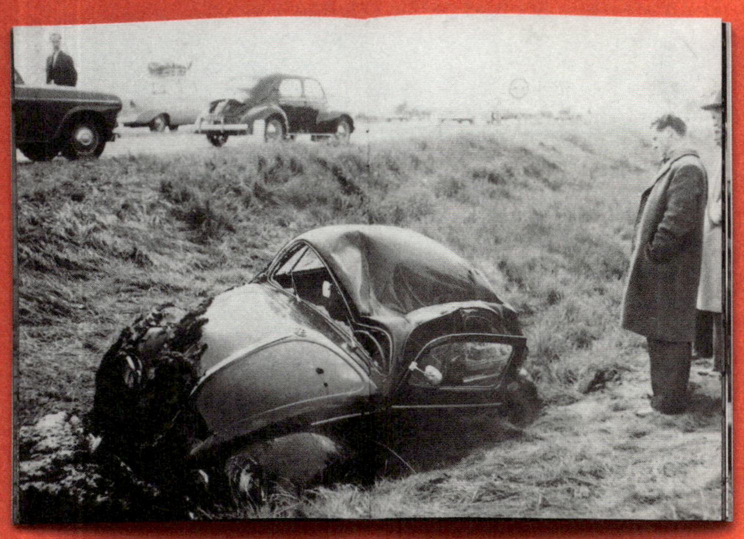
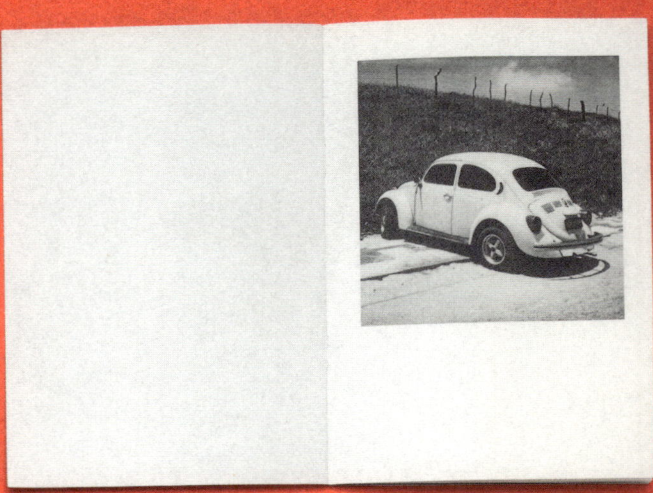
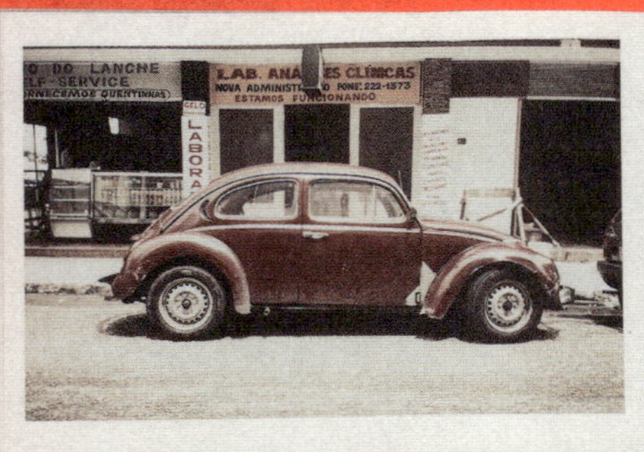
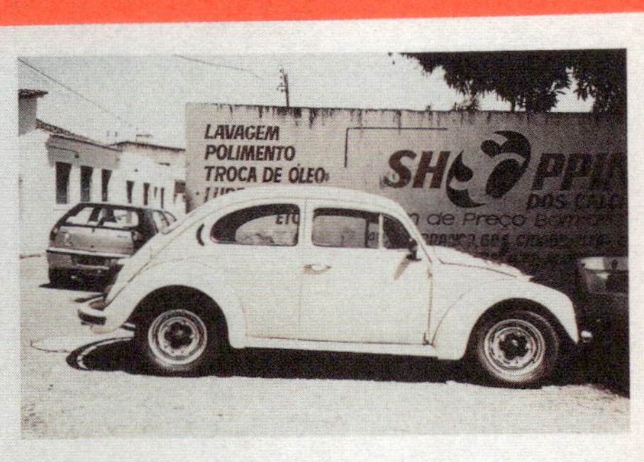
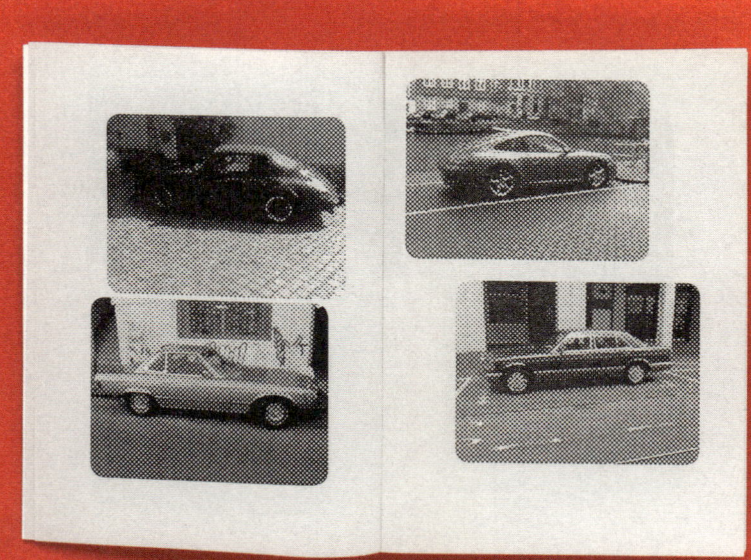
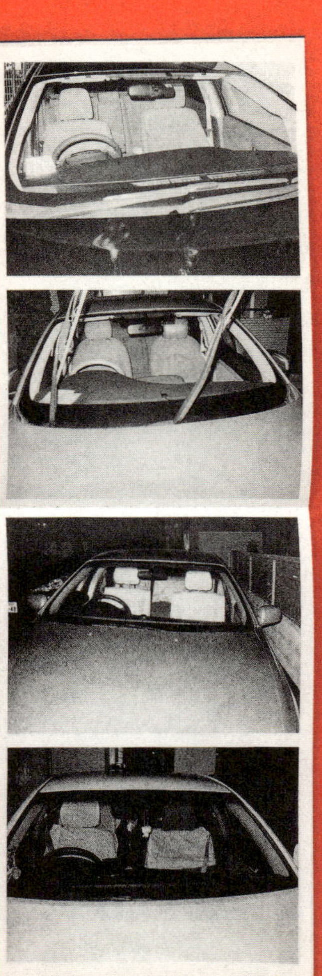

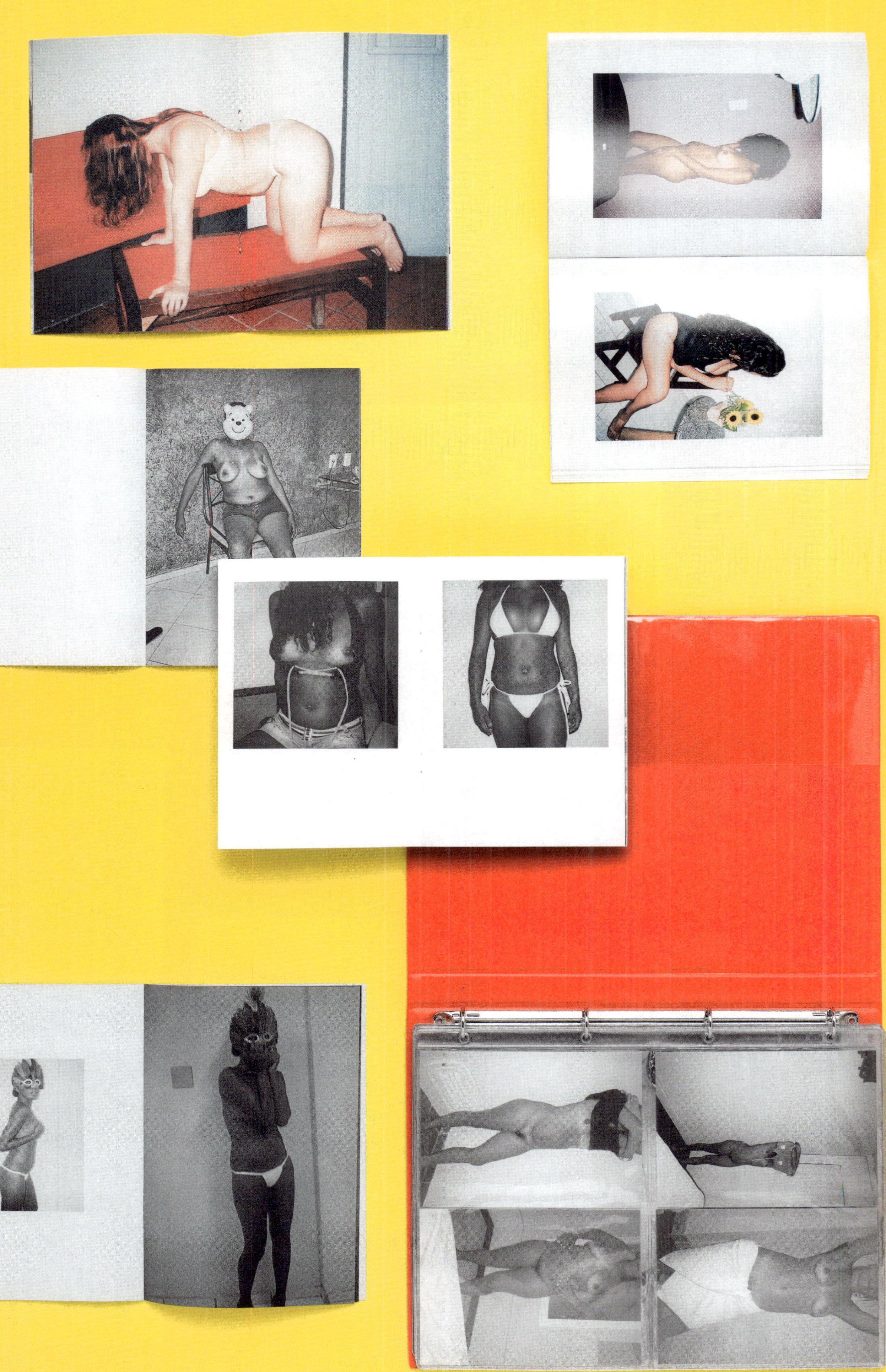

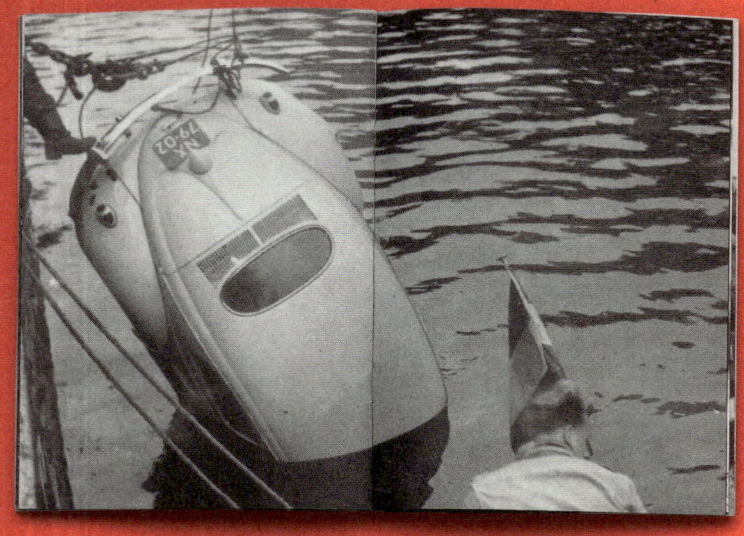
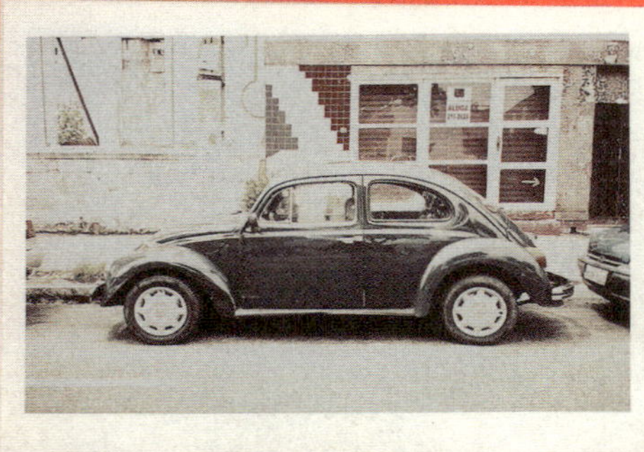
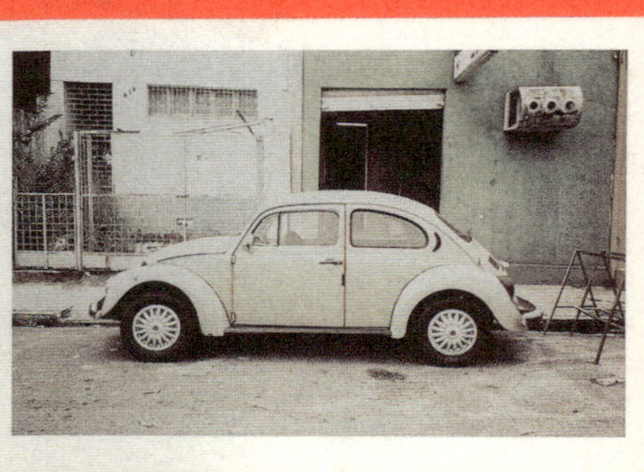
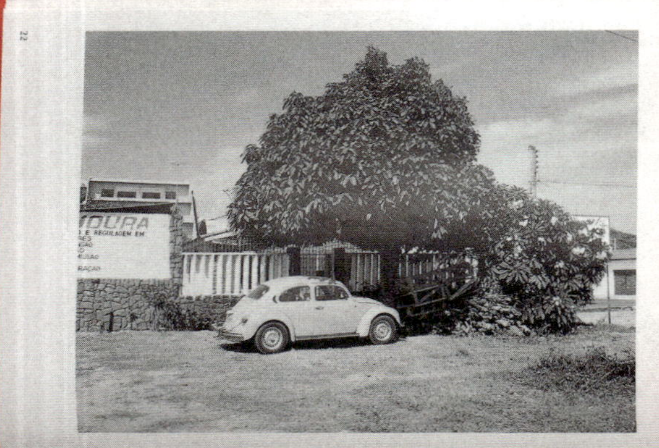
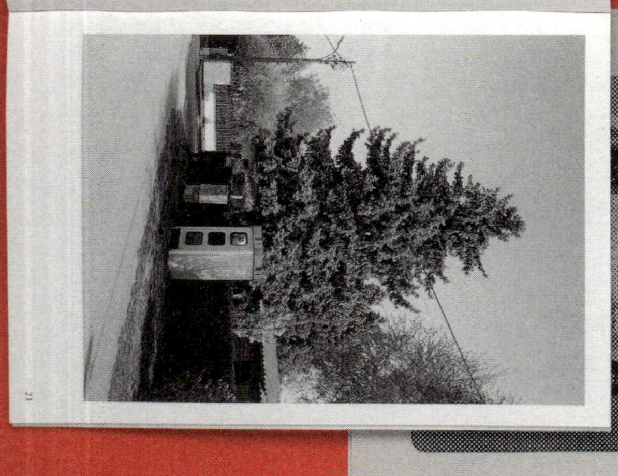
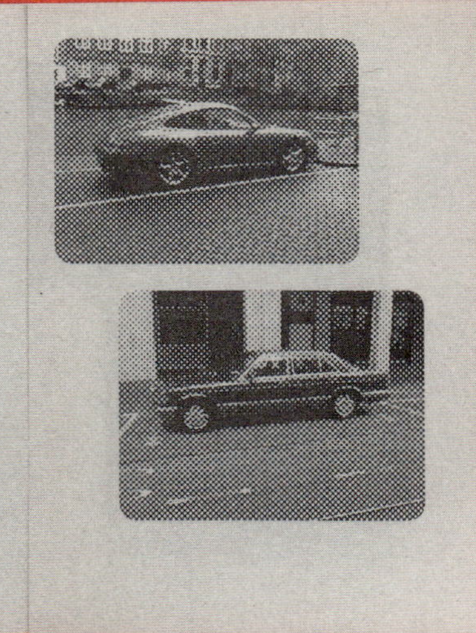
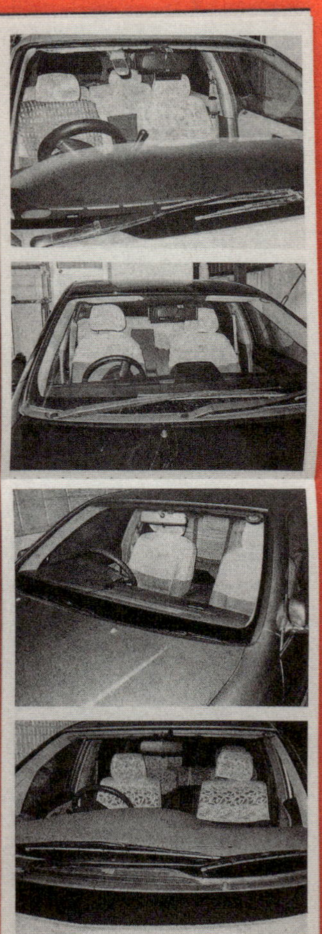

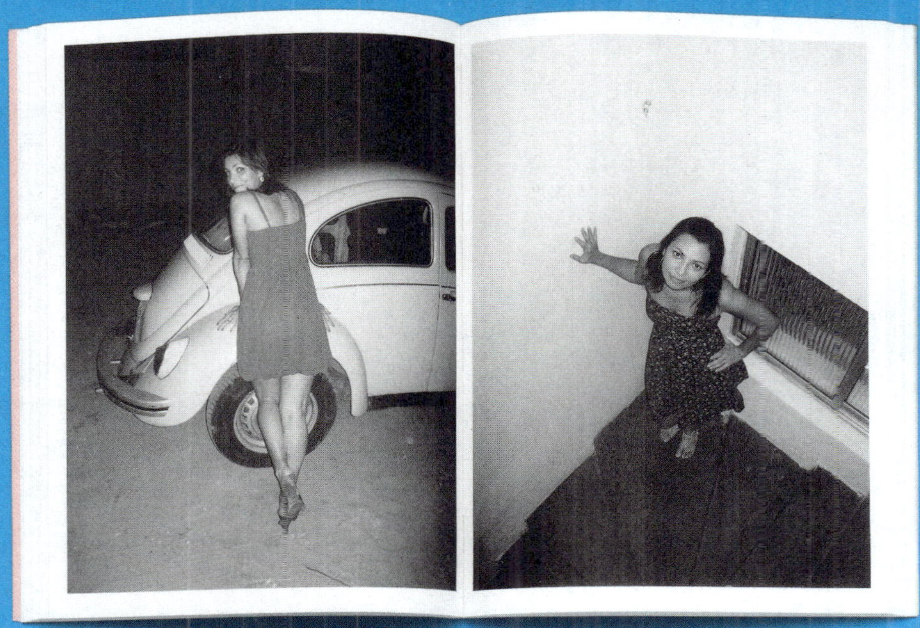

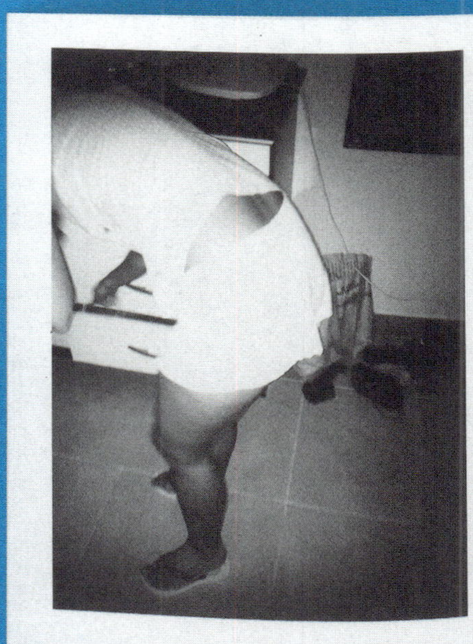

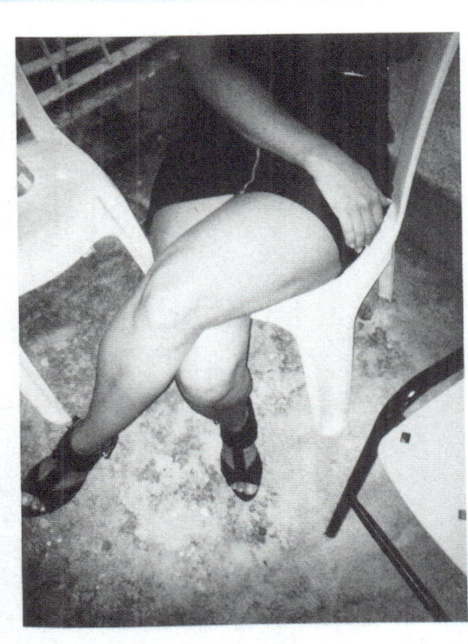

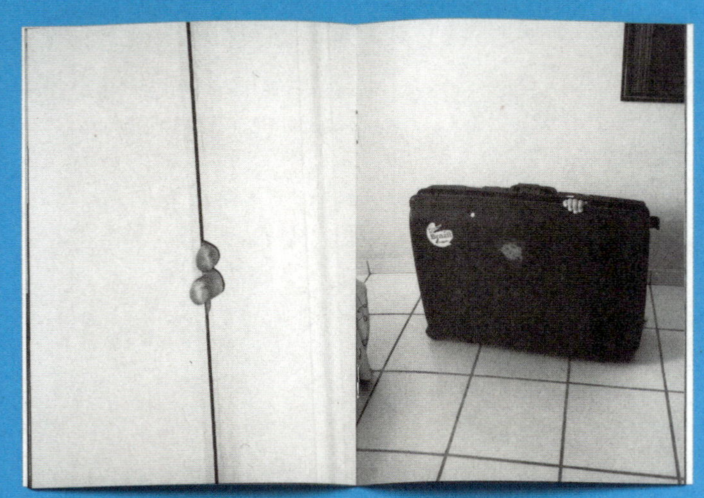
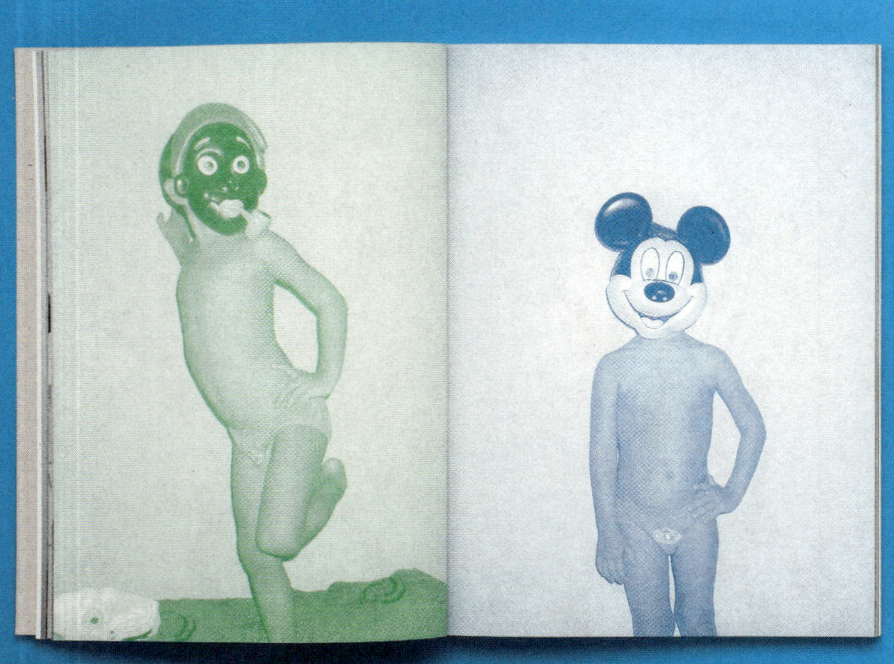
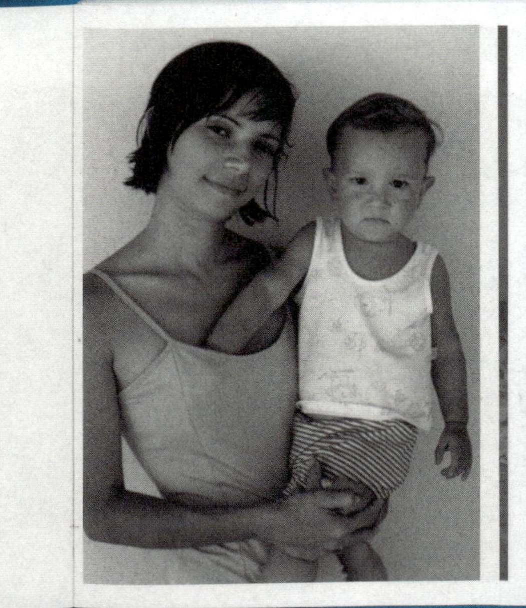
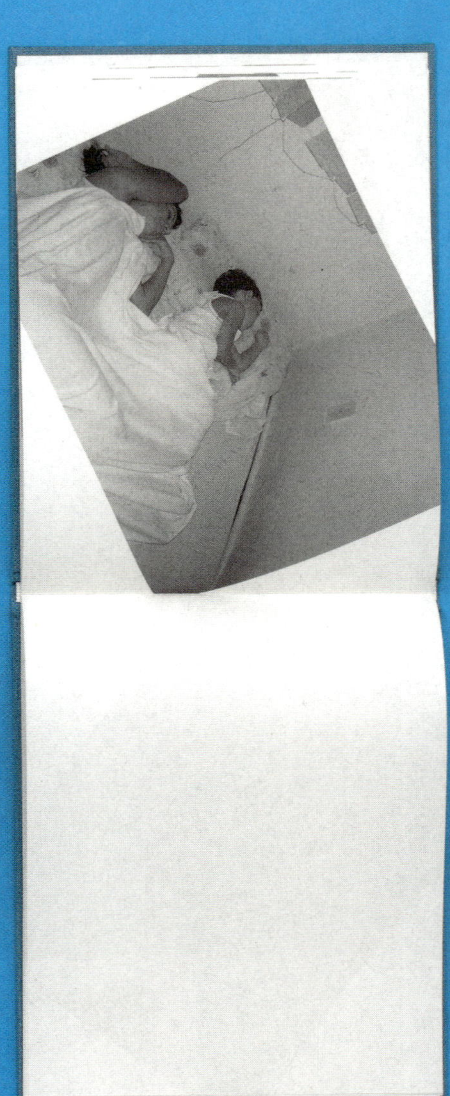

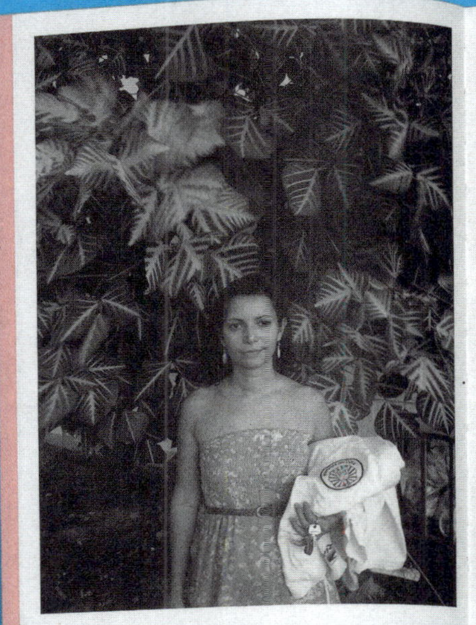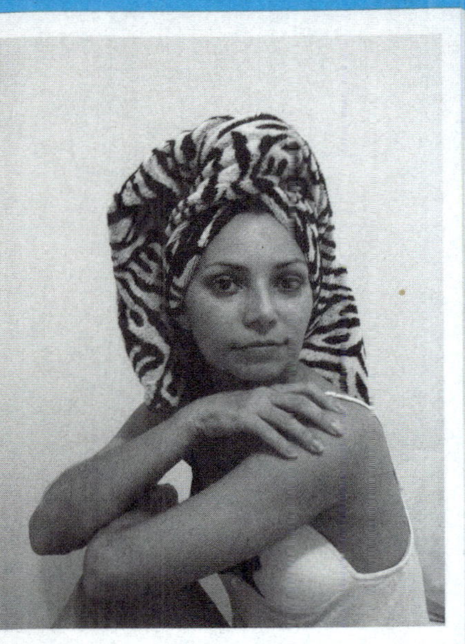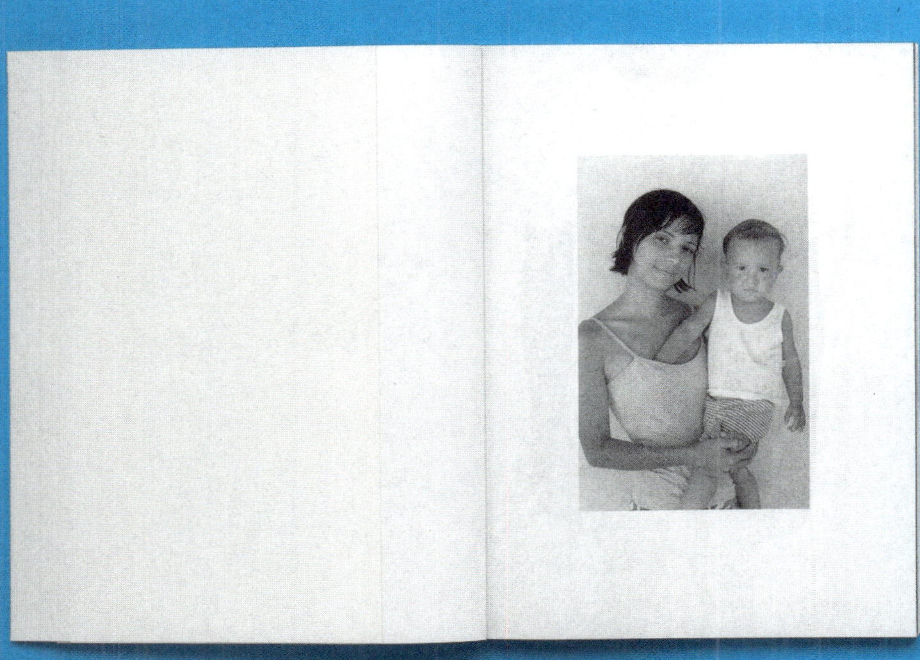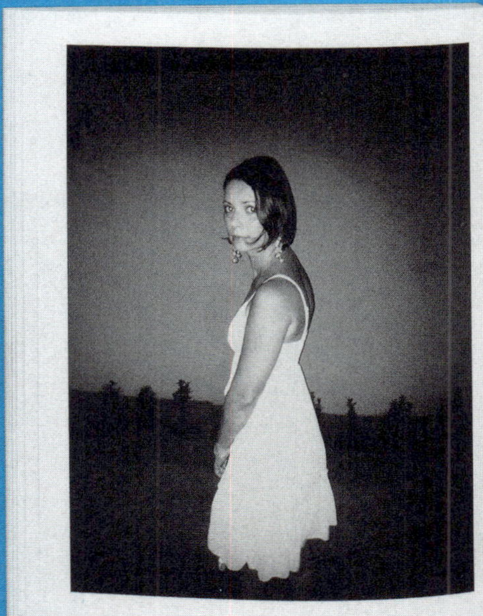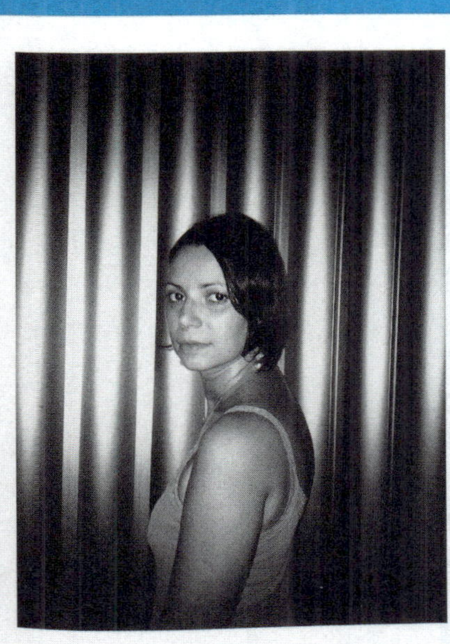

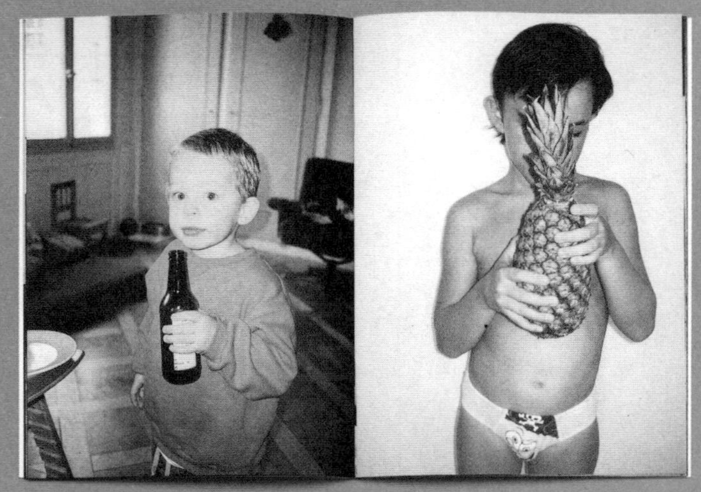

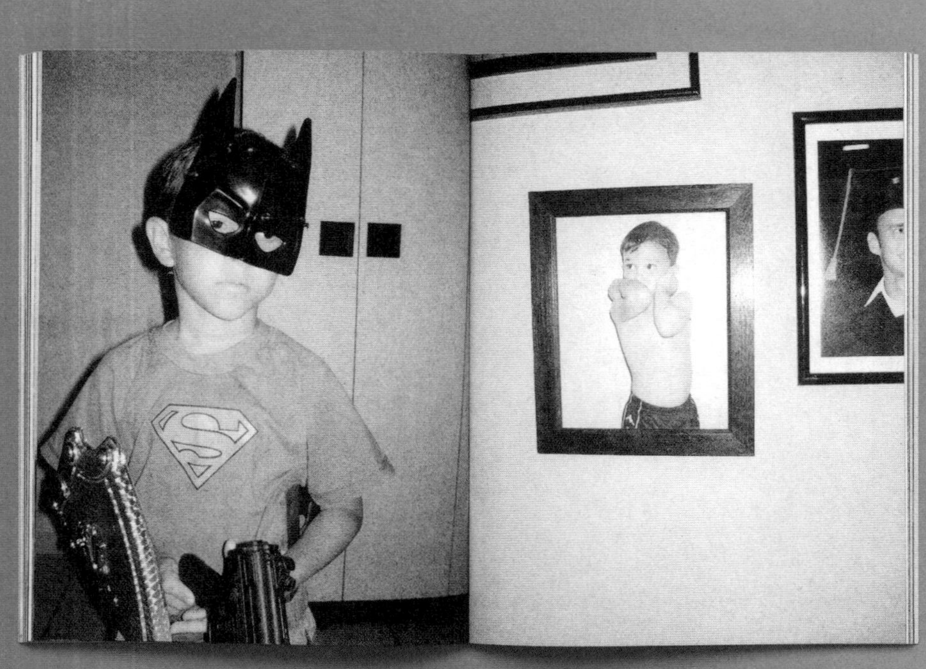

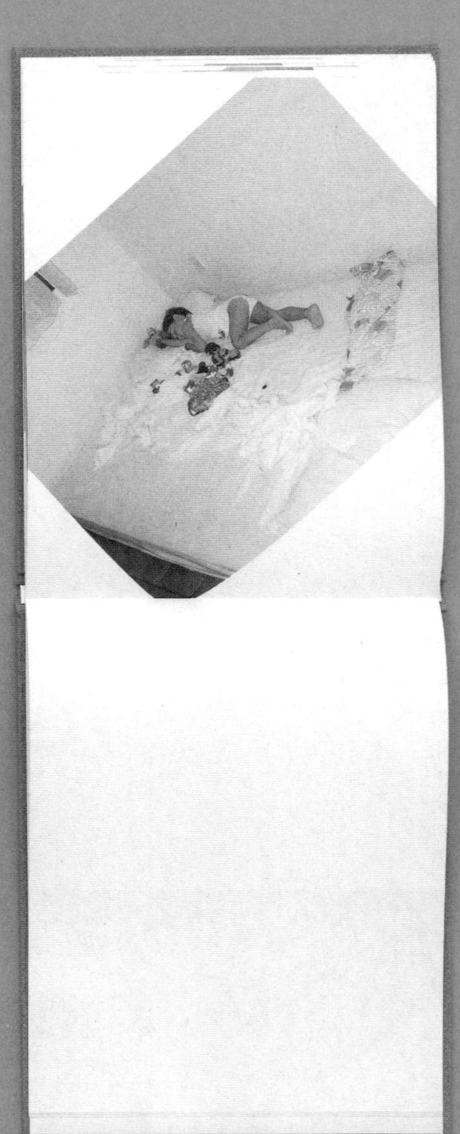

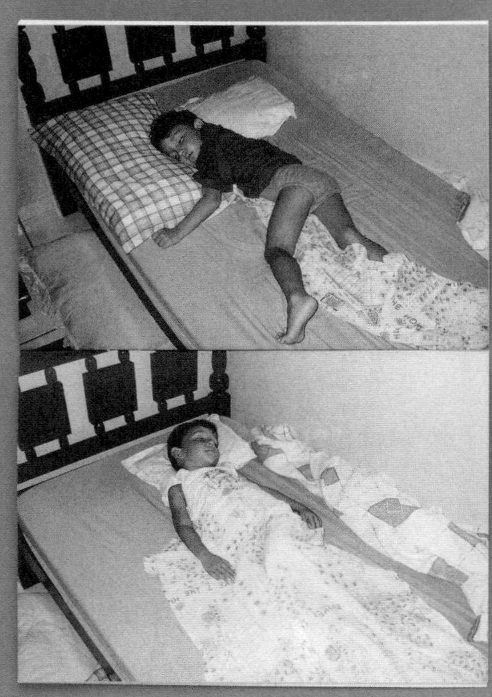

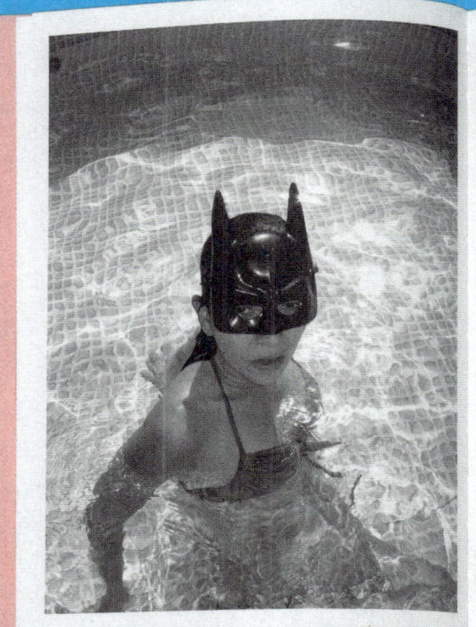
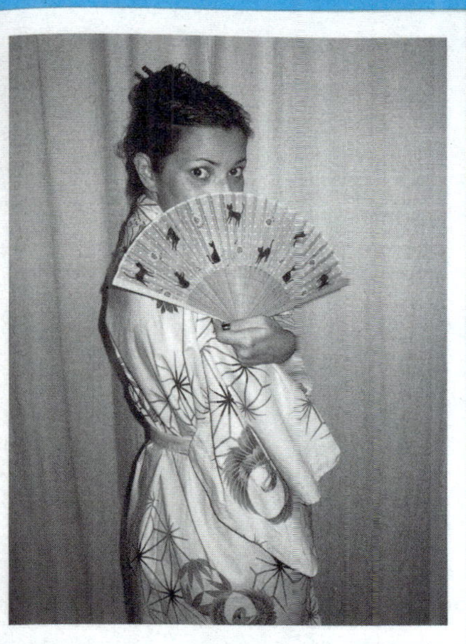
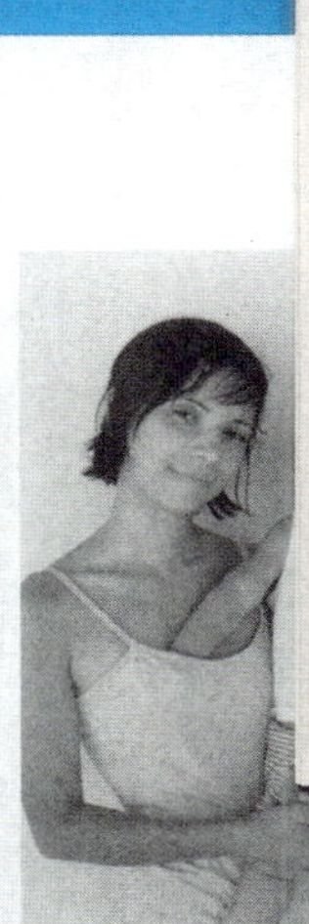
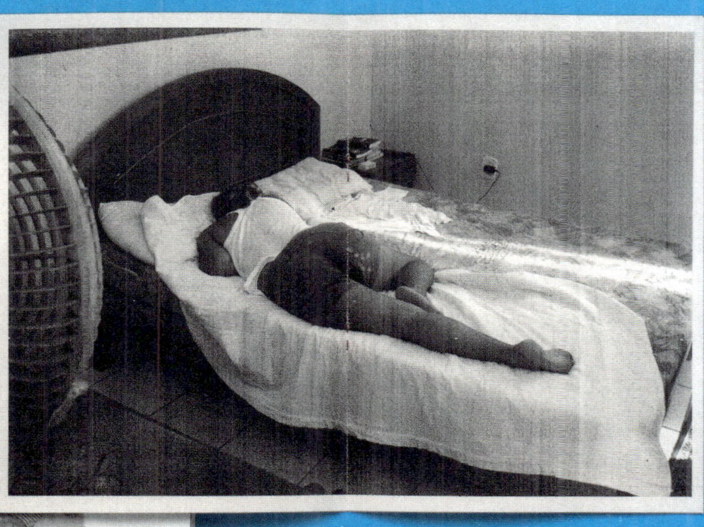
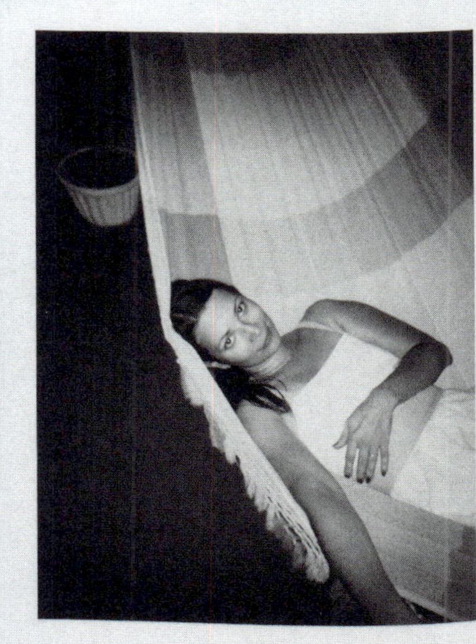
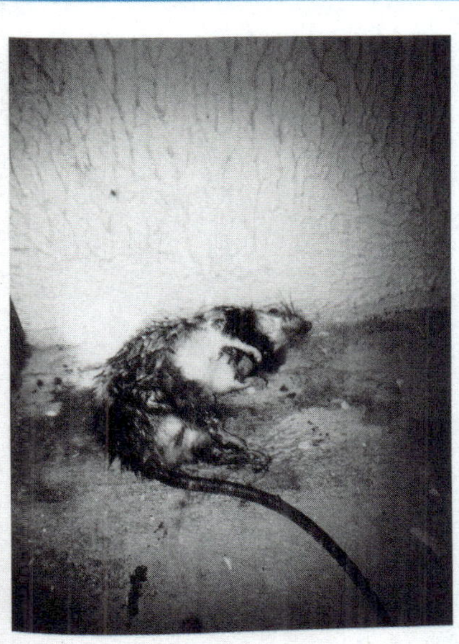

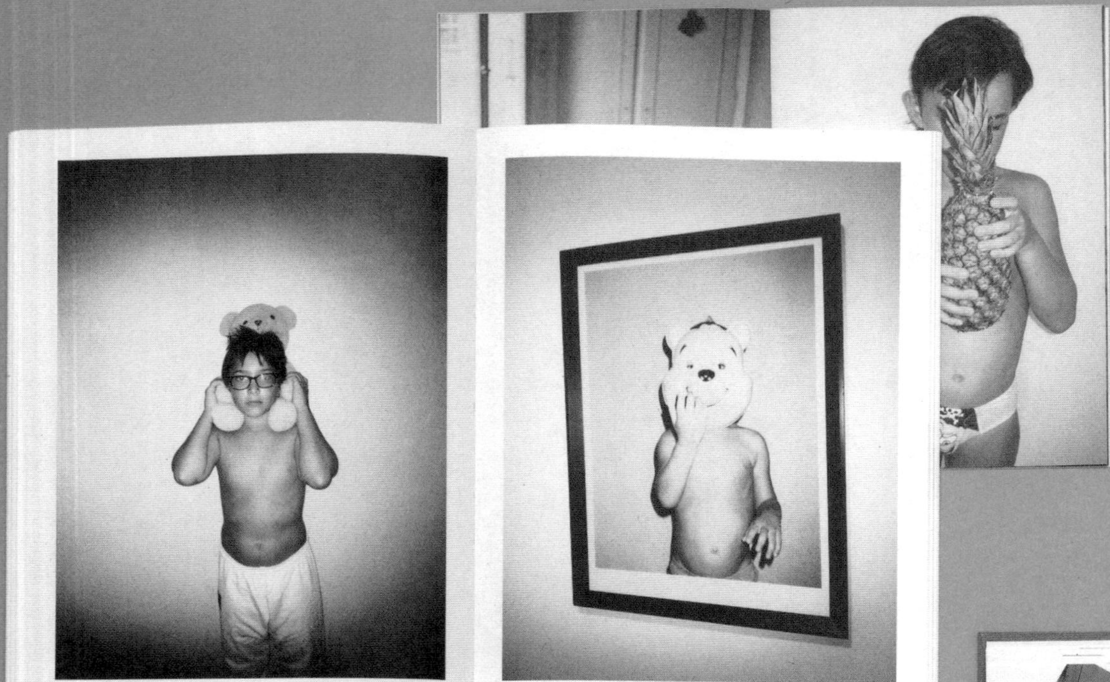

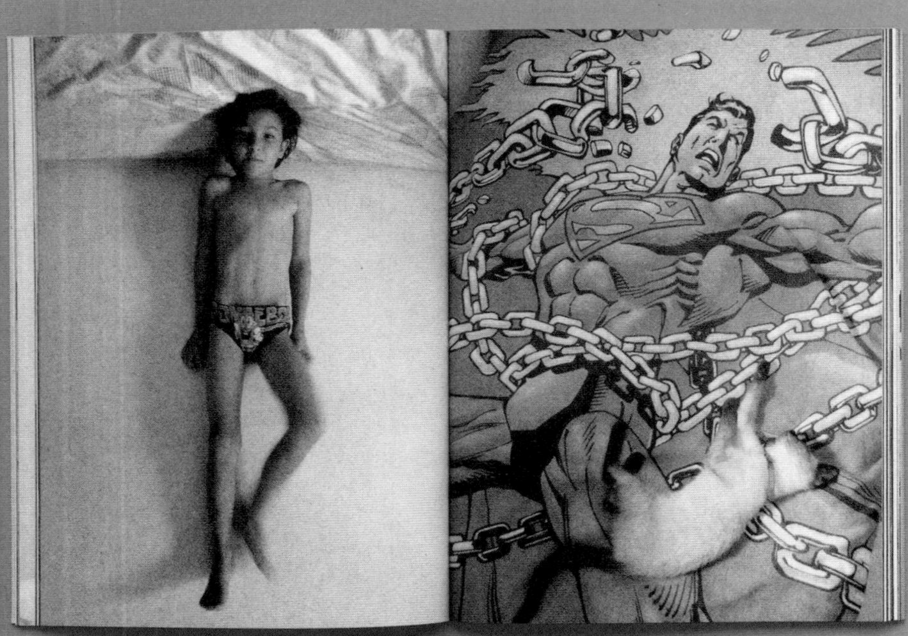

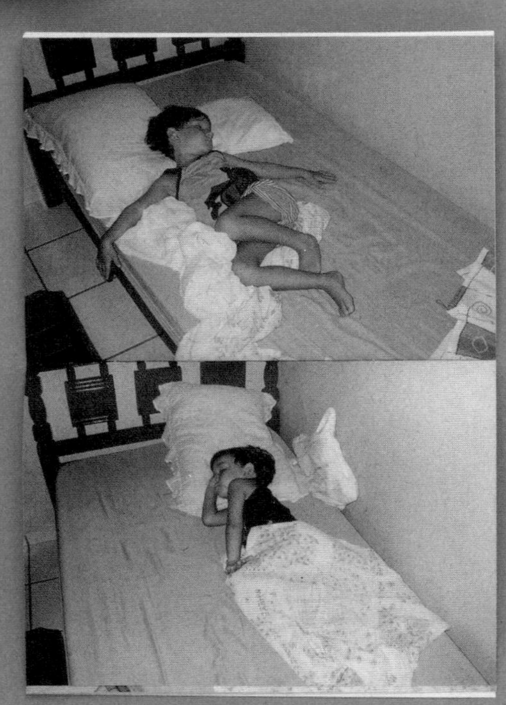

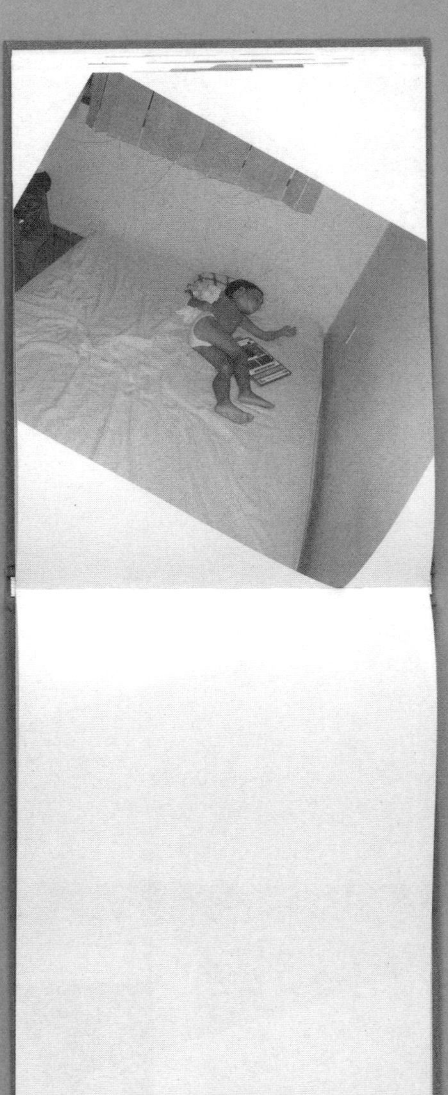

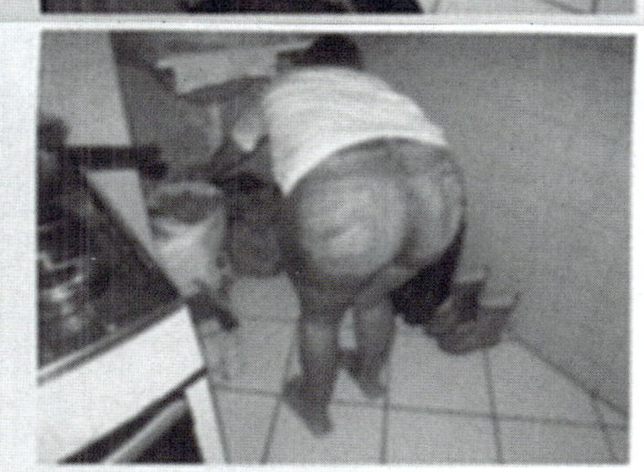

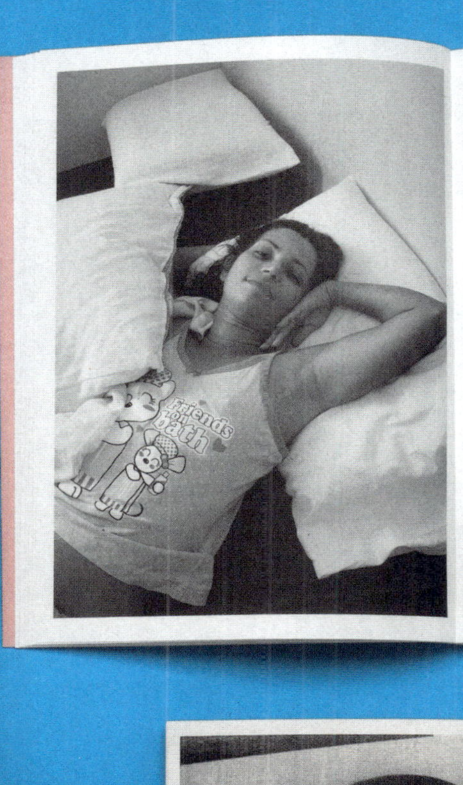

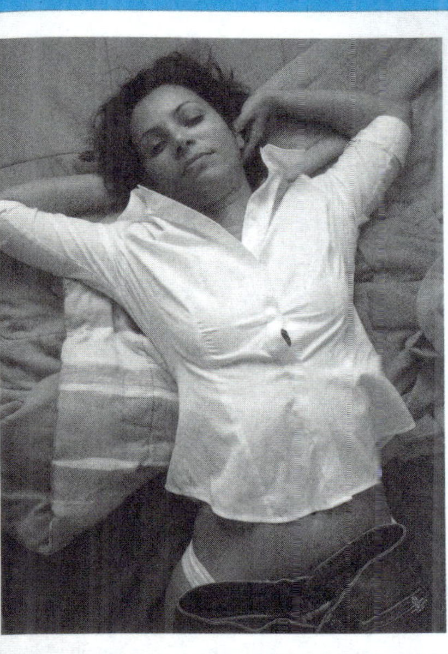

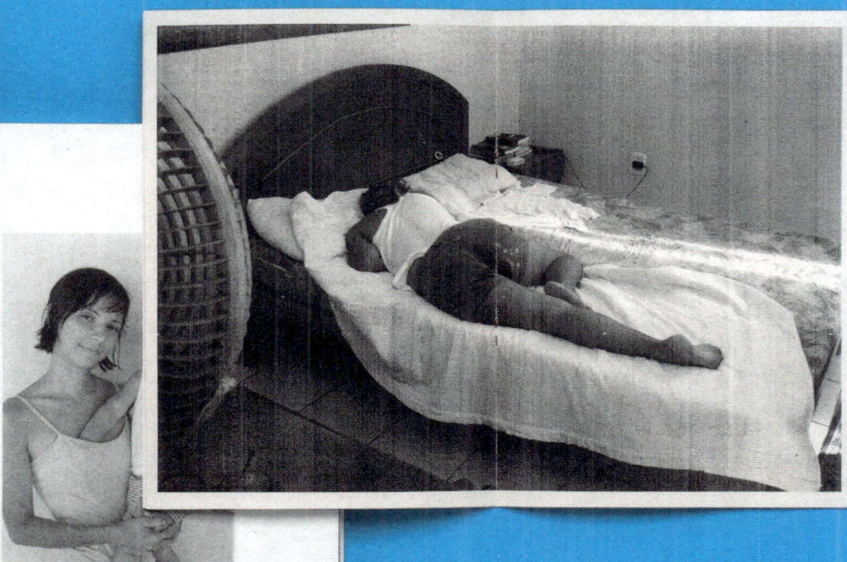

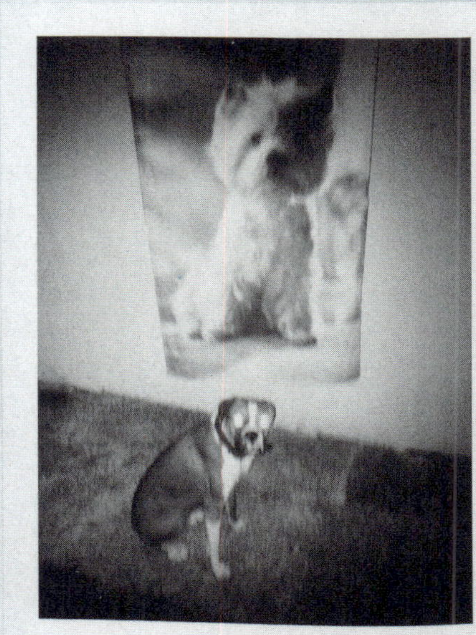

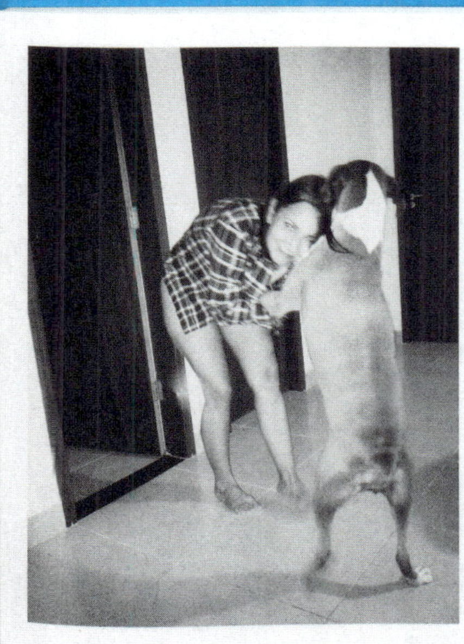

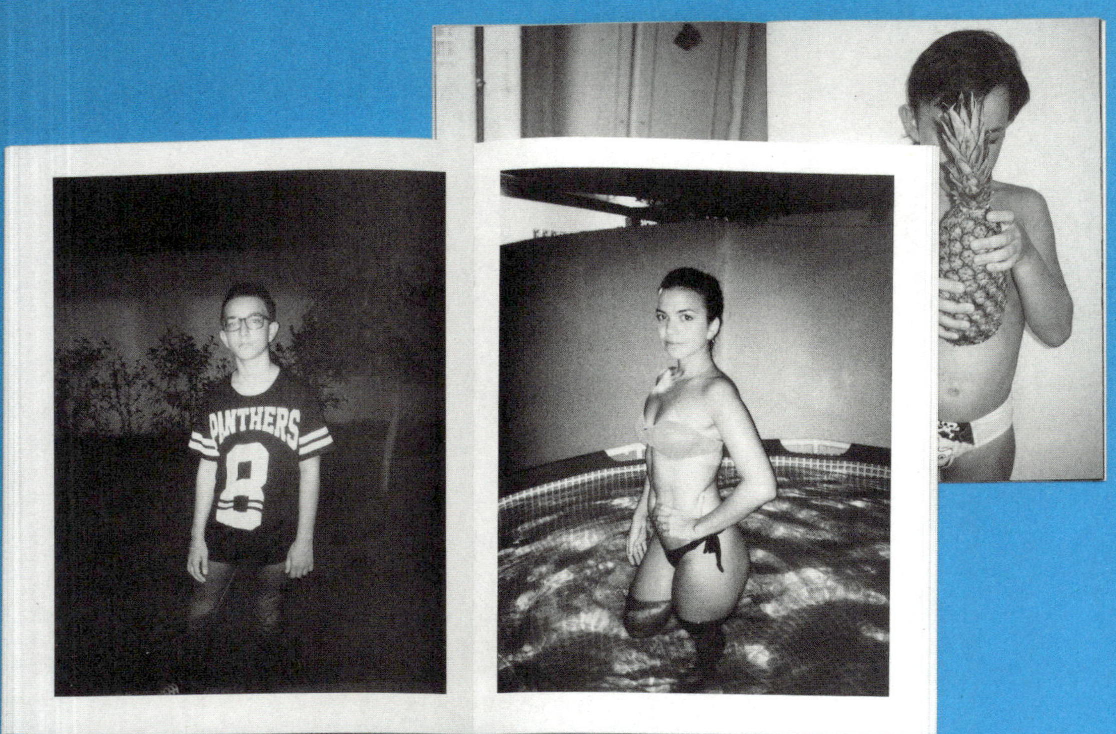
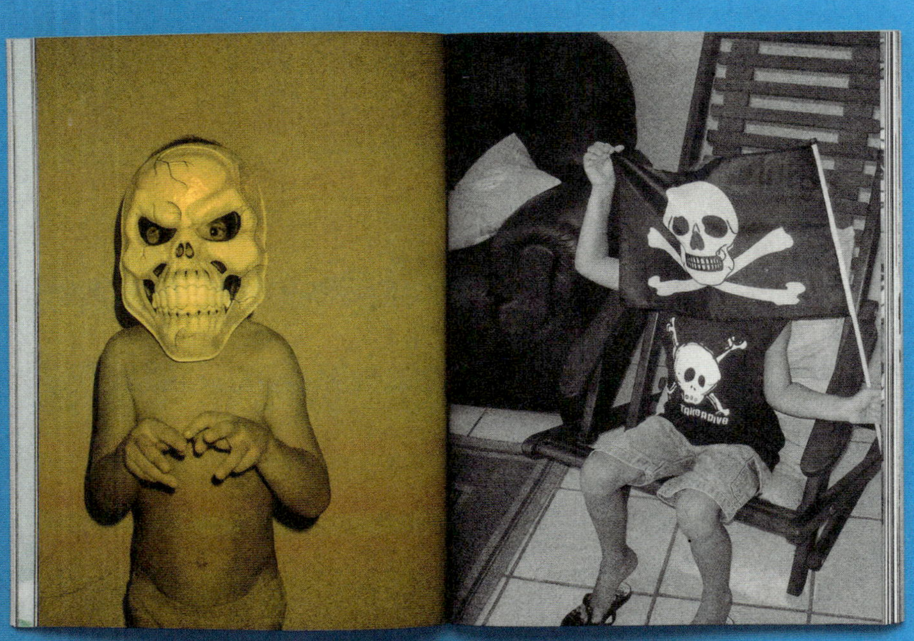
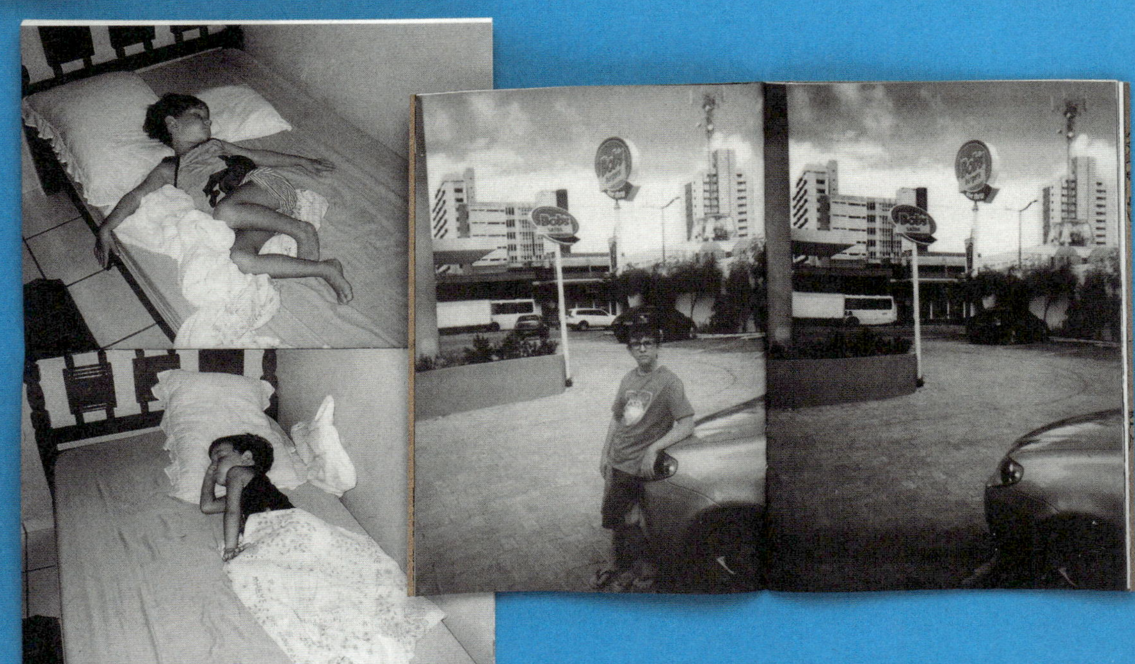

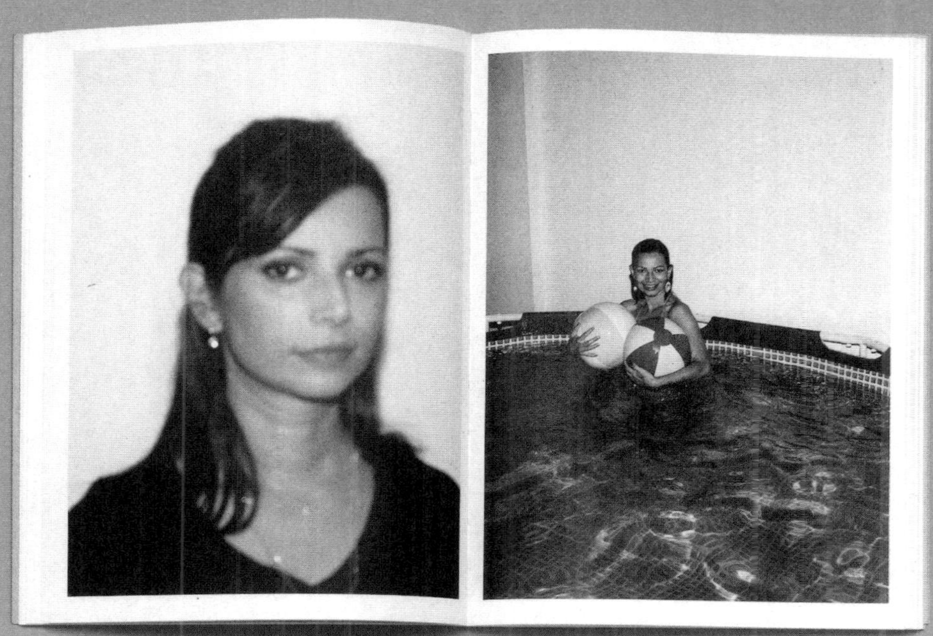

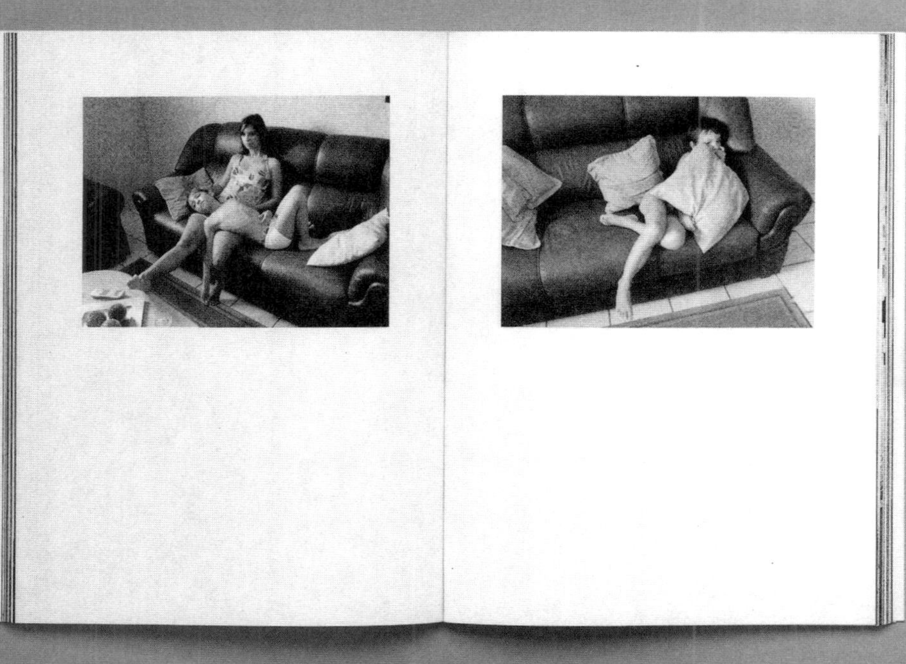

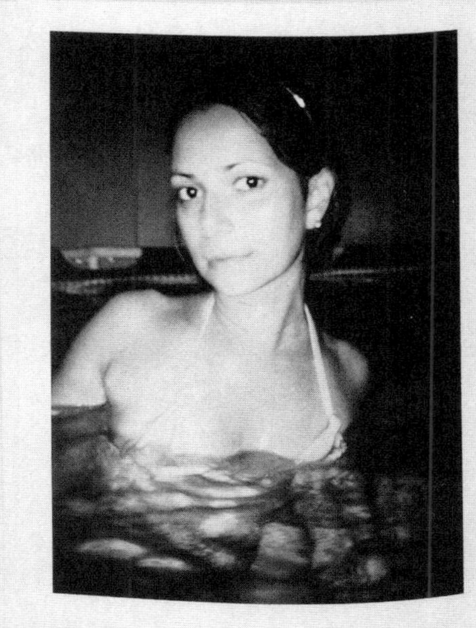

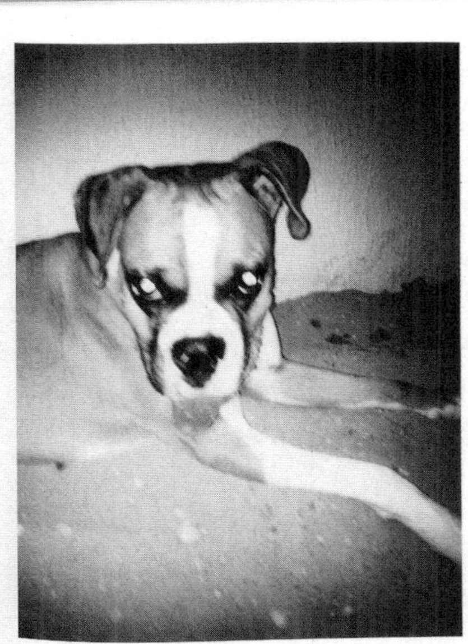

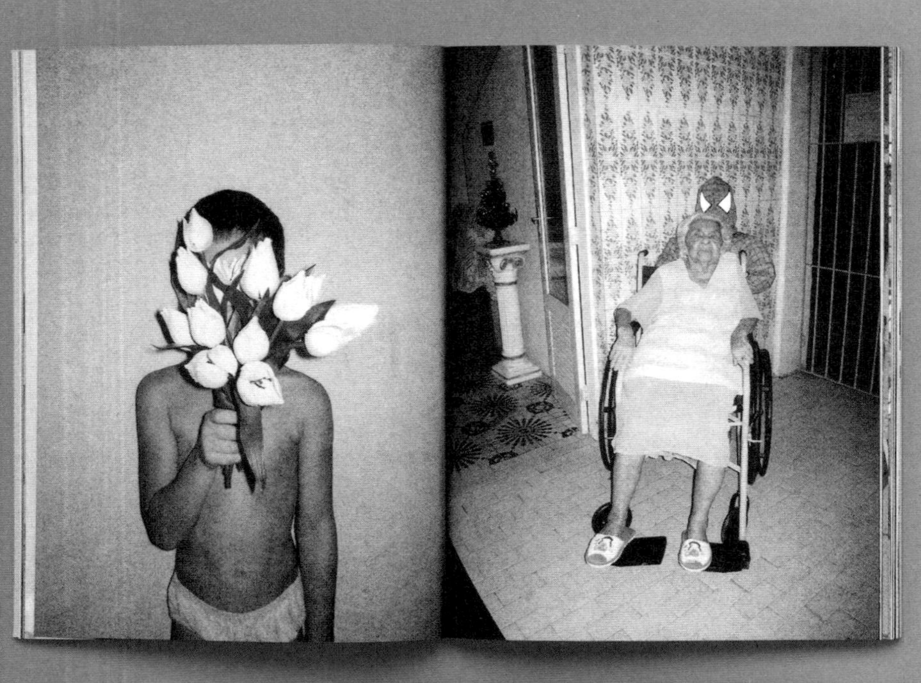
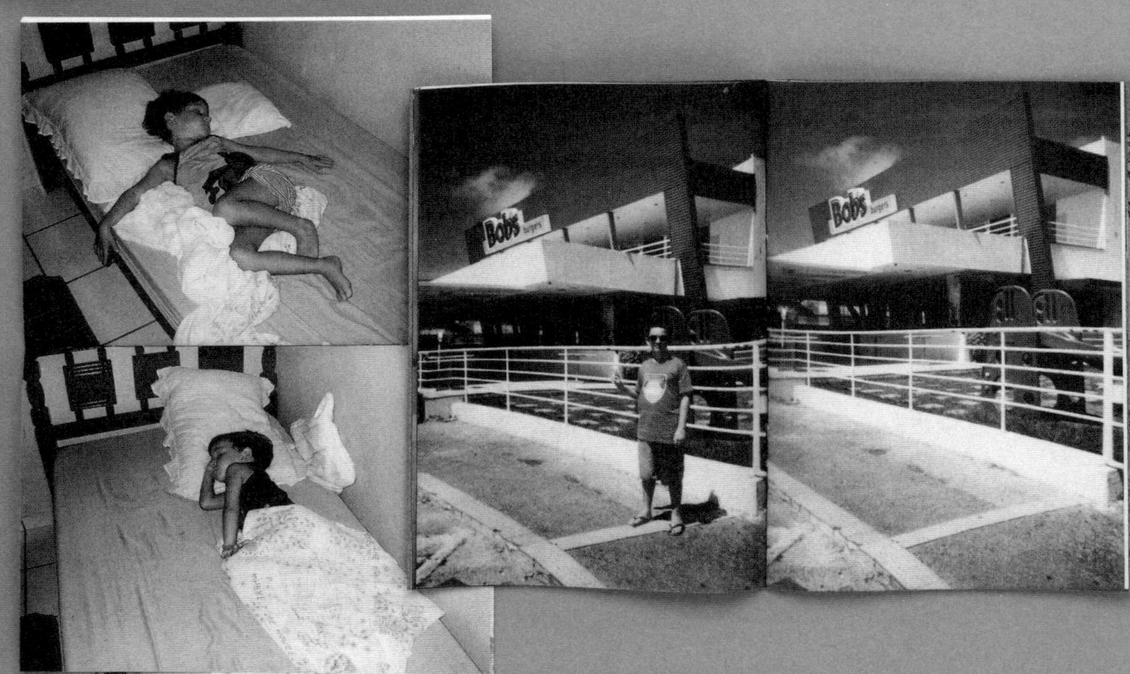

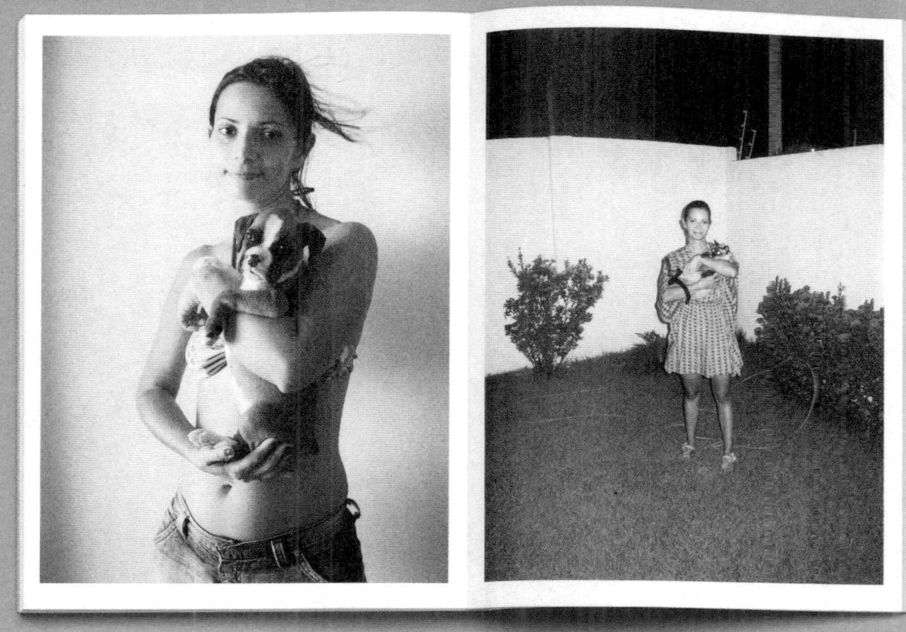

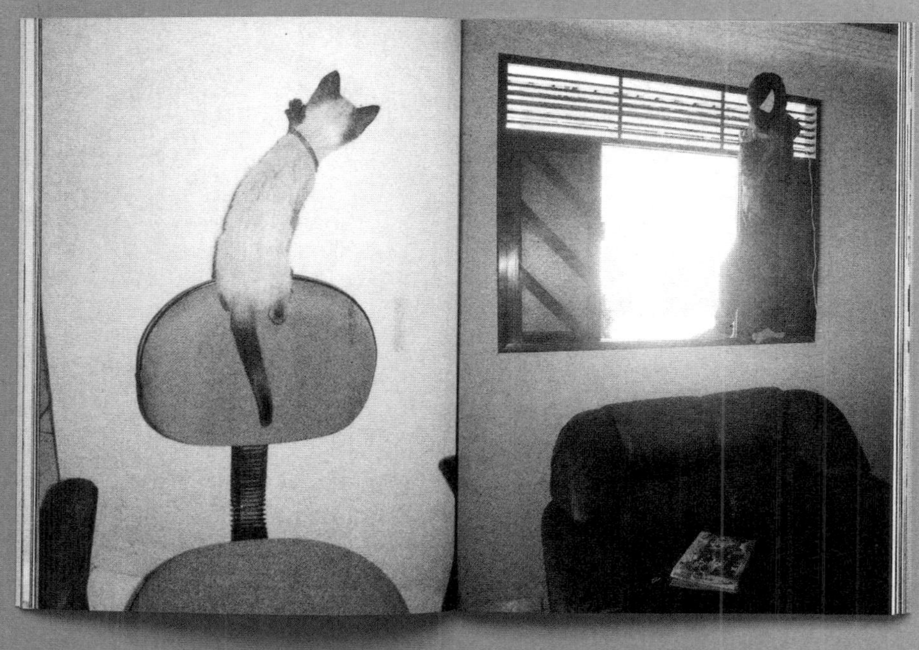

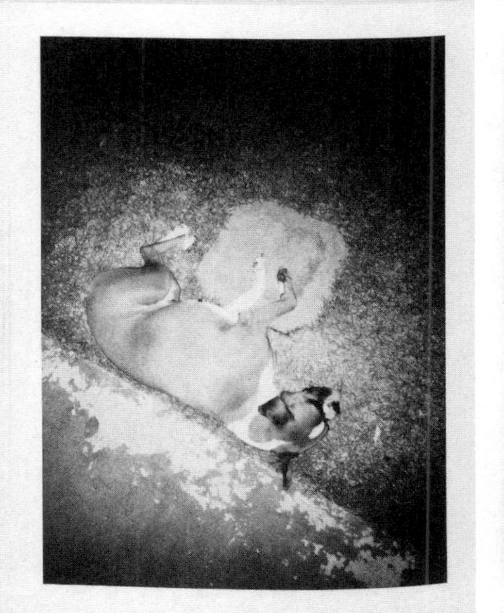

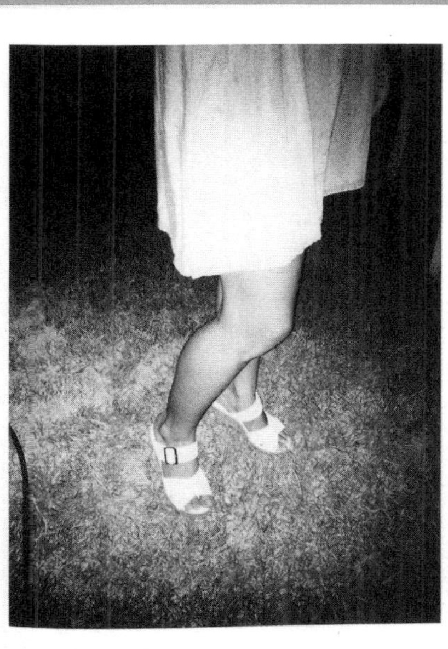

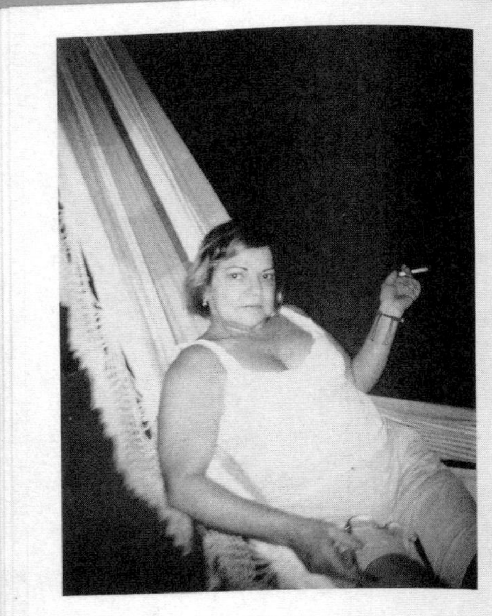
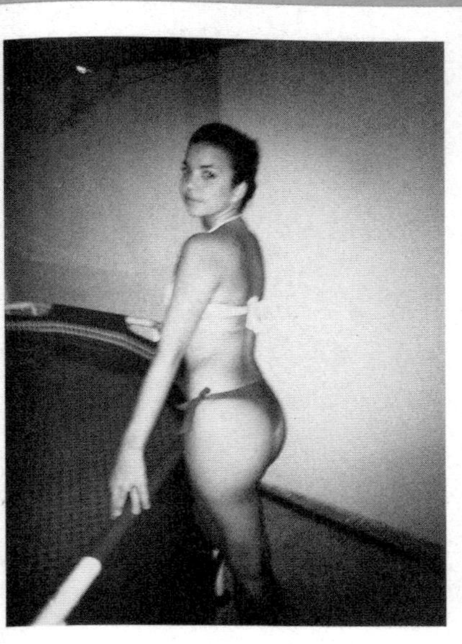
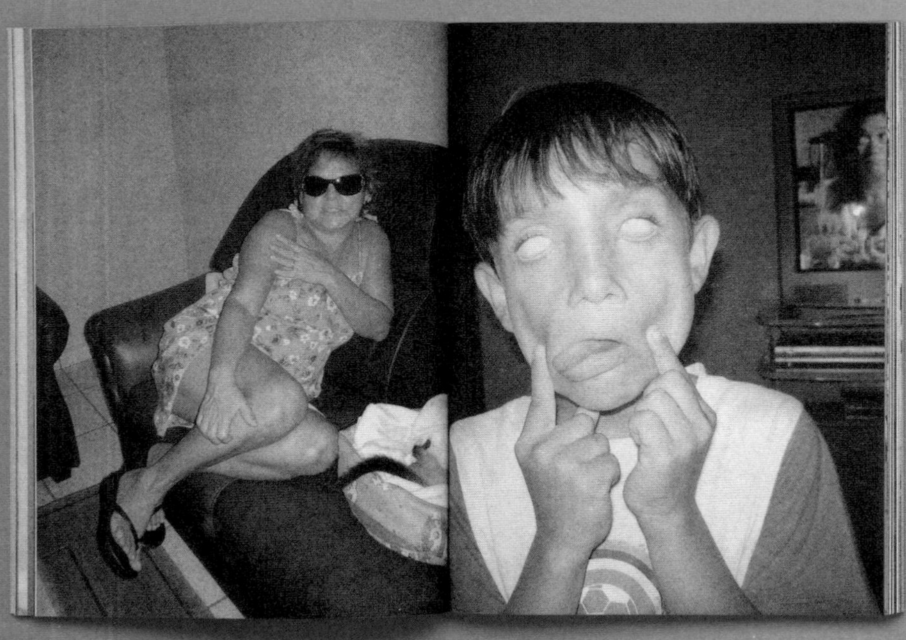
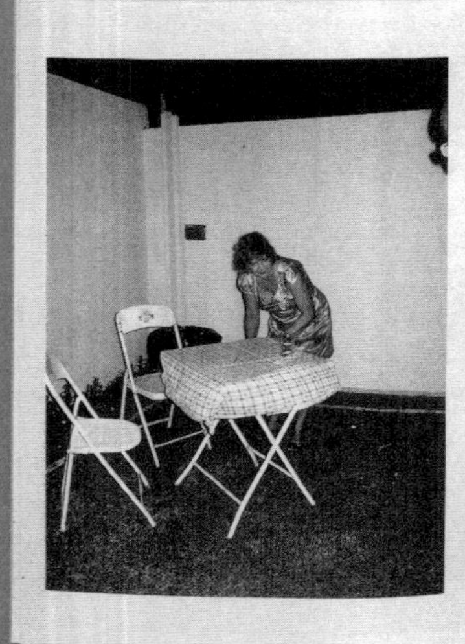
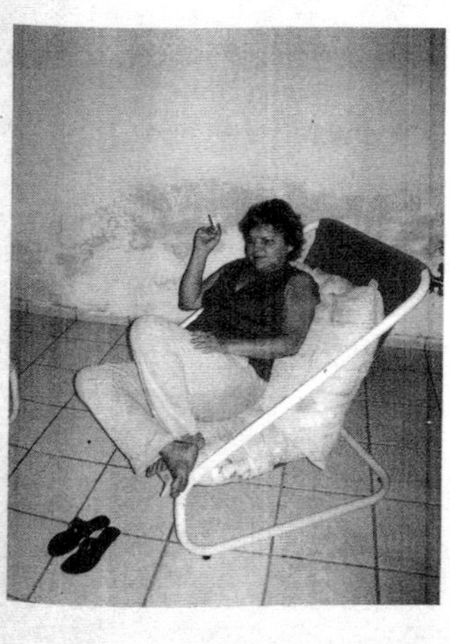

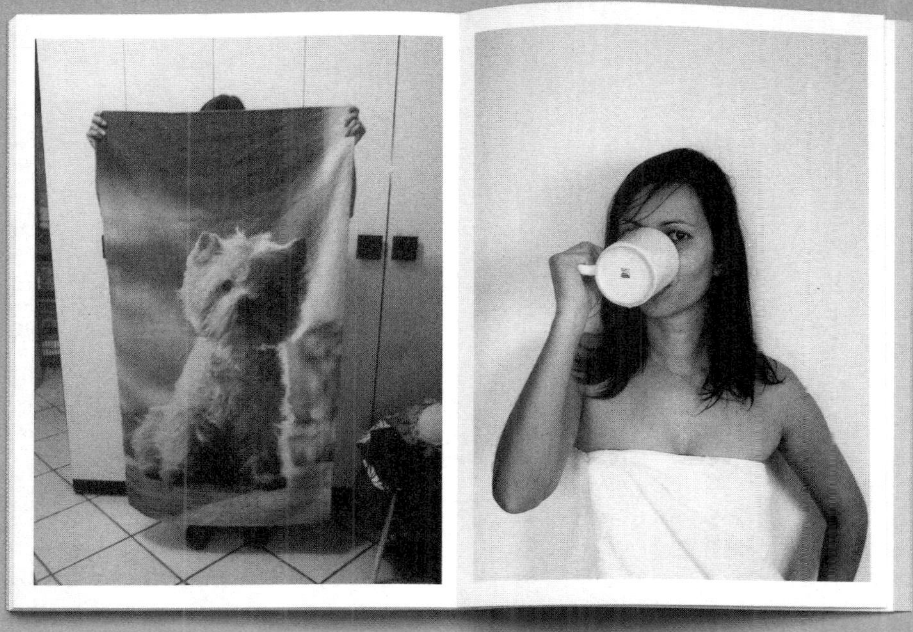

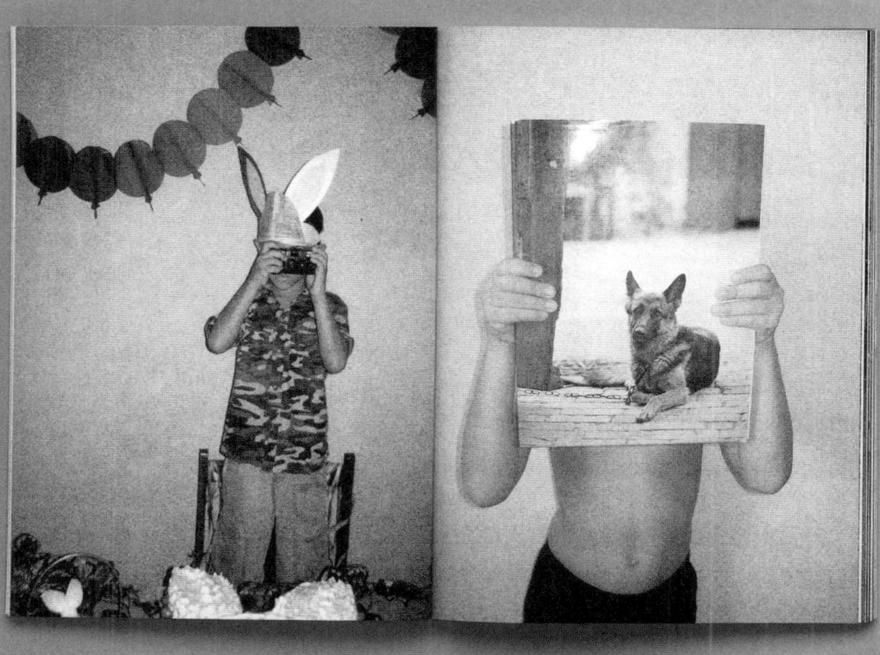

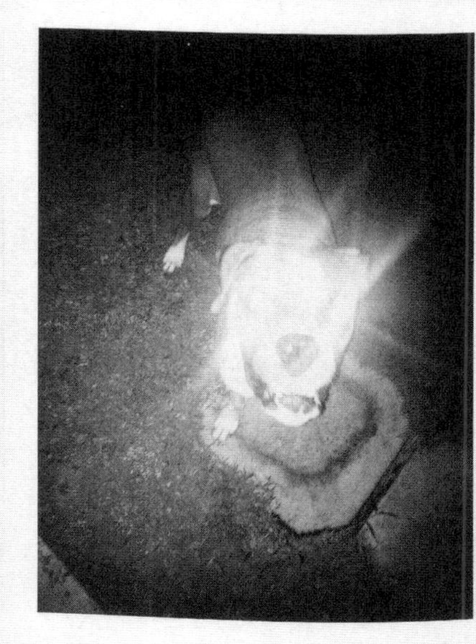

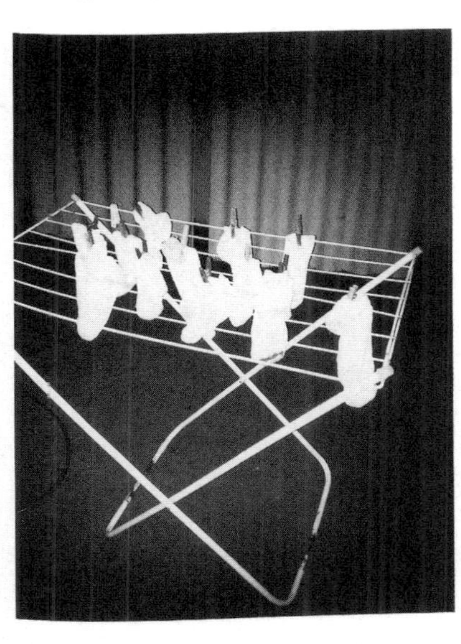

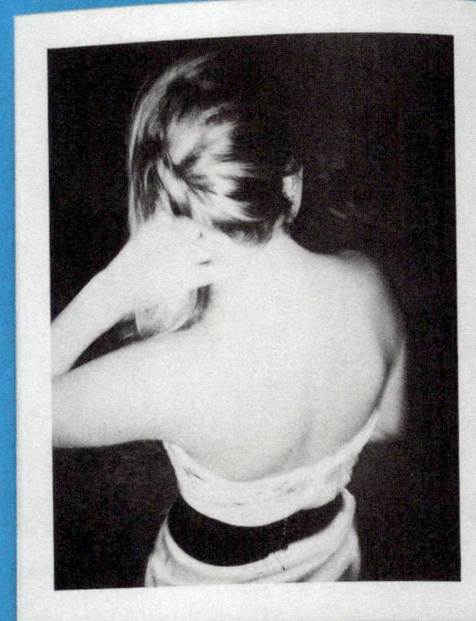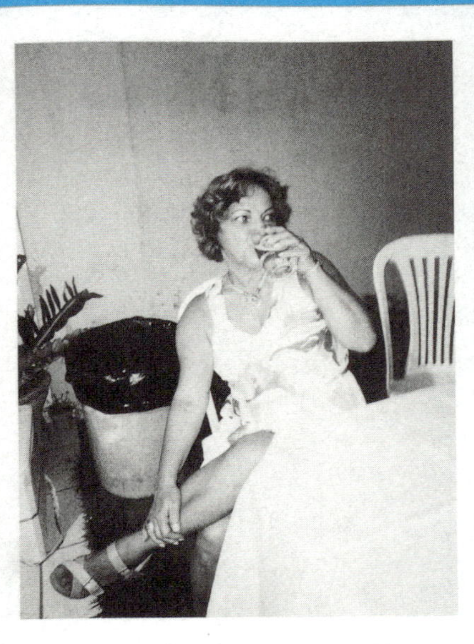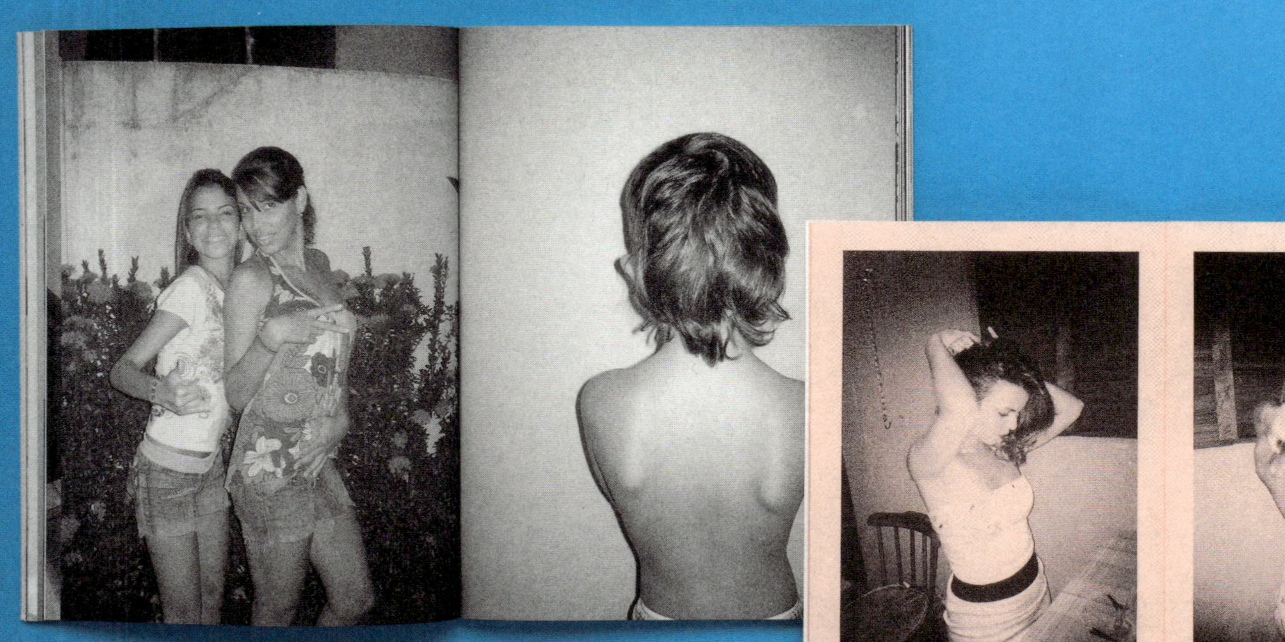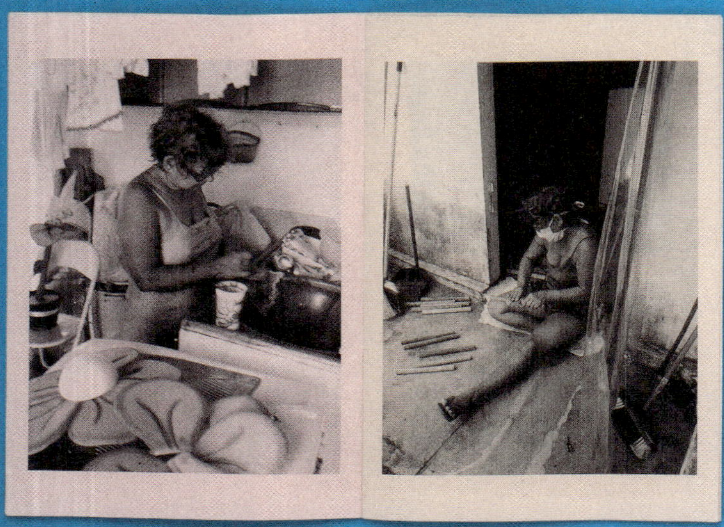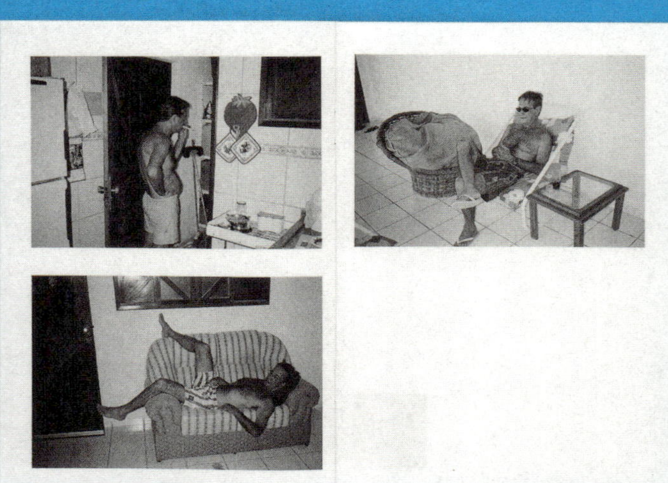

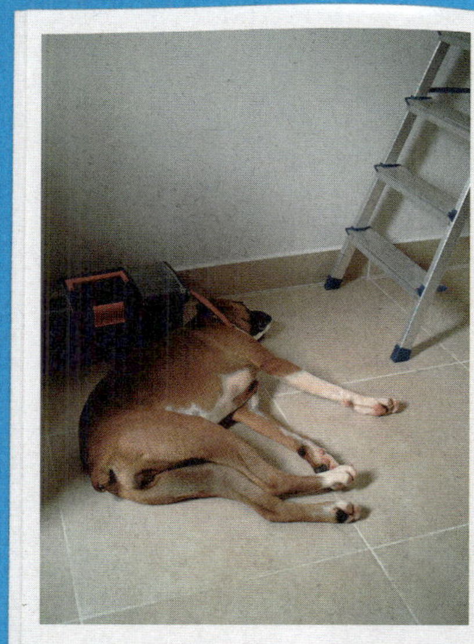
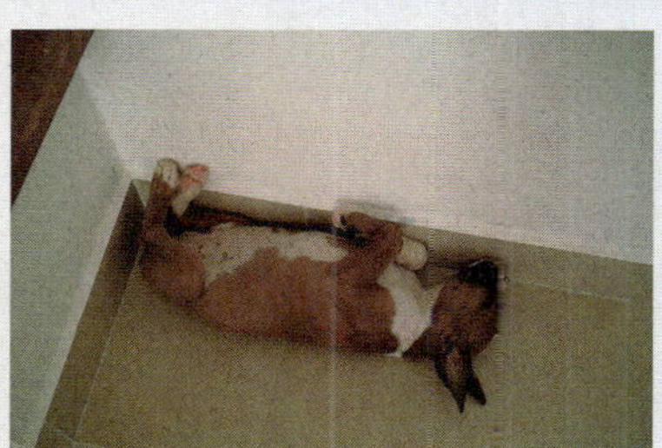
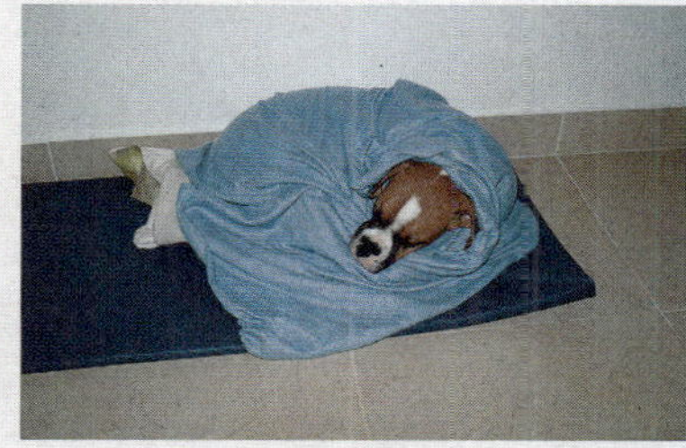
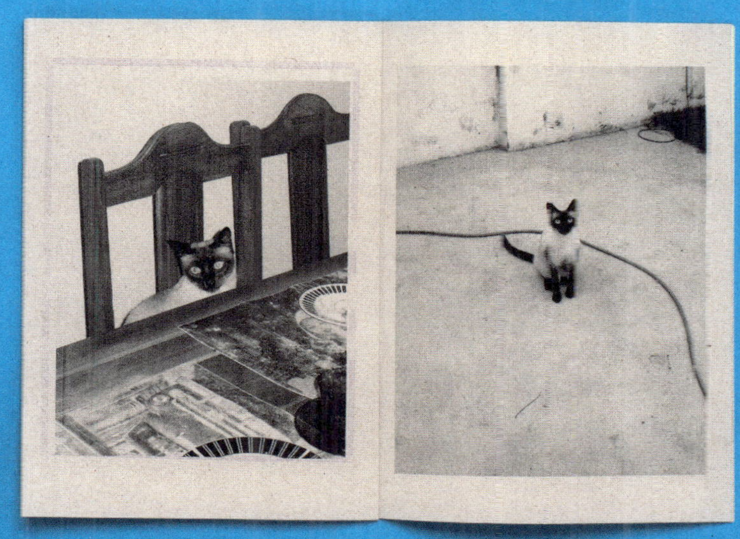
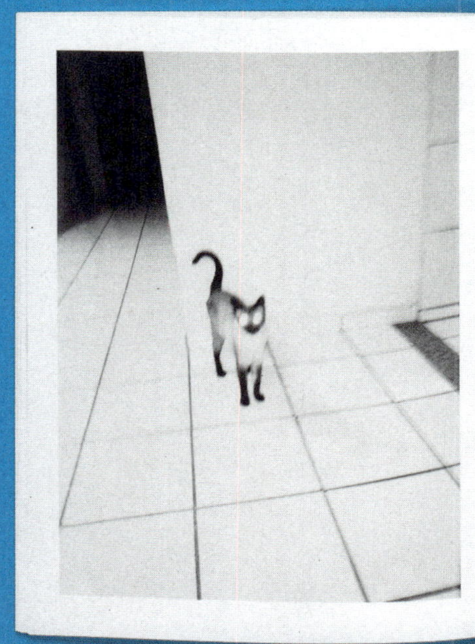

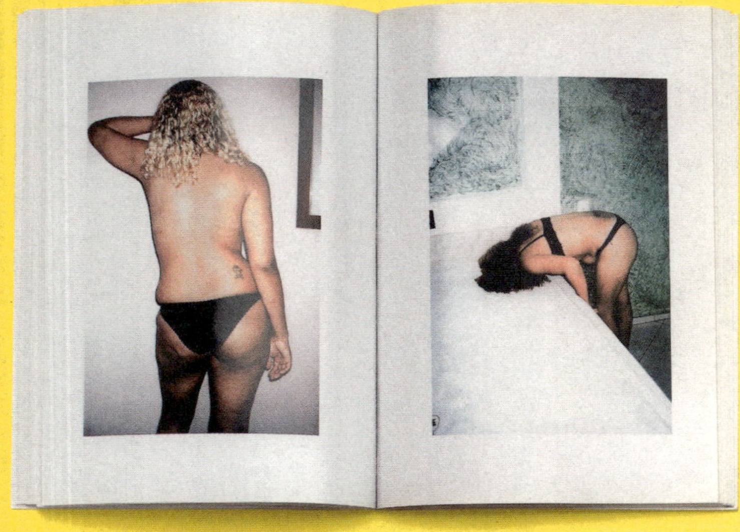

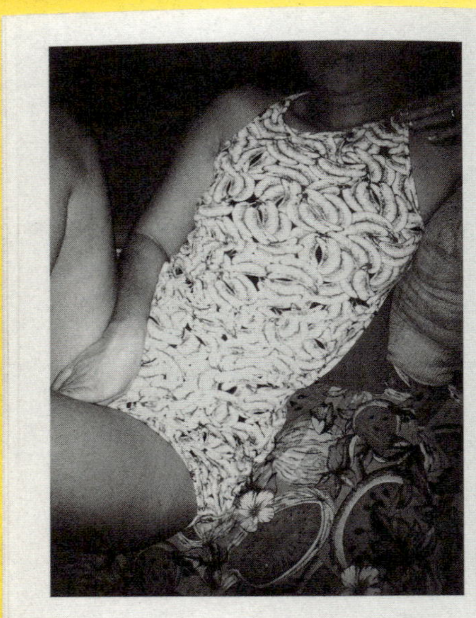

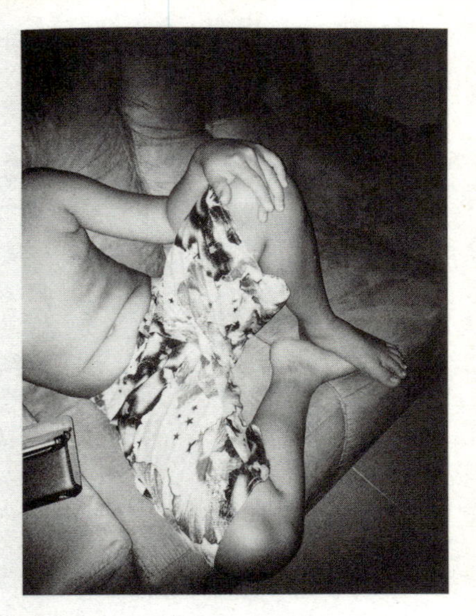

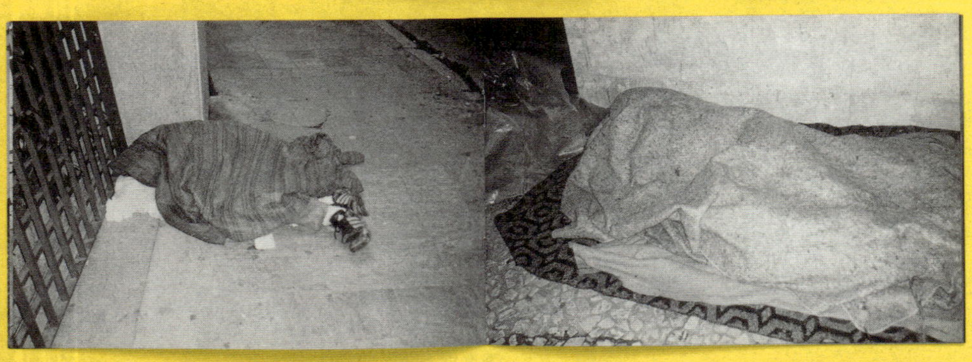

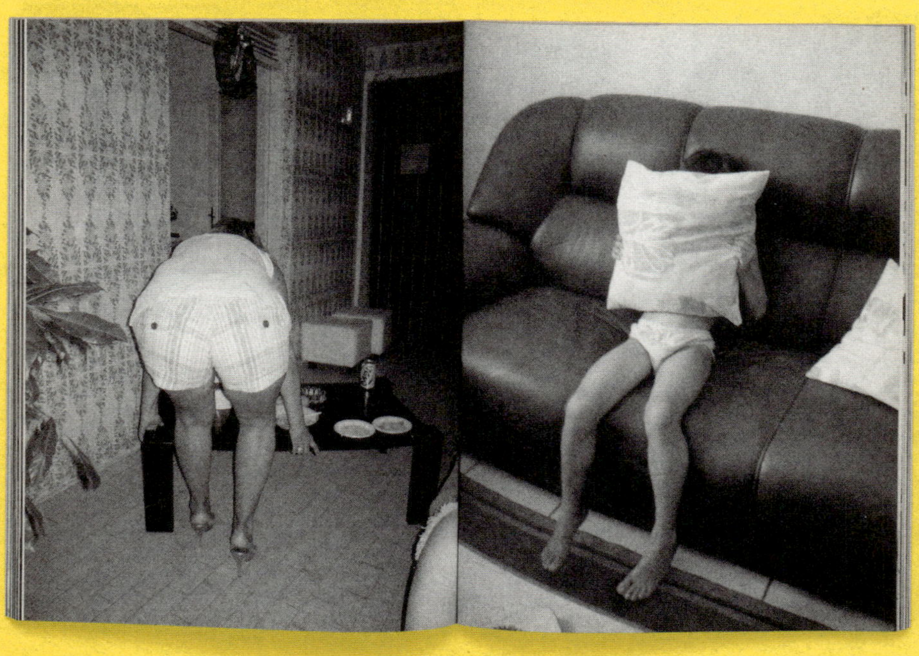

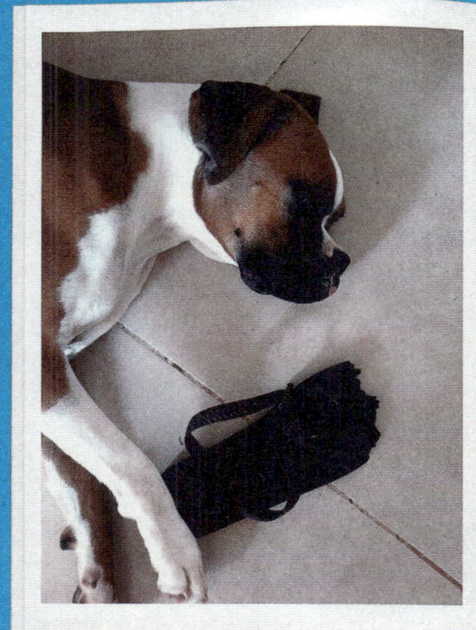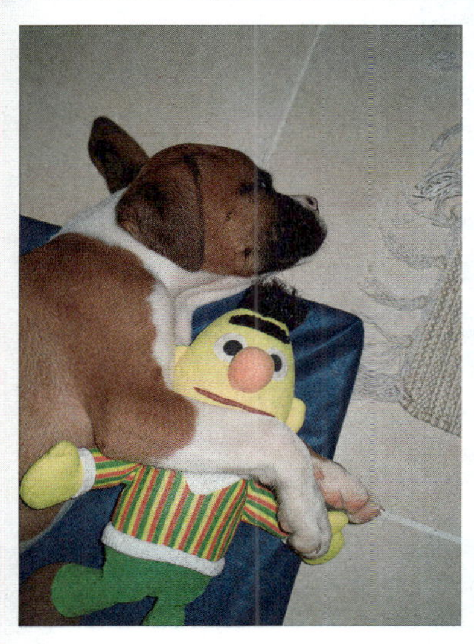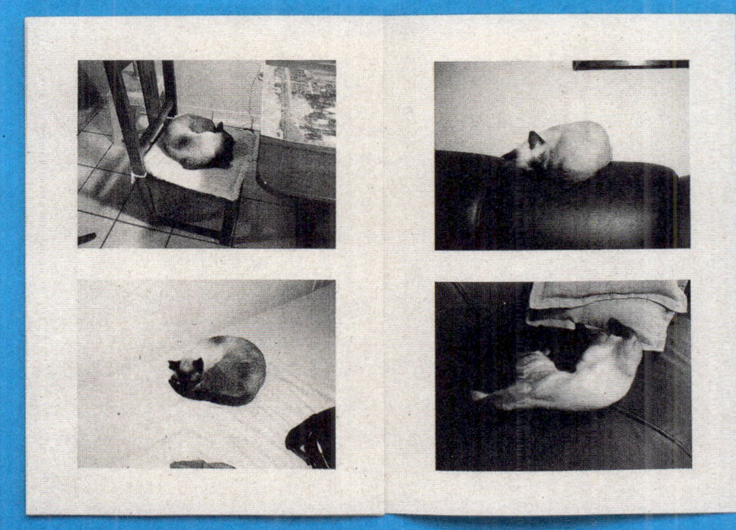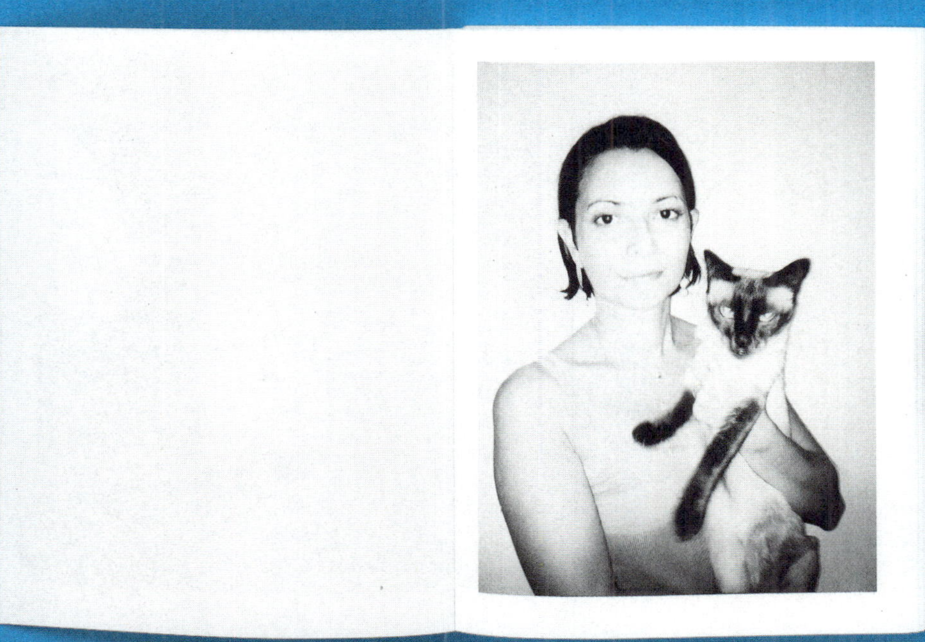

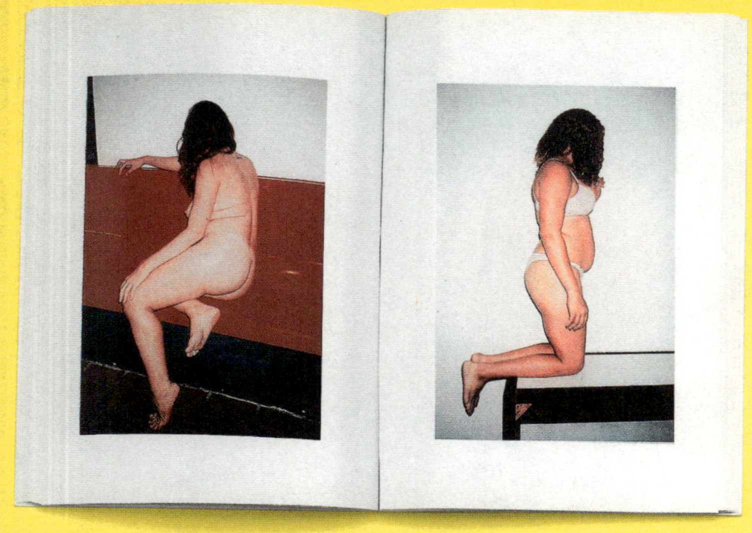

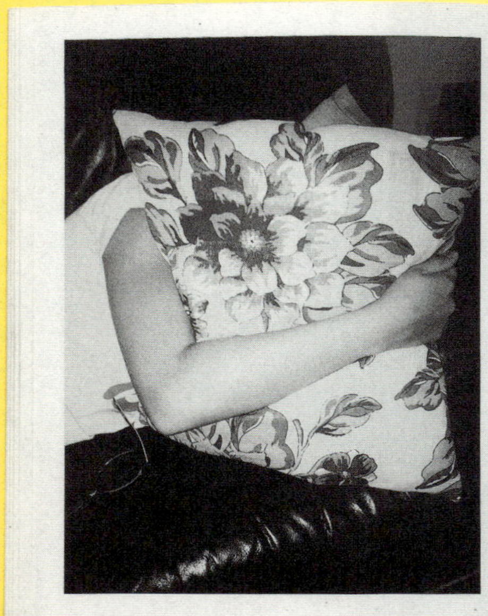

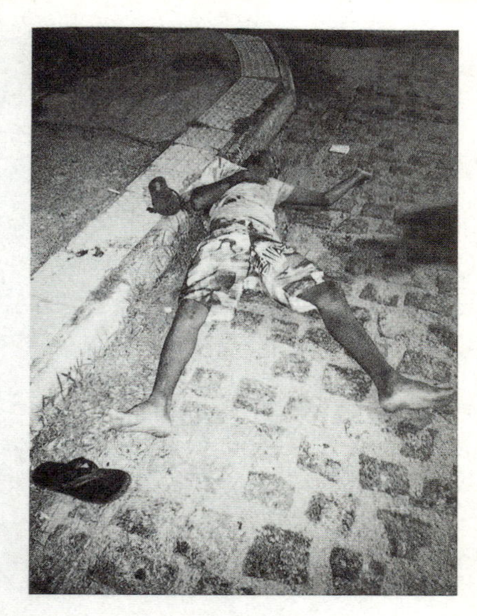

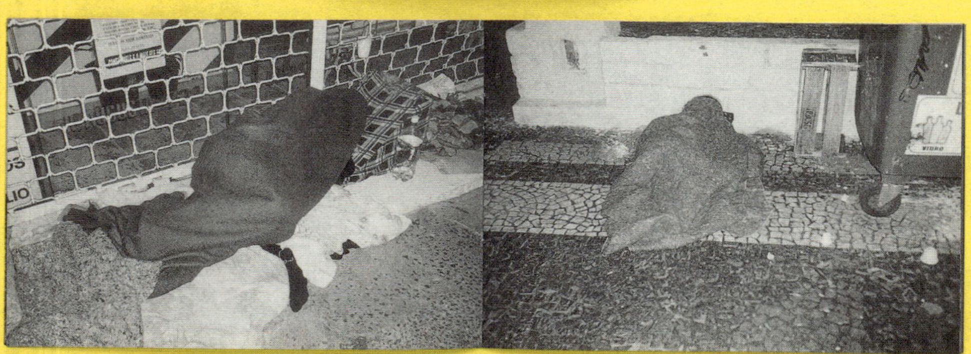

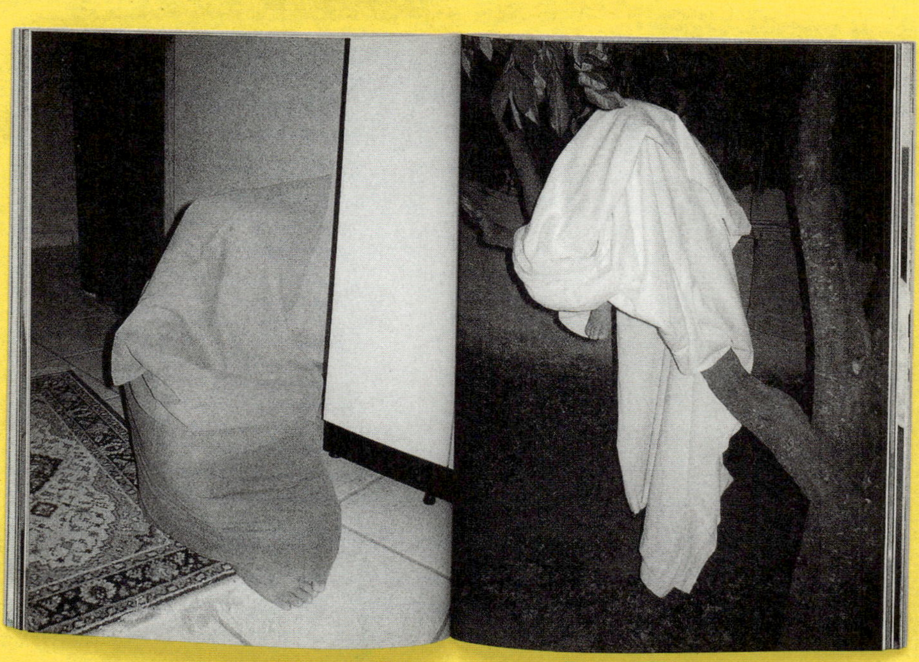

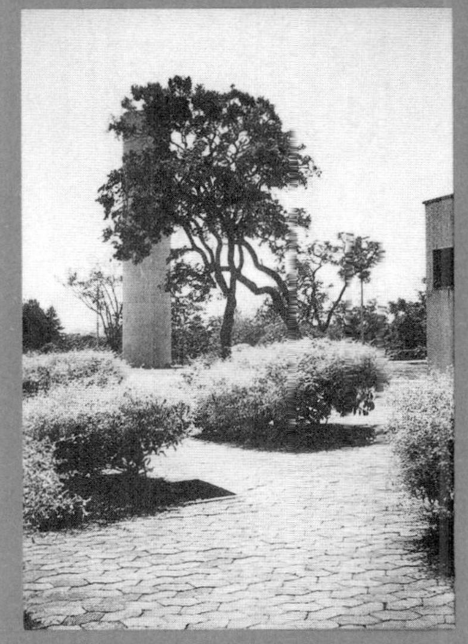

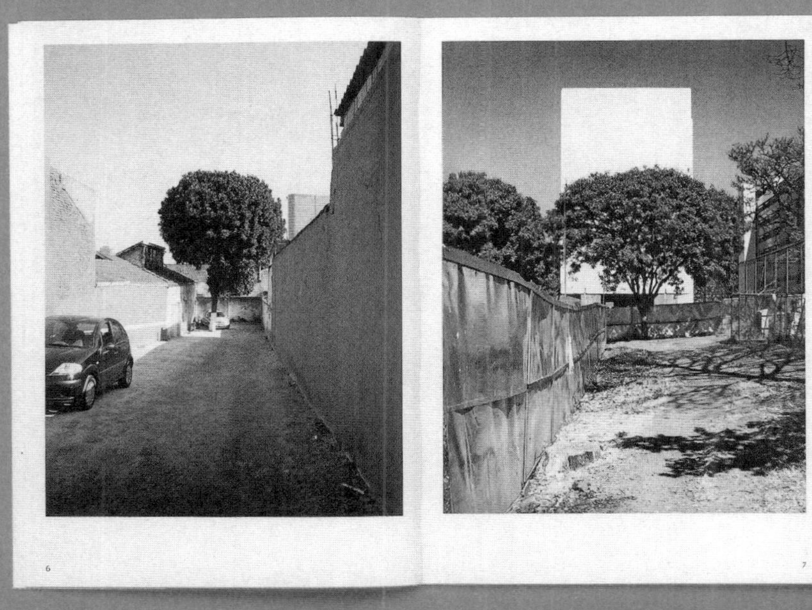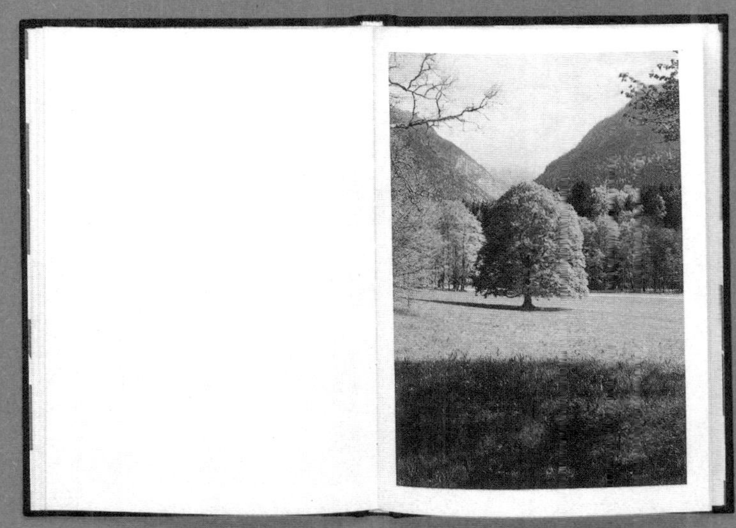

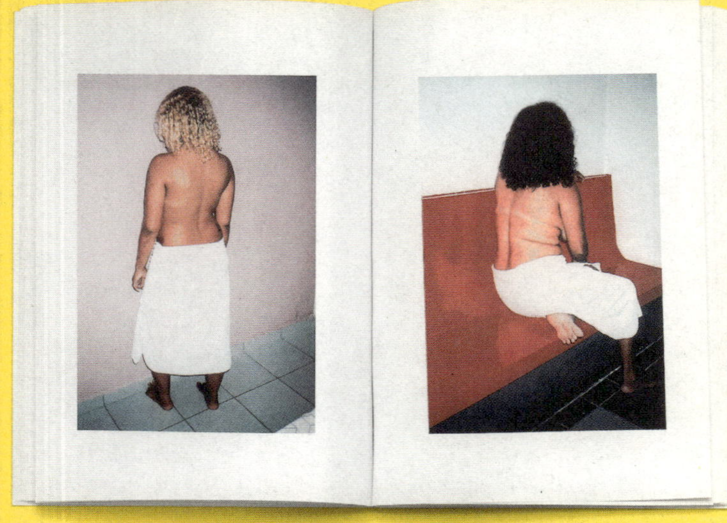

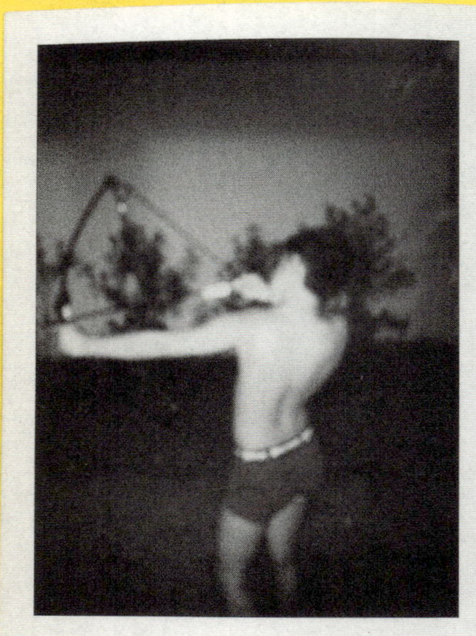

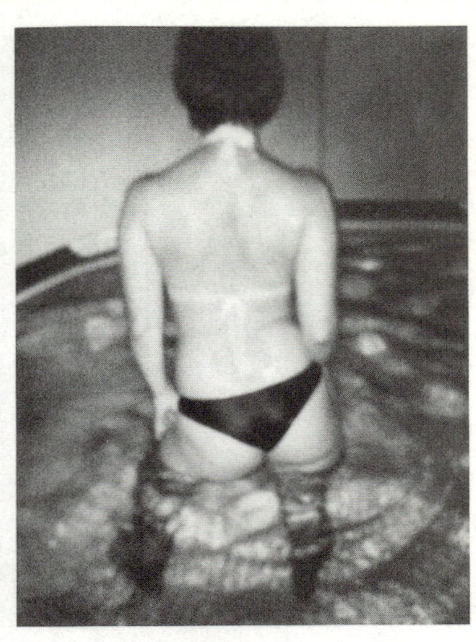

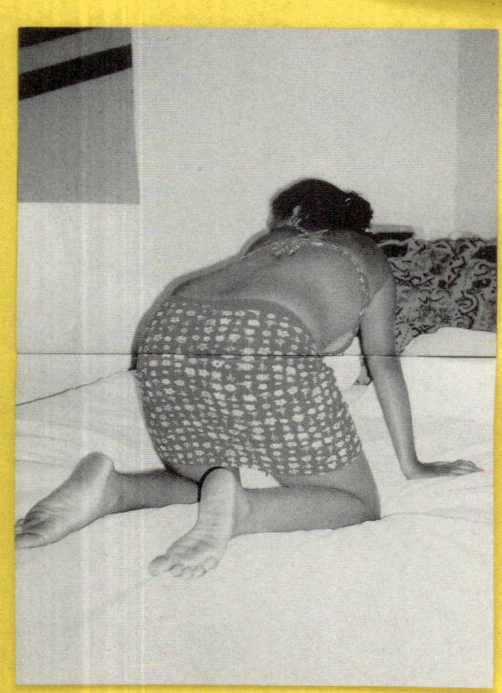

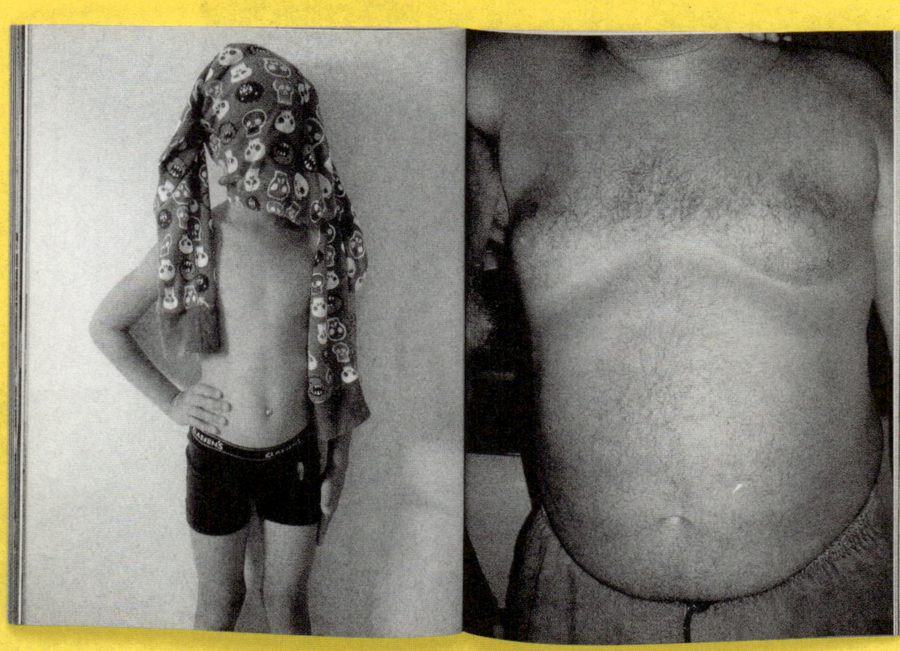

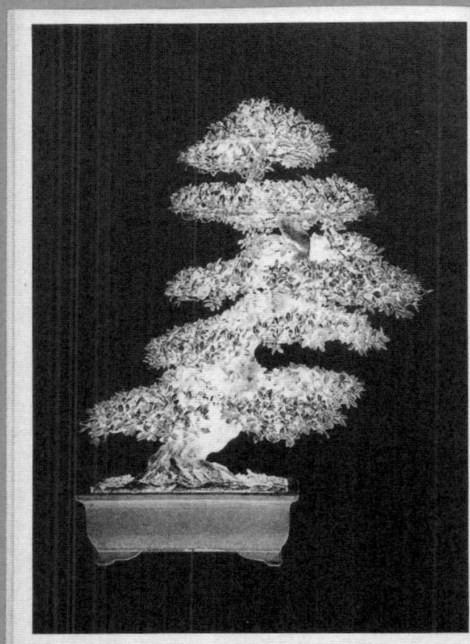
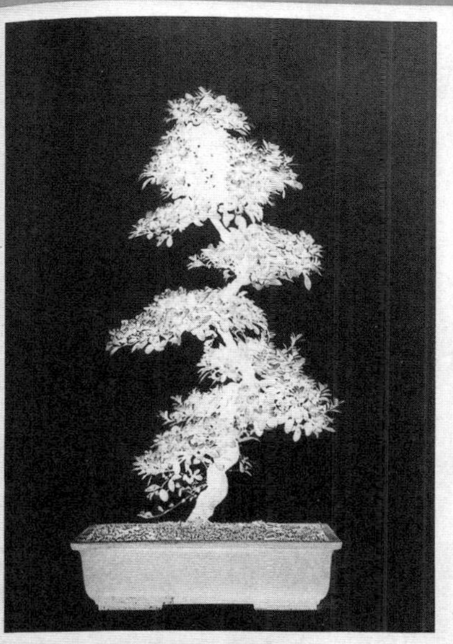
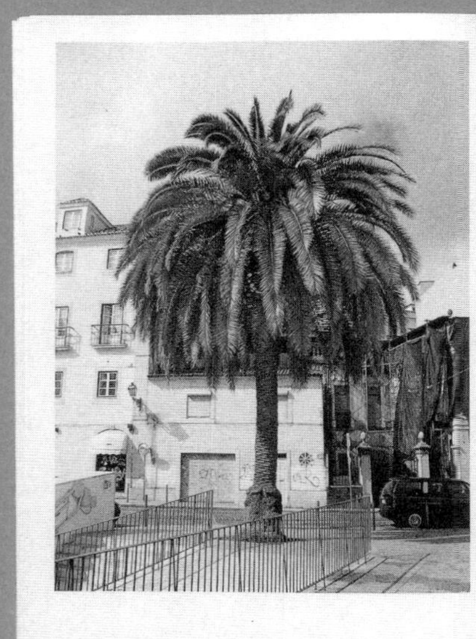
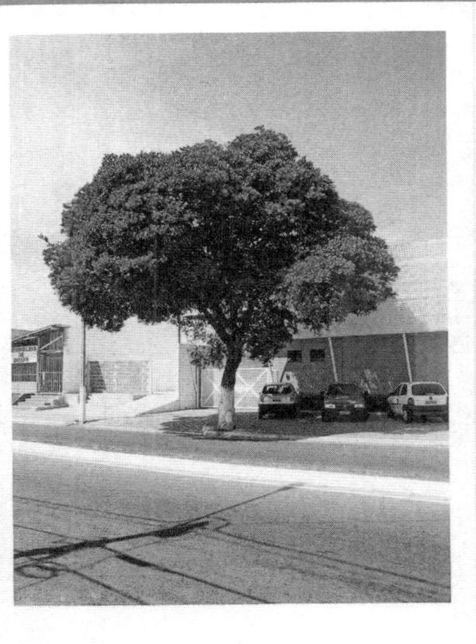
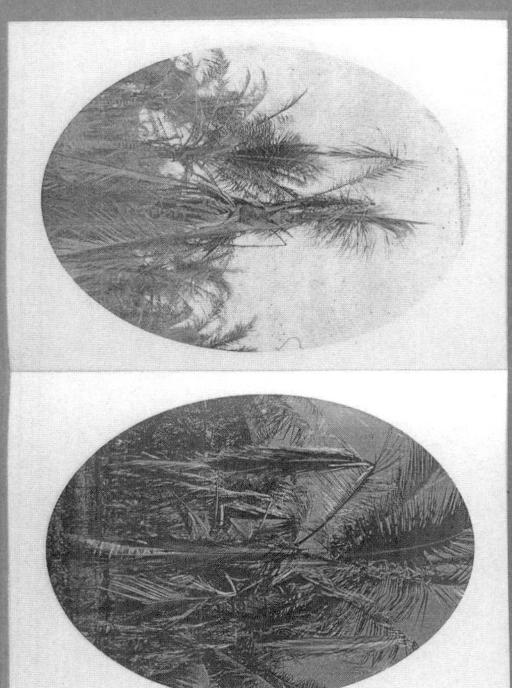
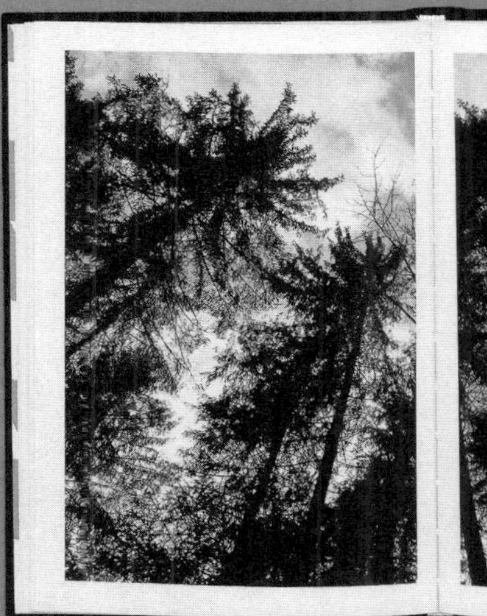
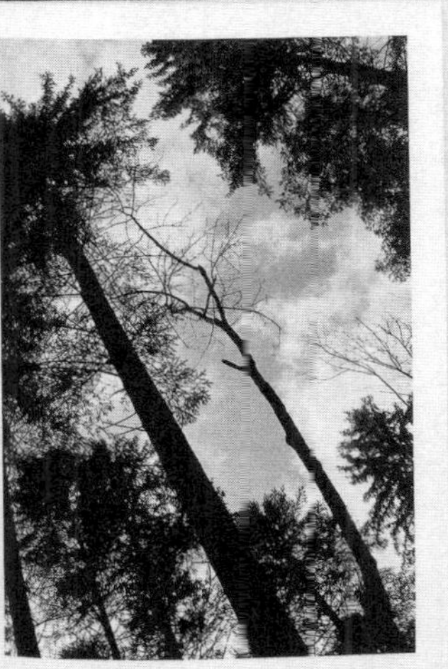

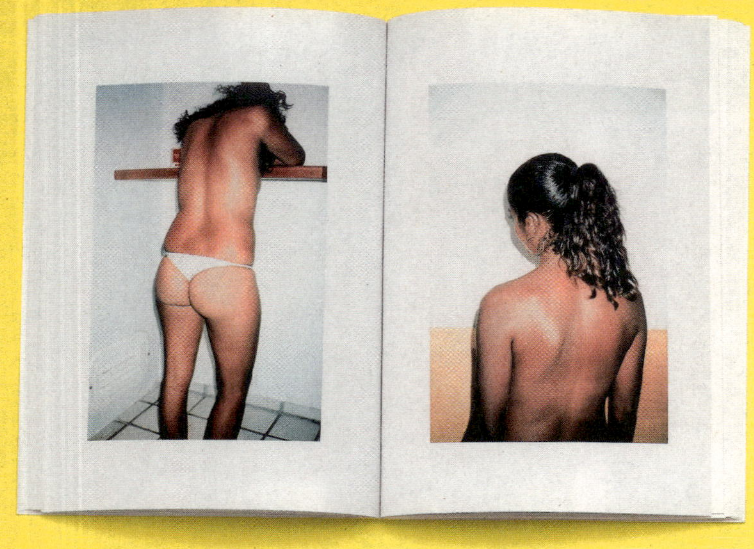
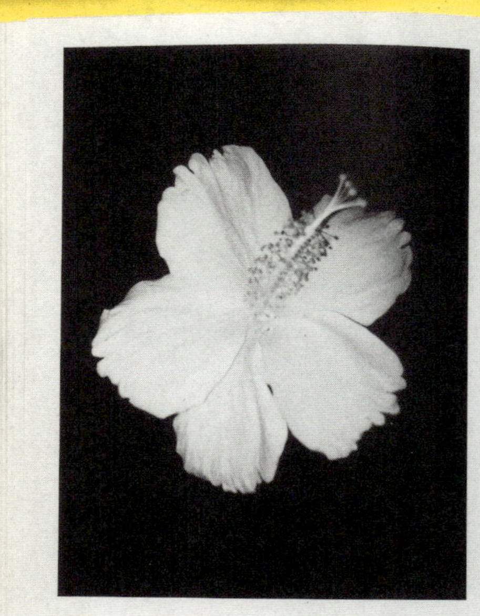
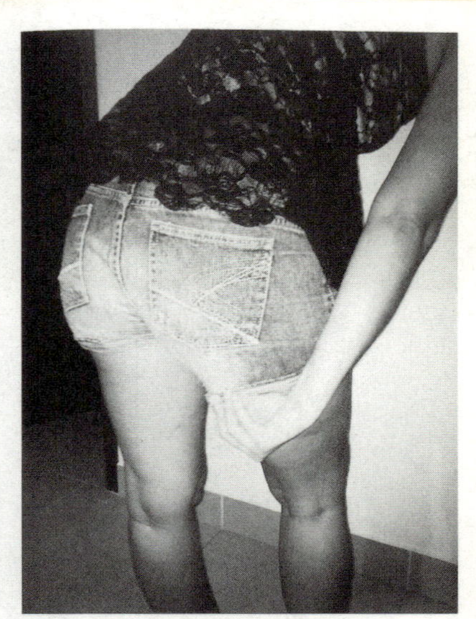
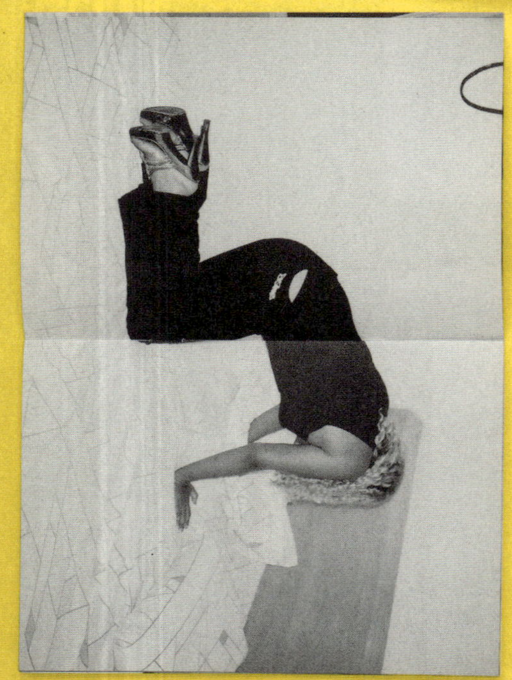
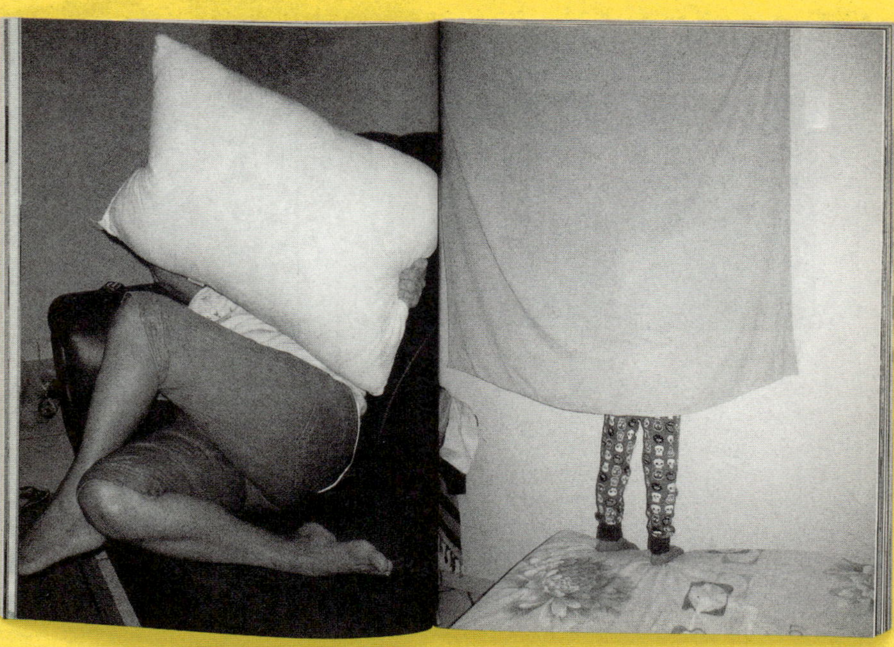

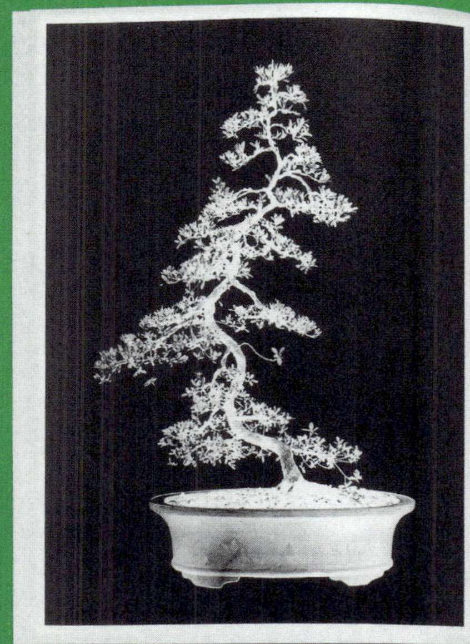
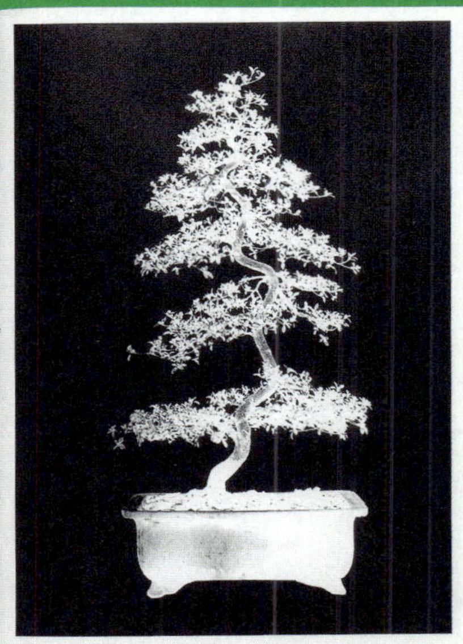

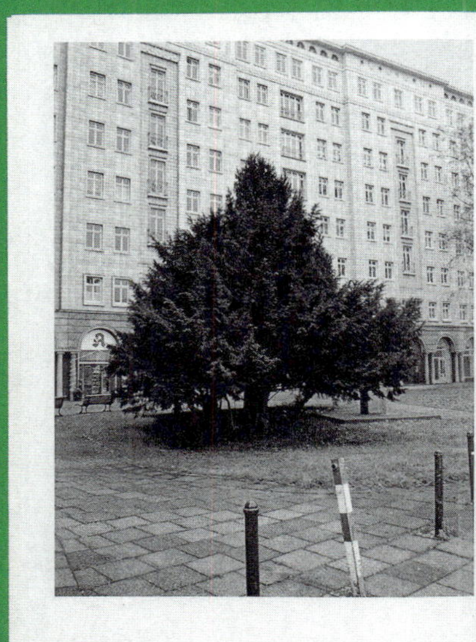
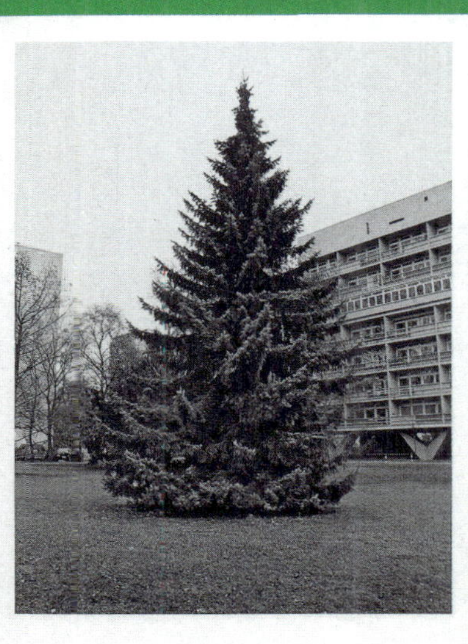

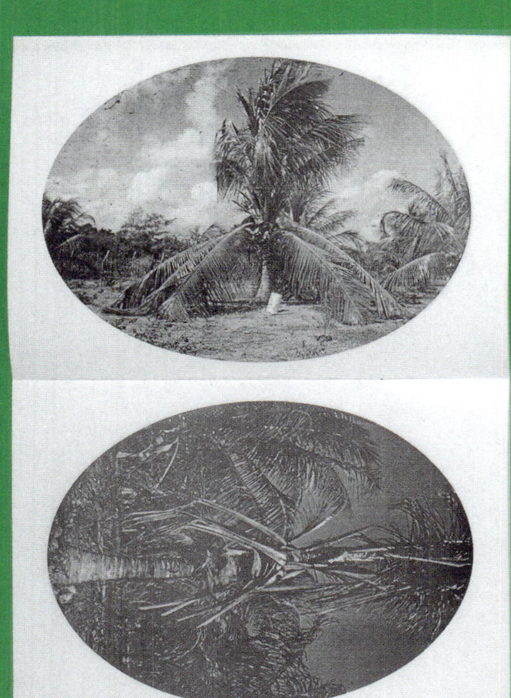

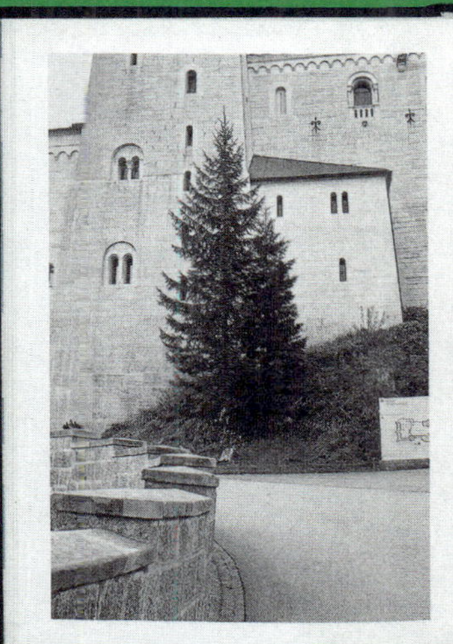
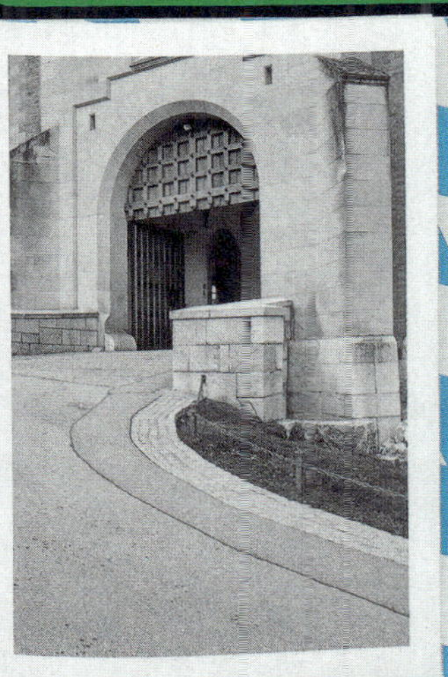

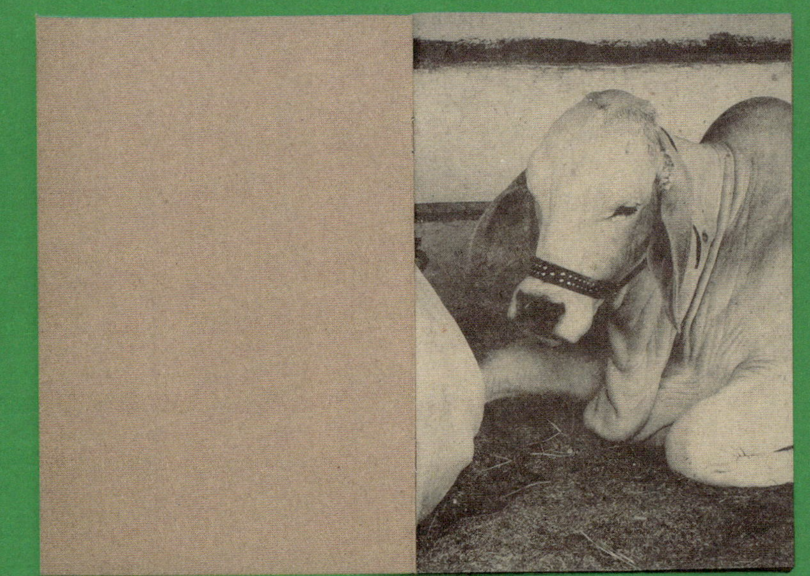

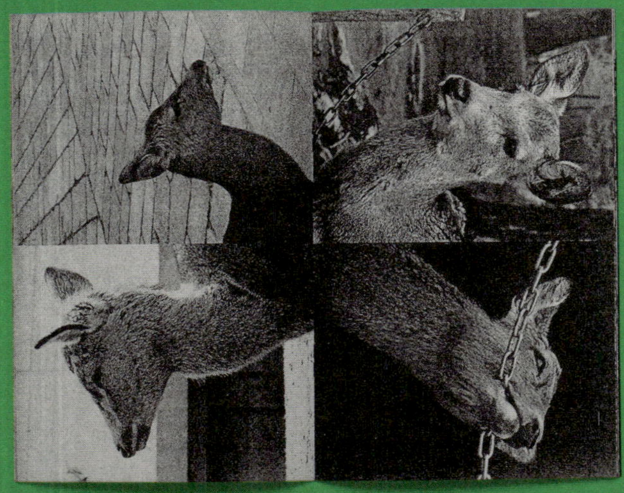

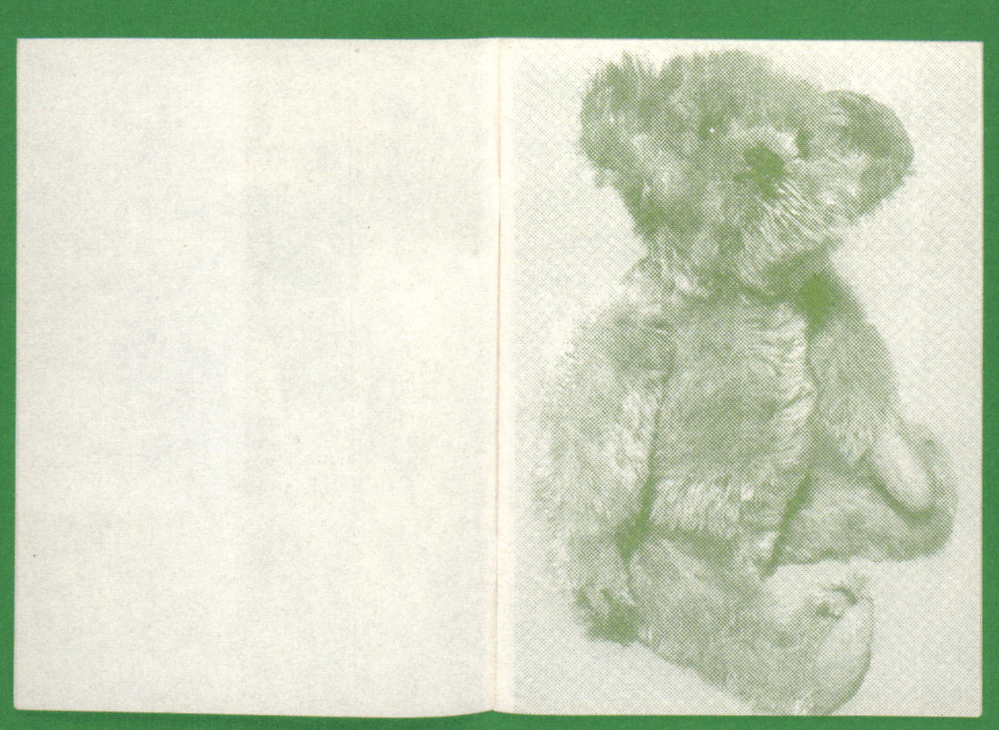

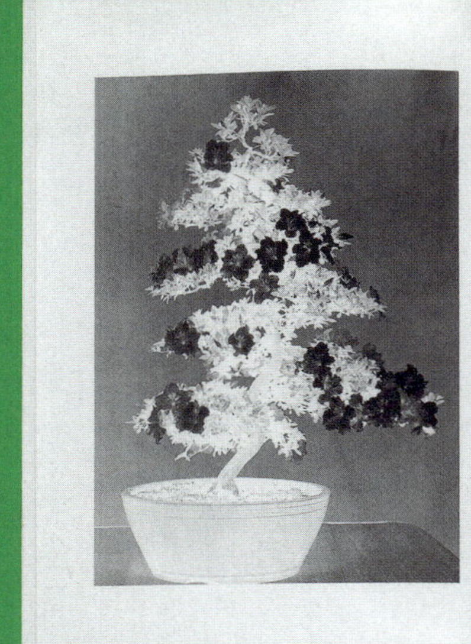
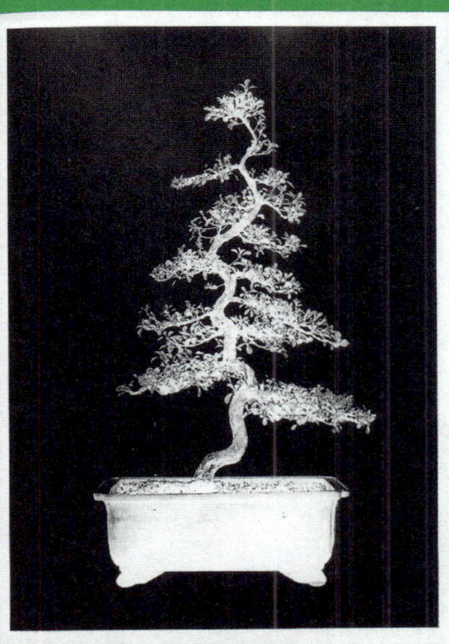
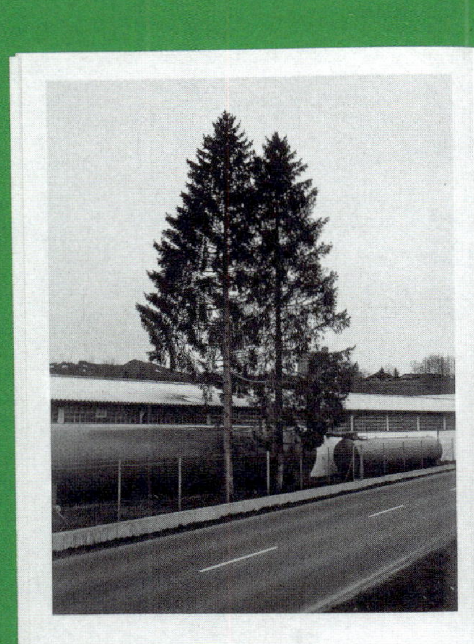
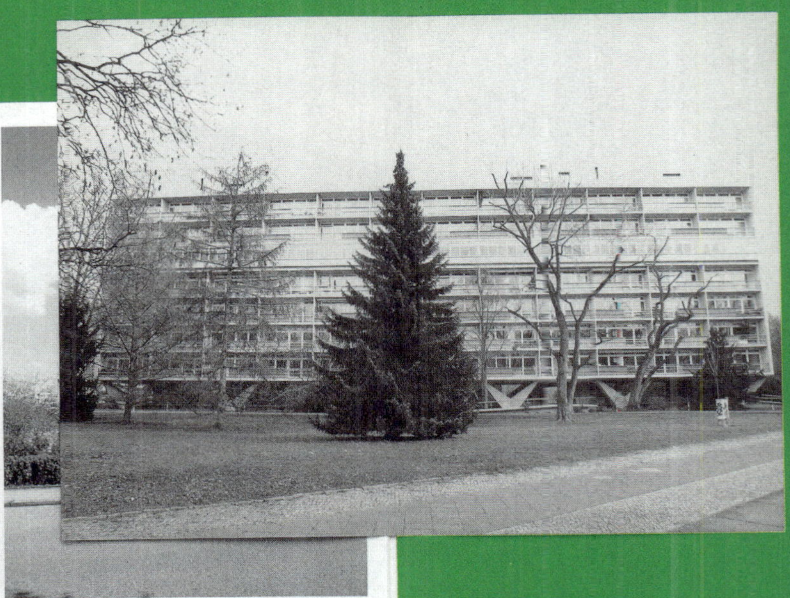
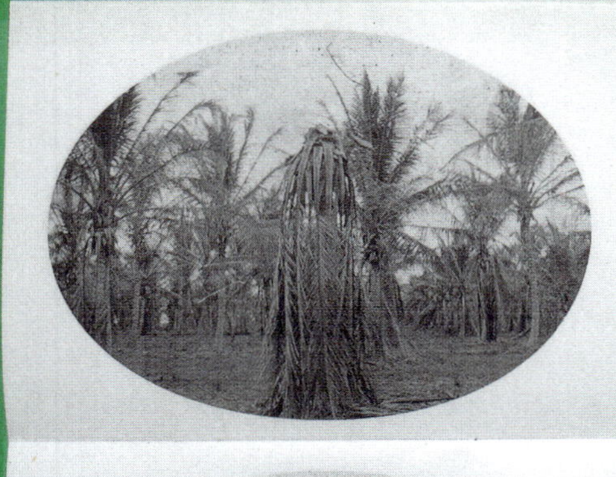
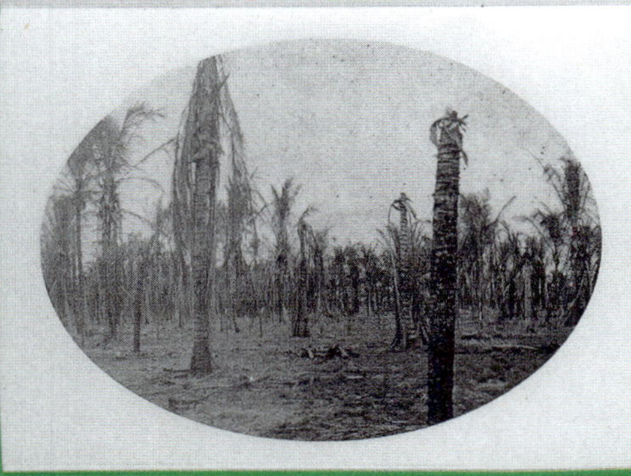
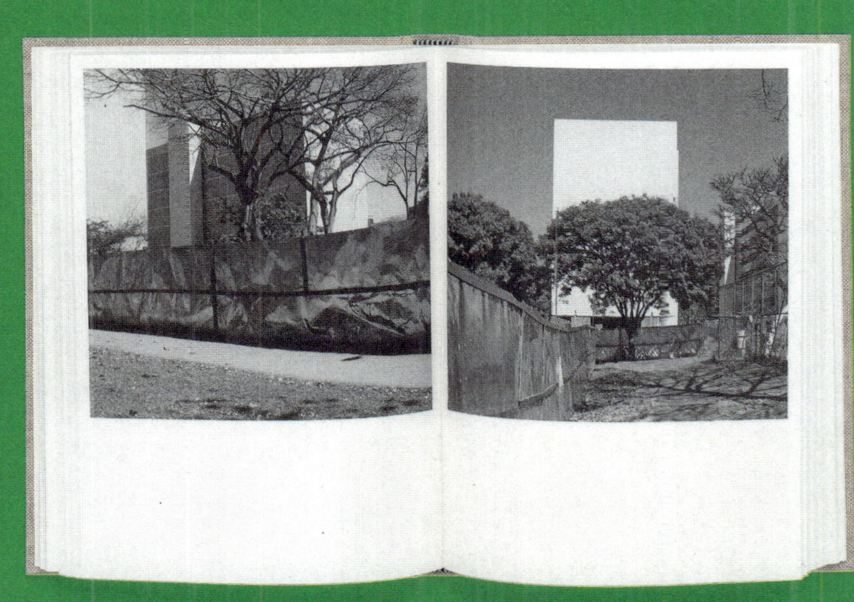

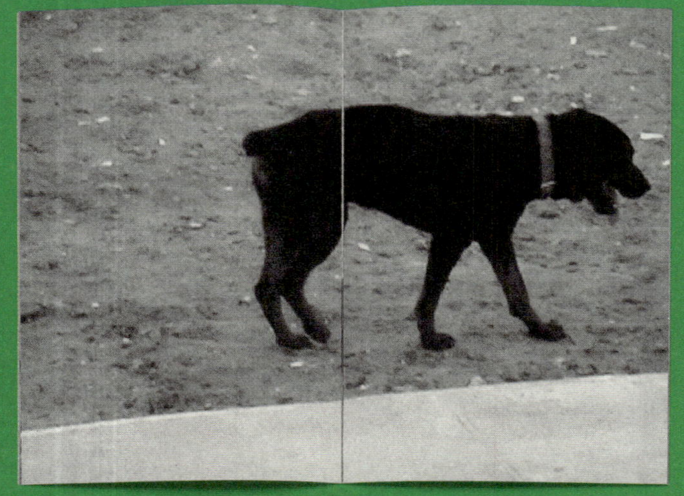
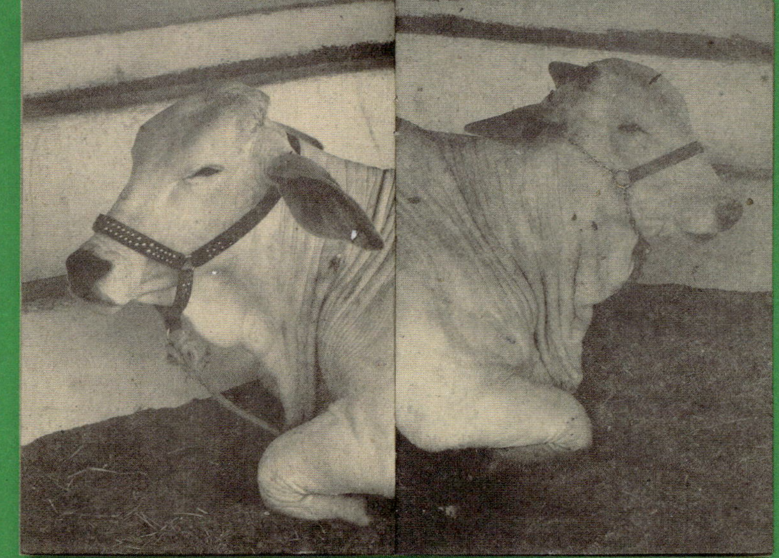
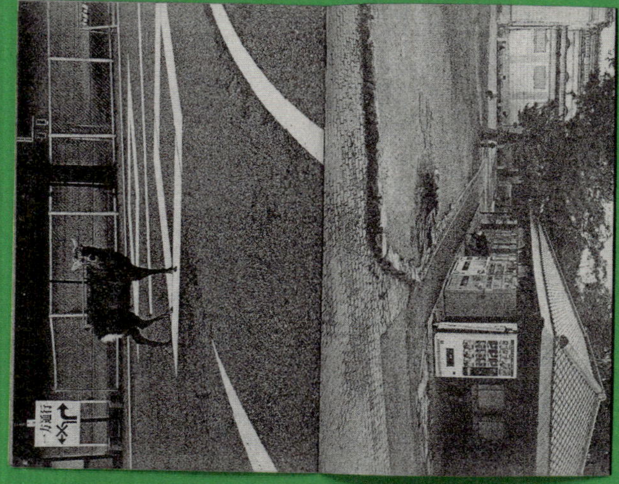
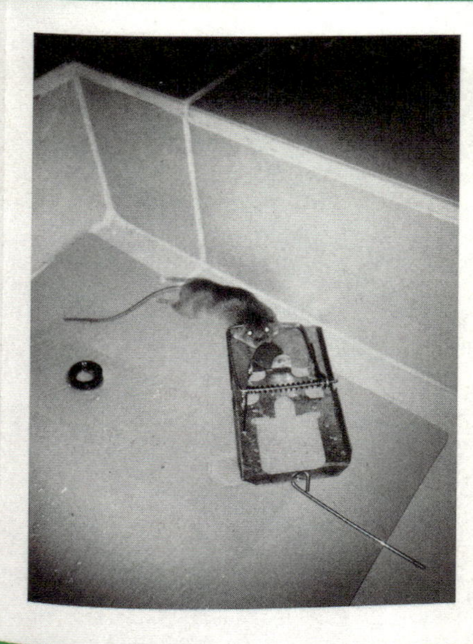
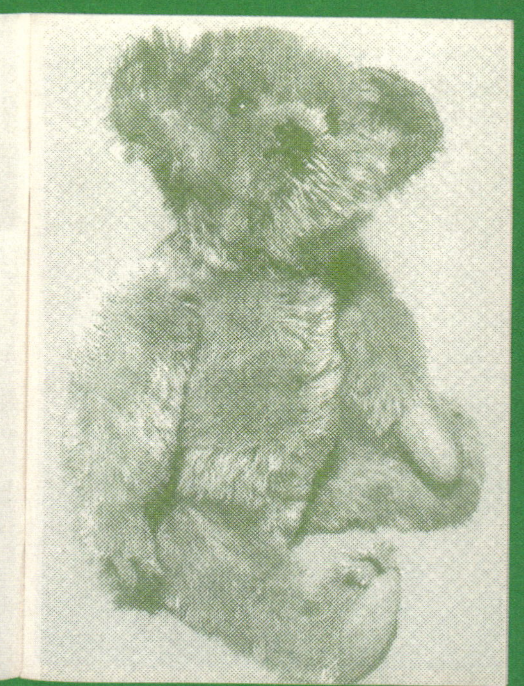

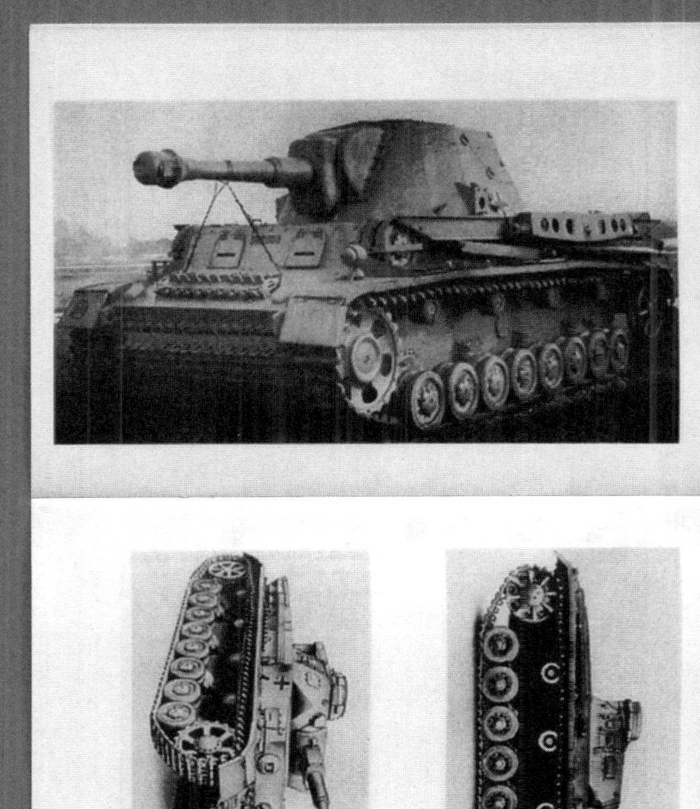

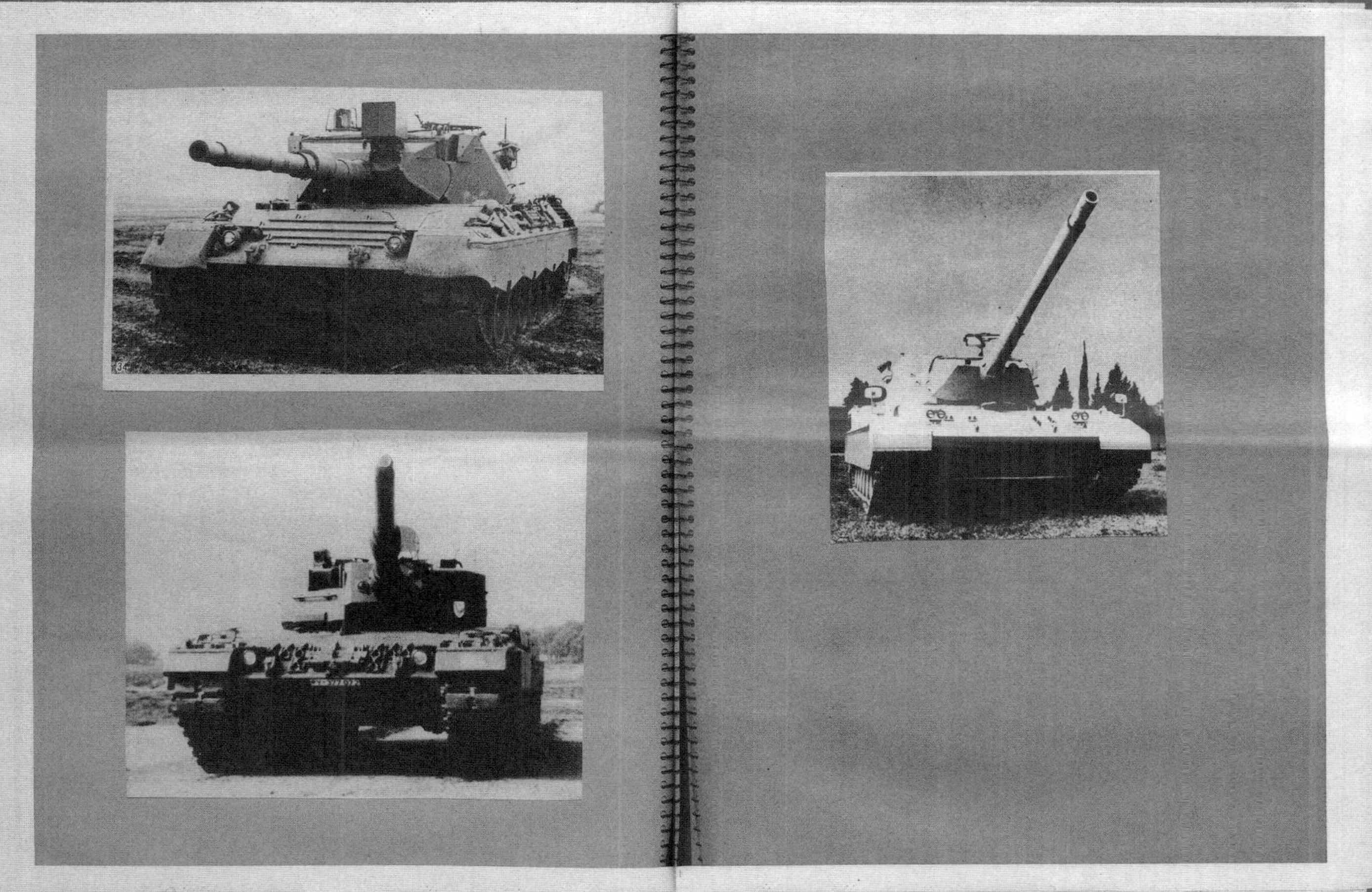

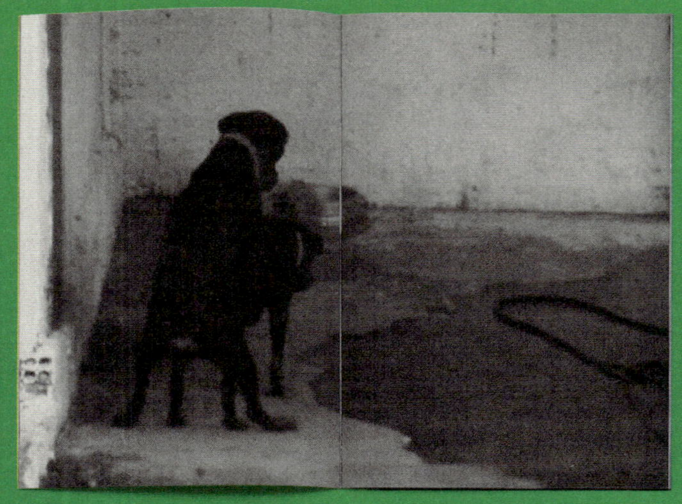
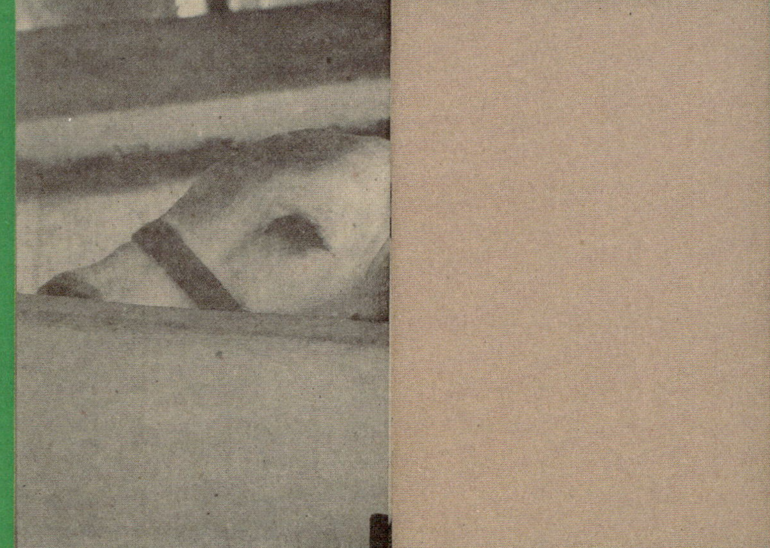
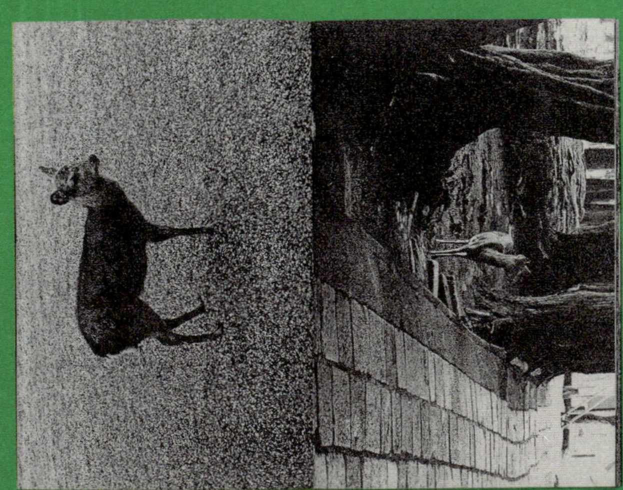
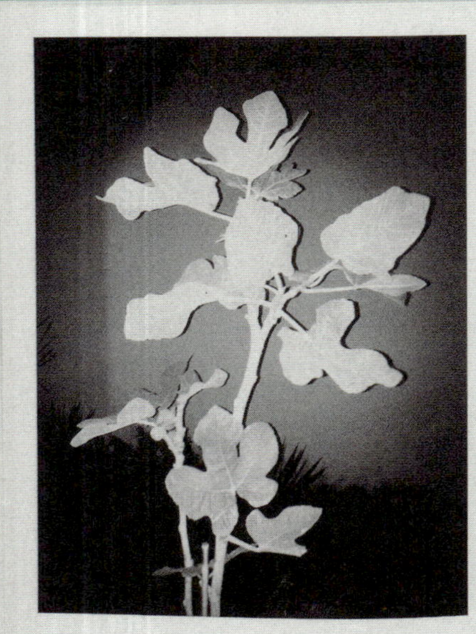
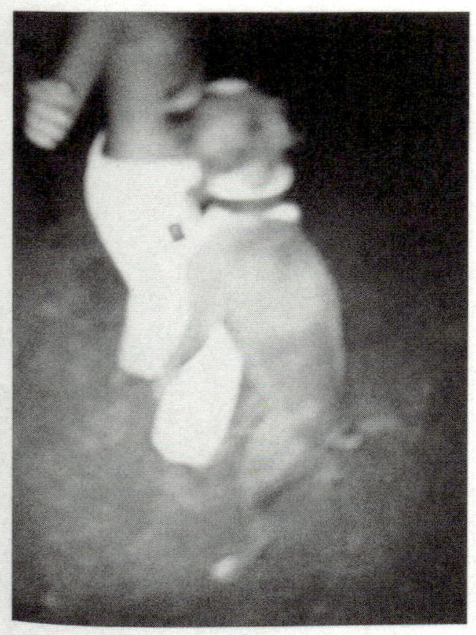
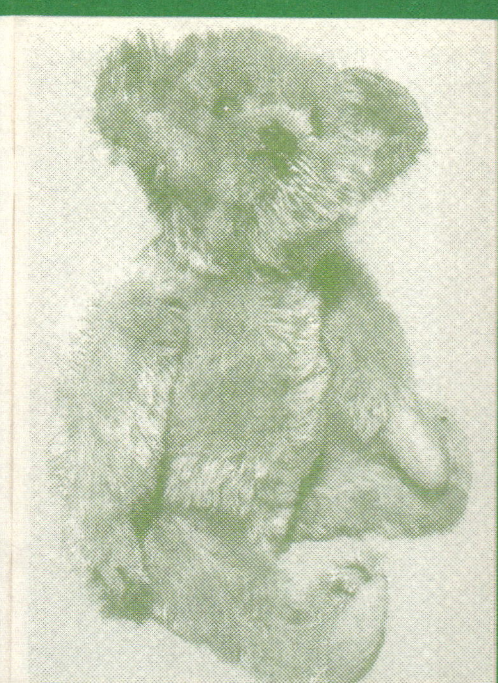

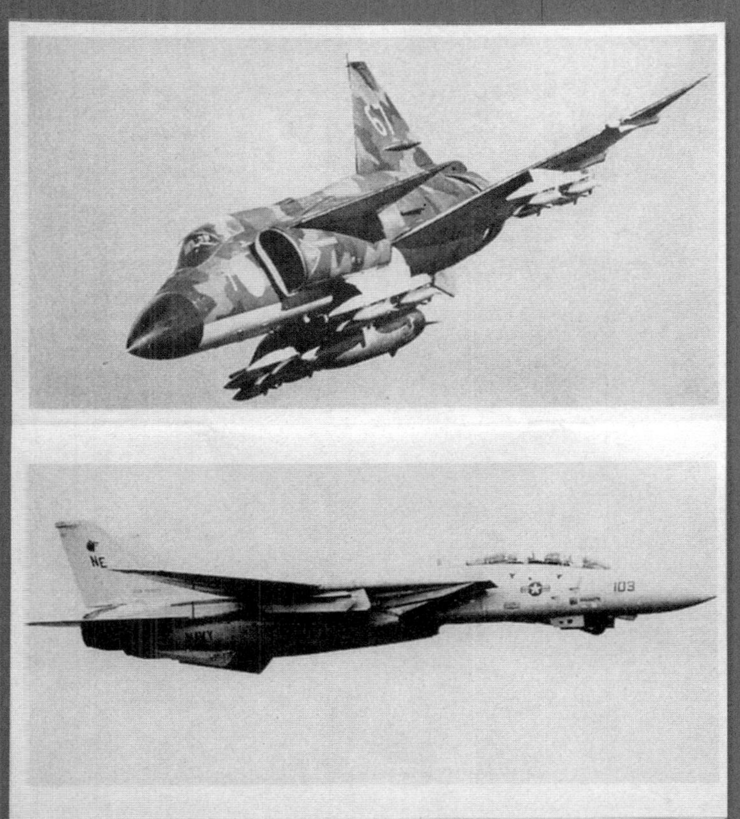

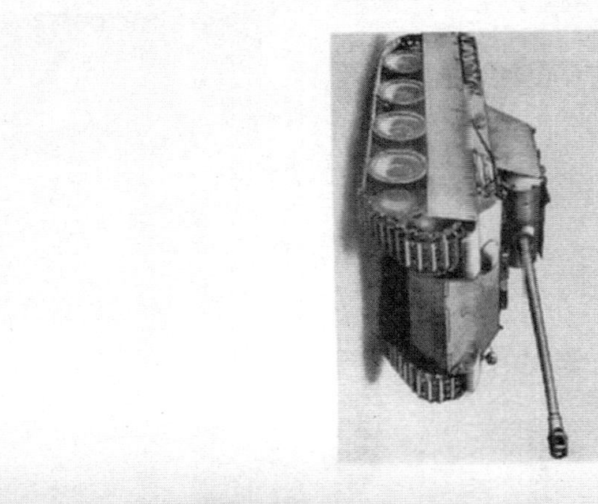

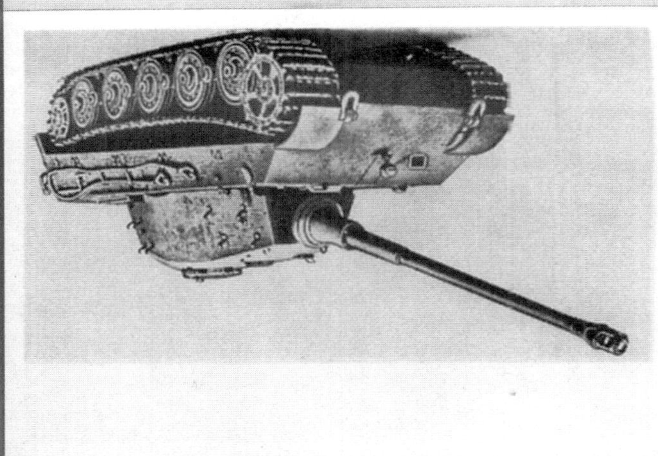

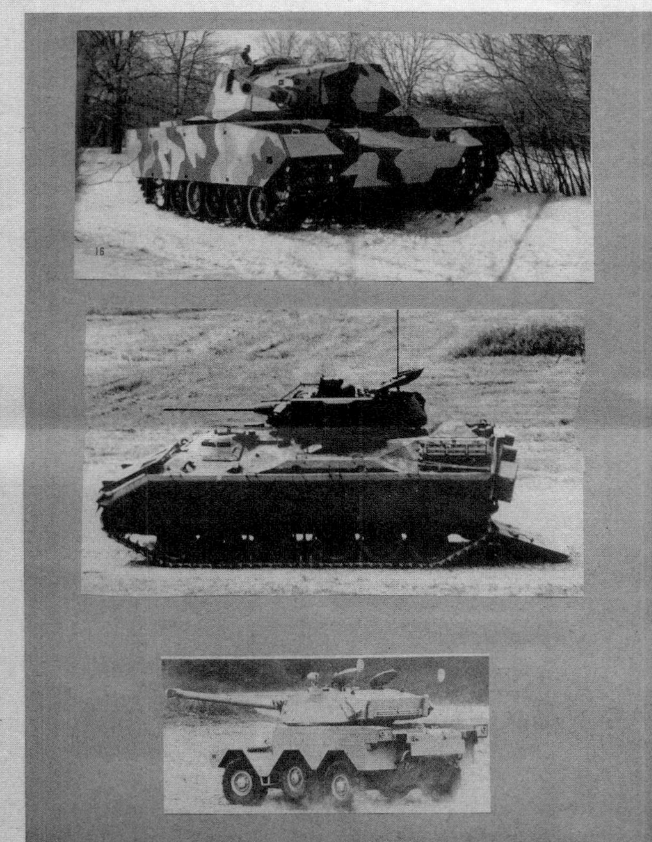

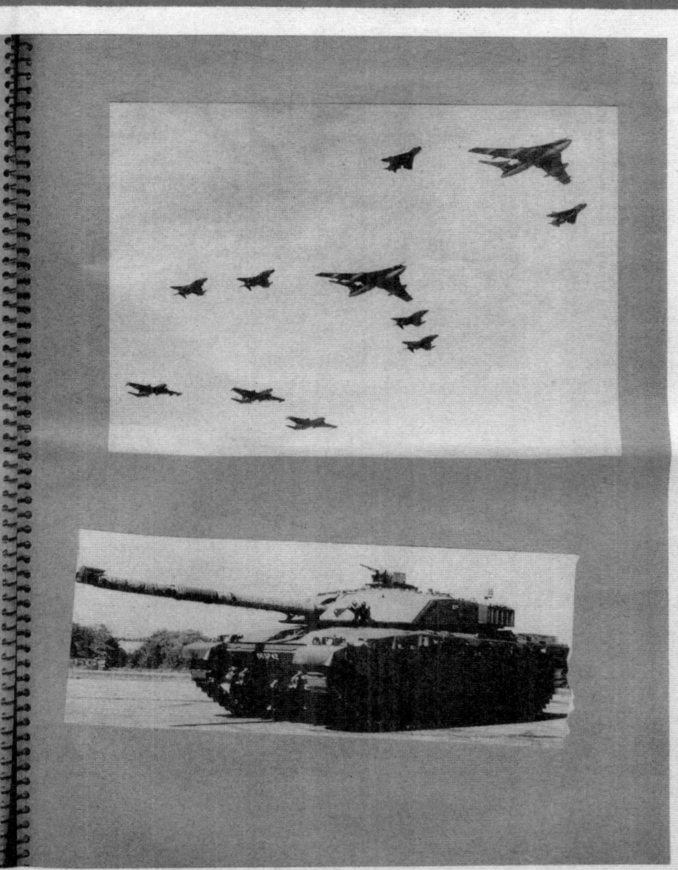

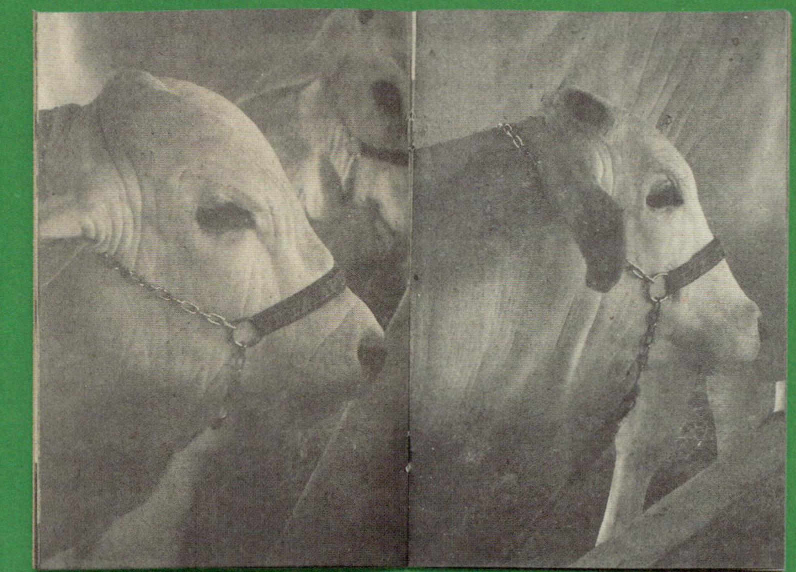

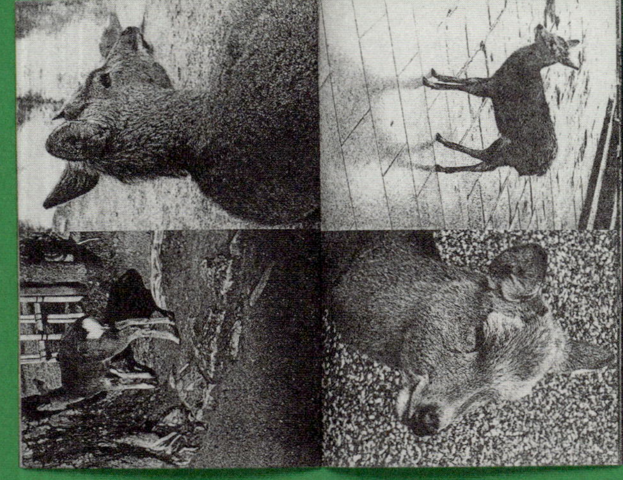

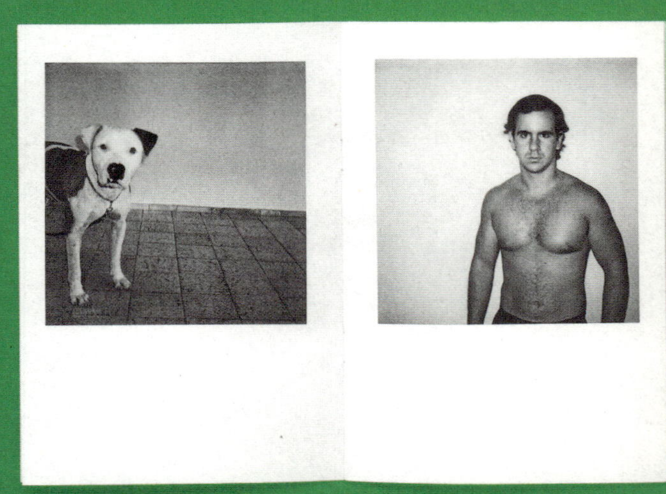

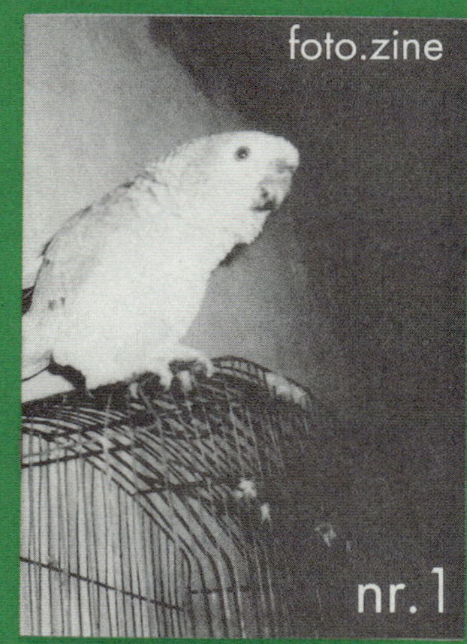
foto.zine
nr. 1

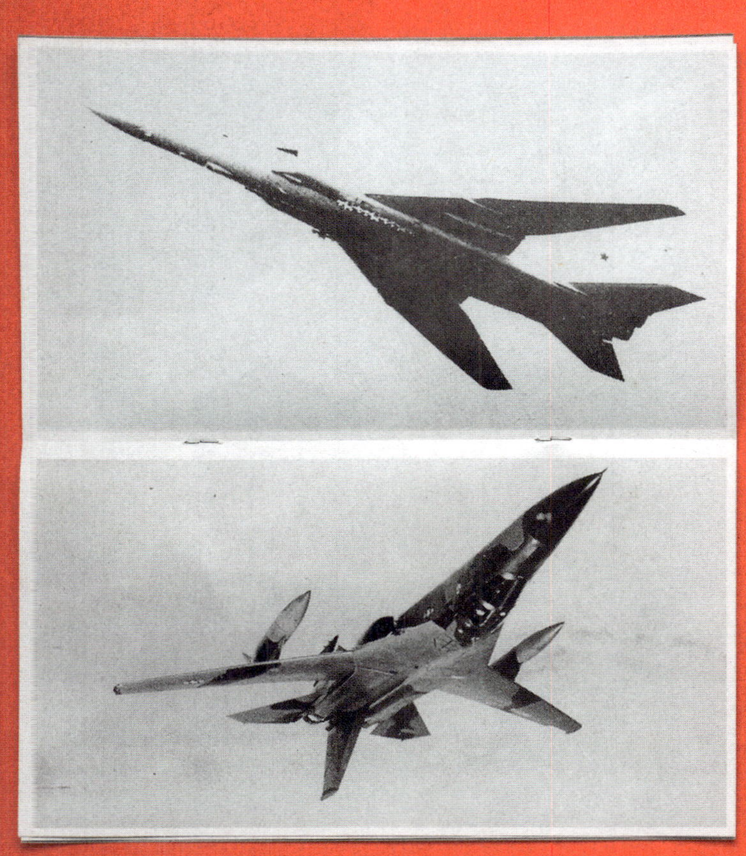

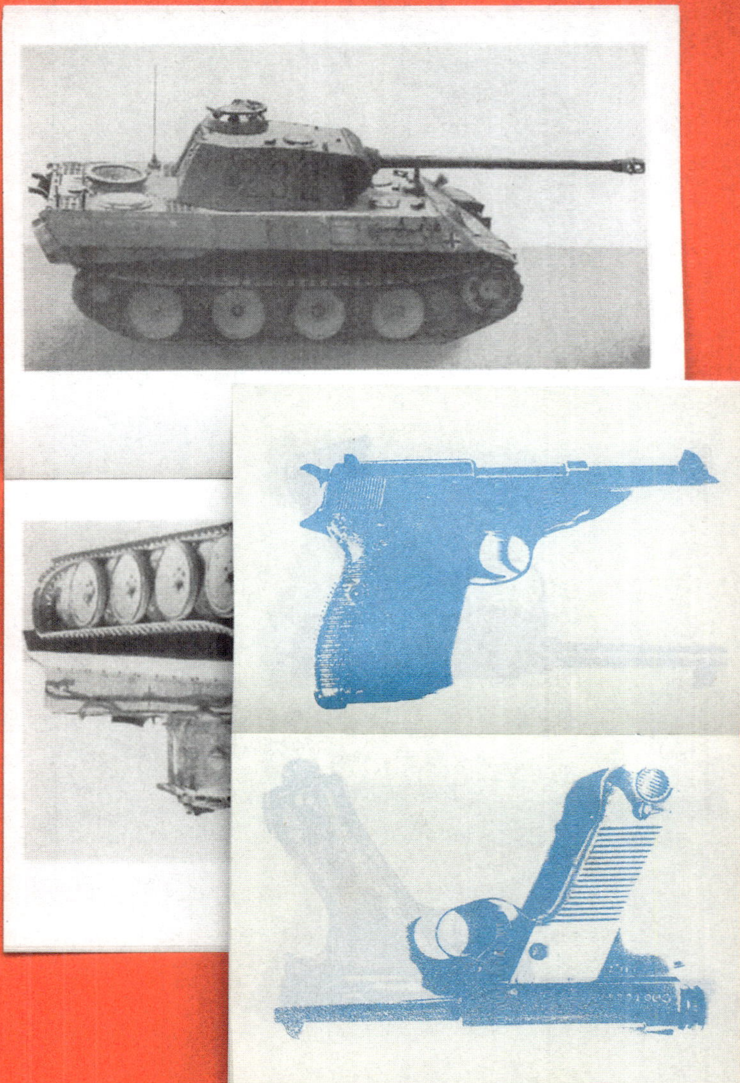

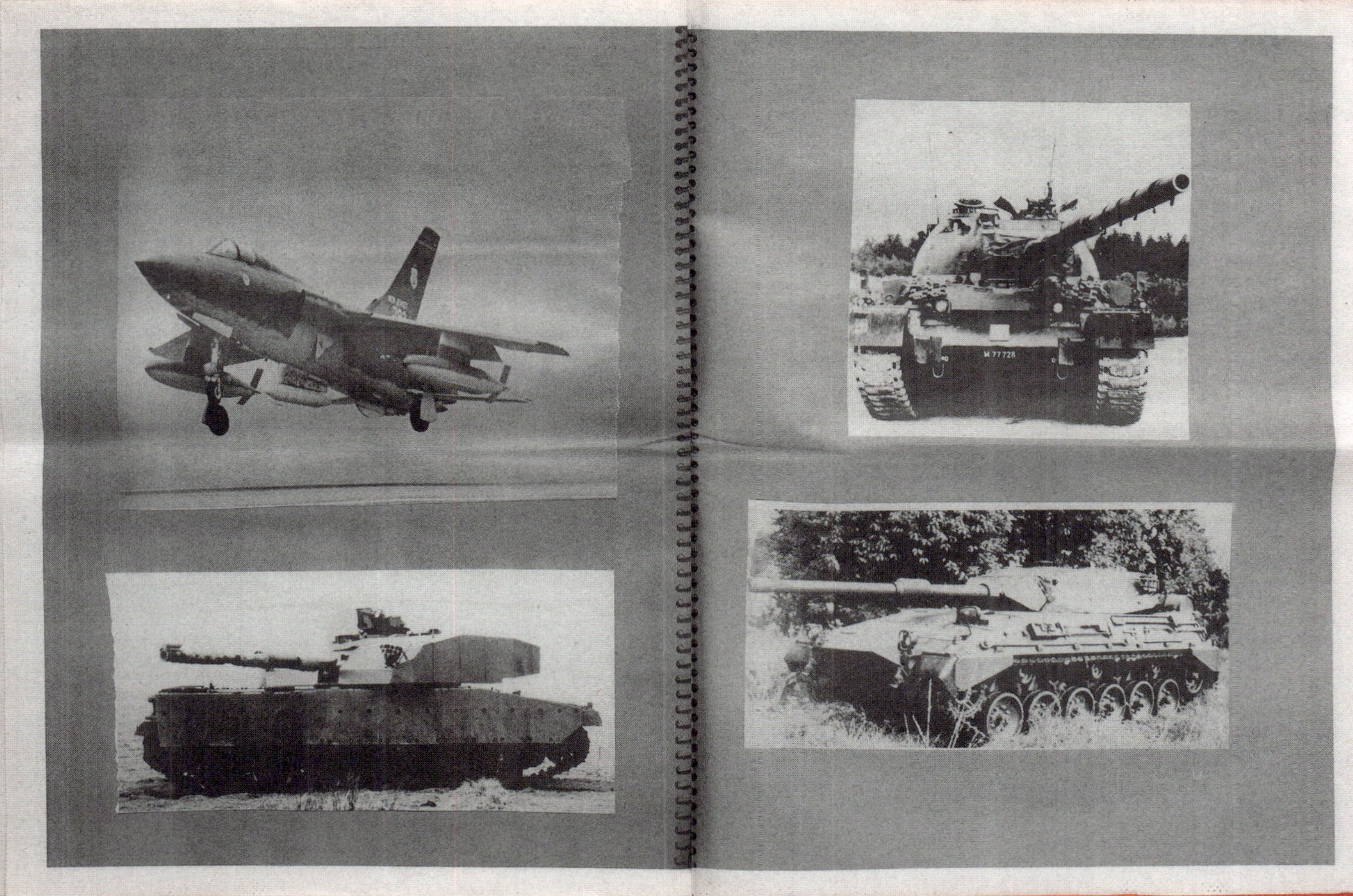

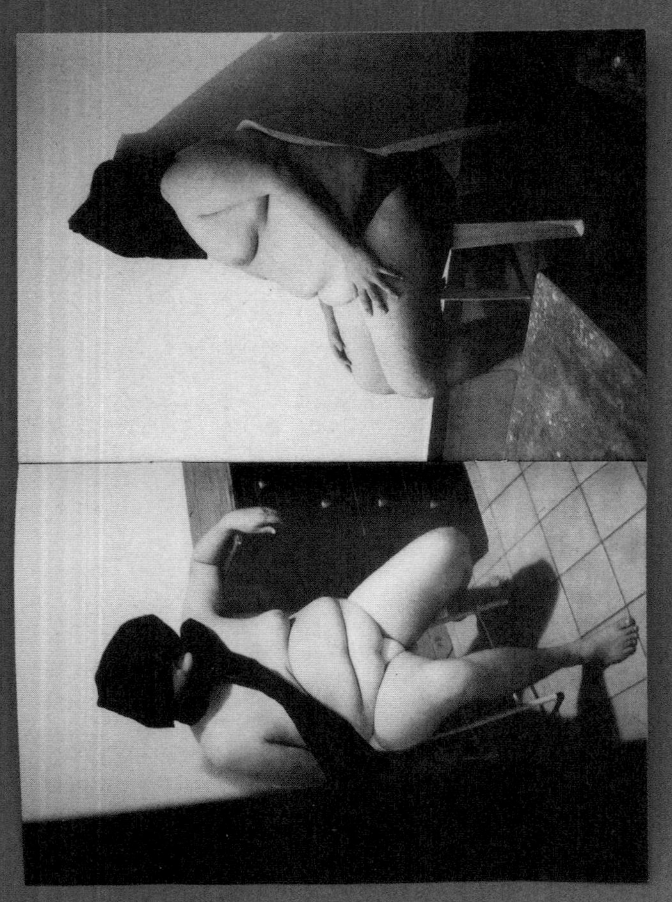

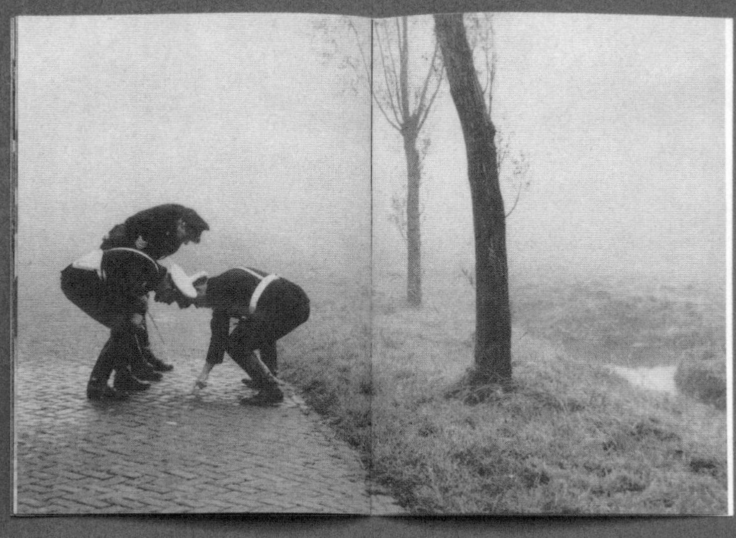

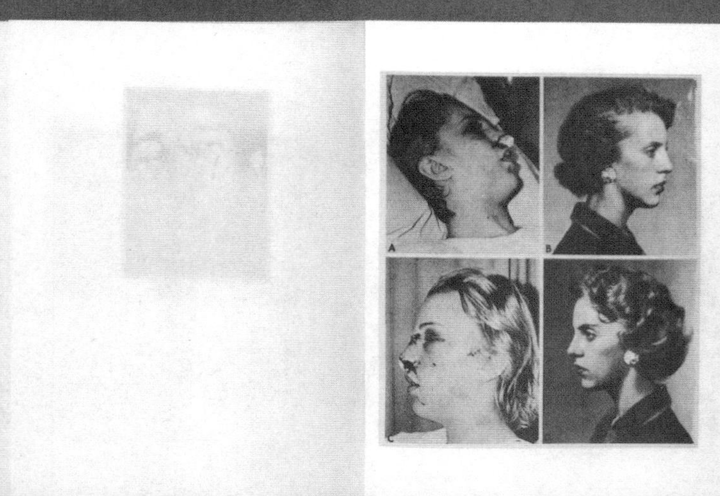

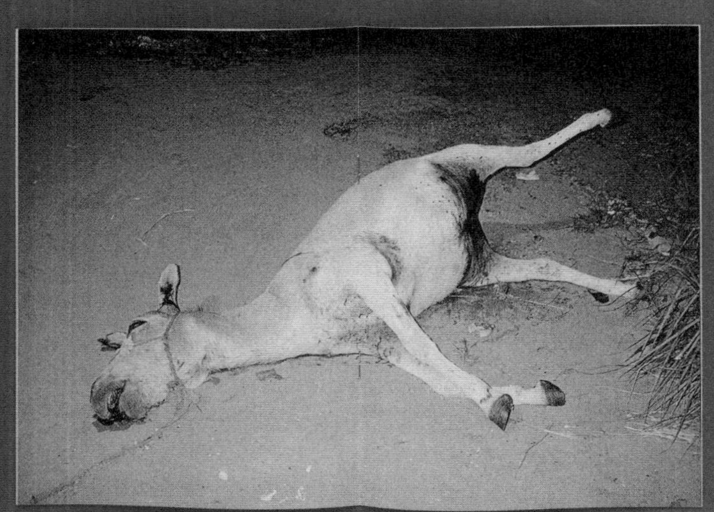

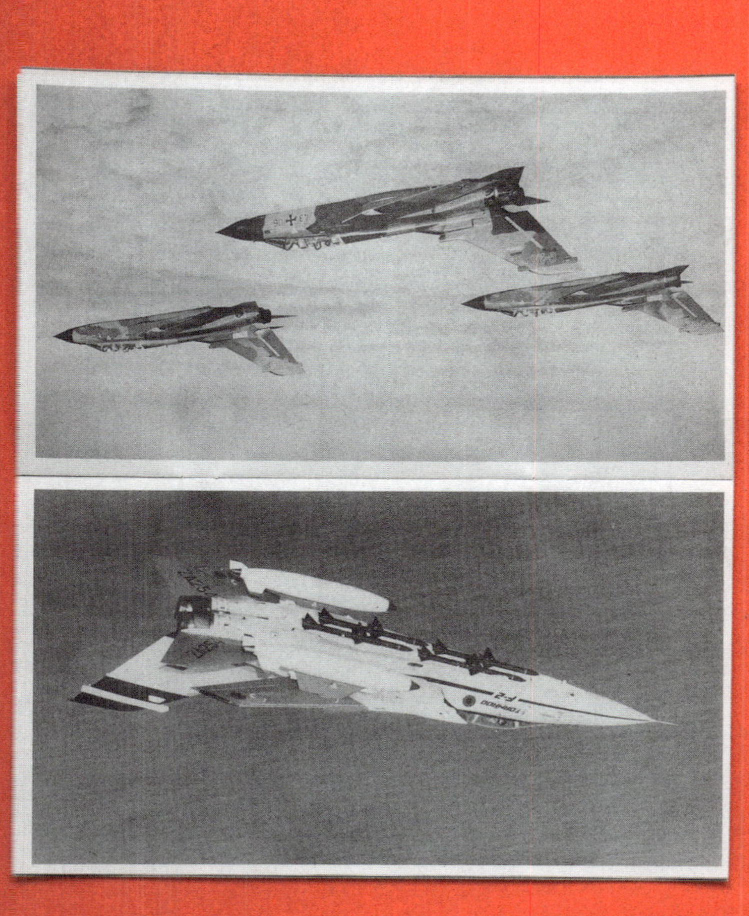

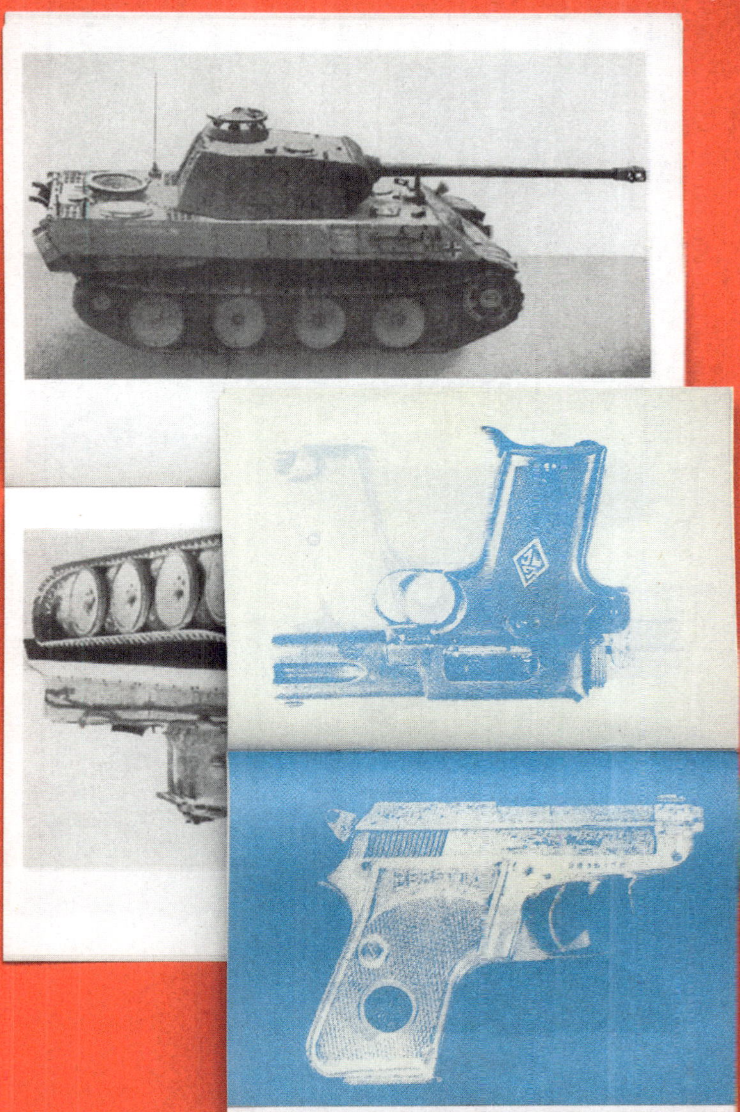

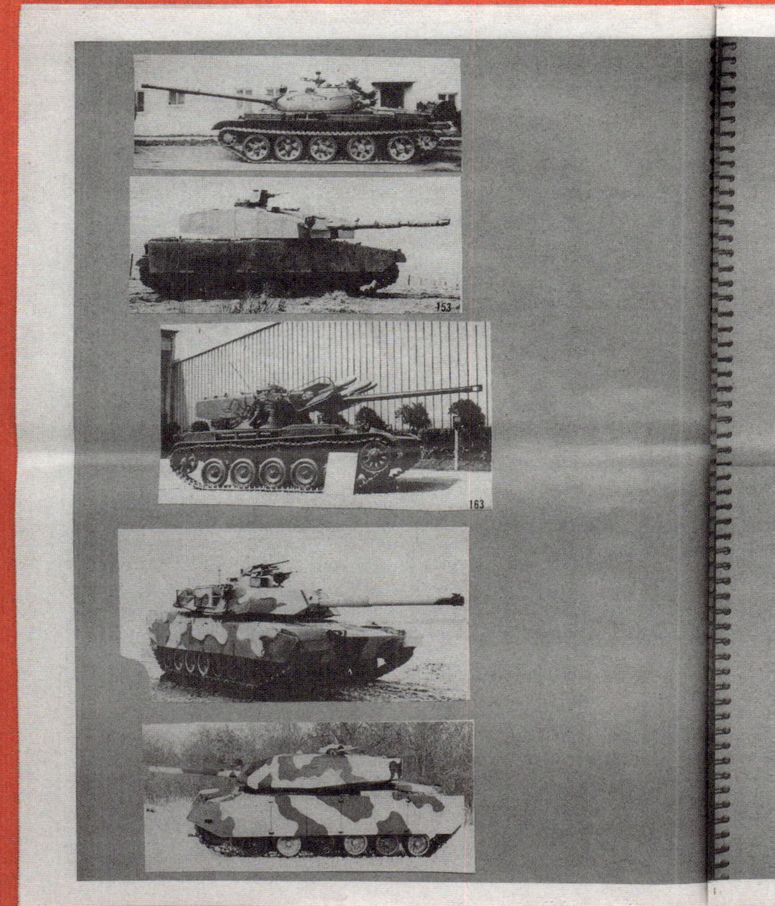

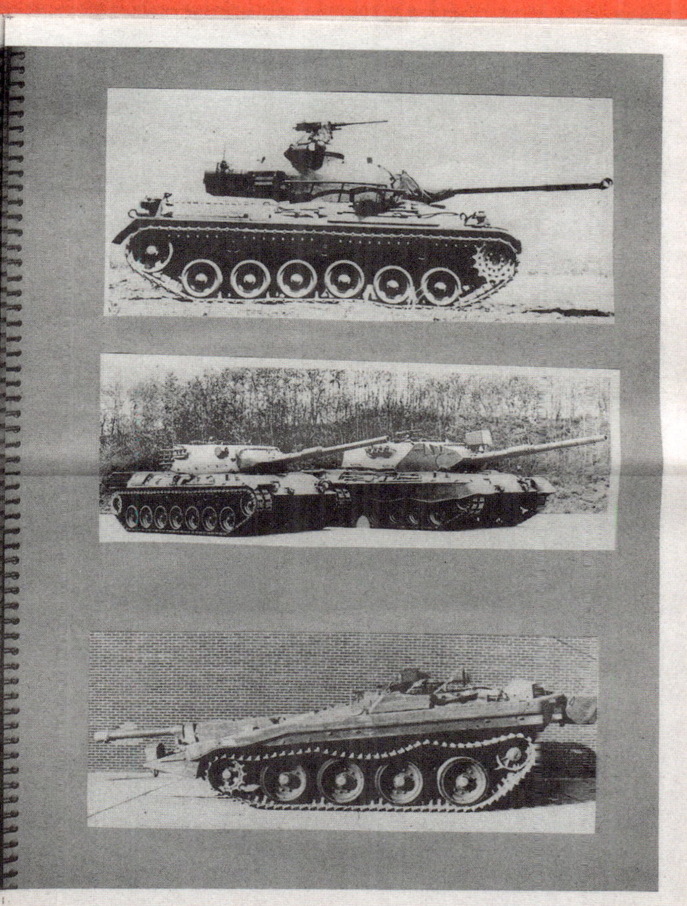

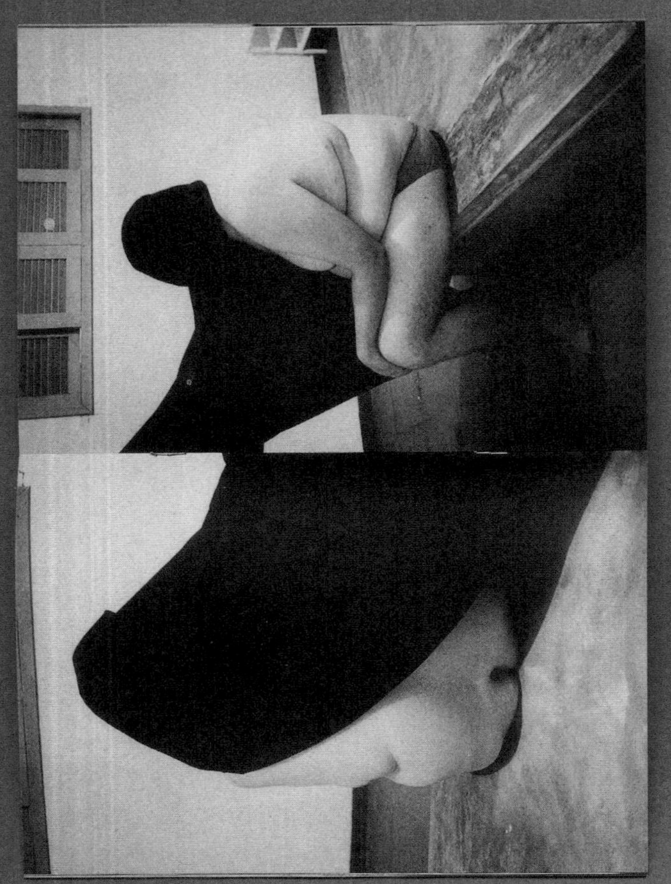
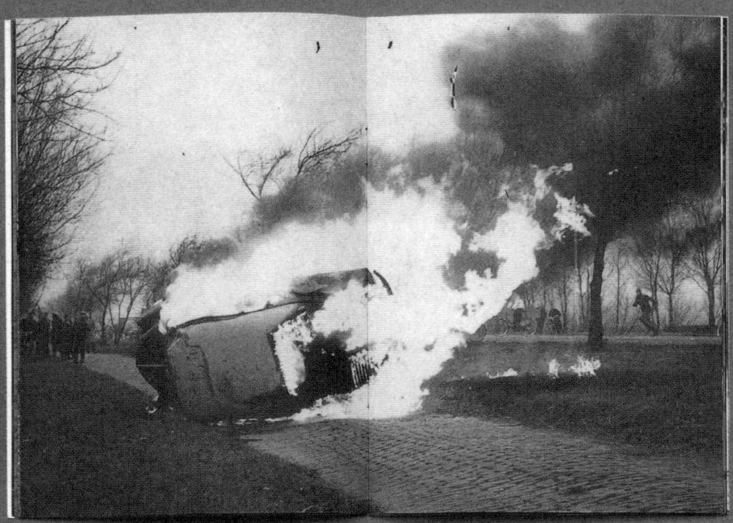
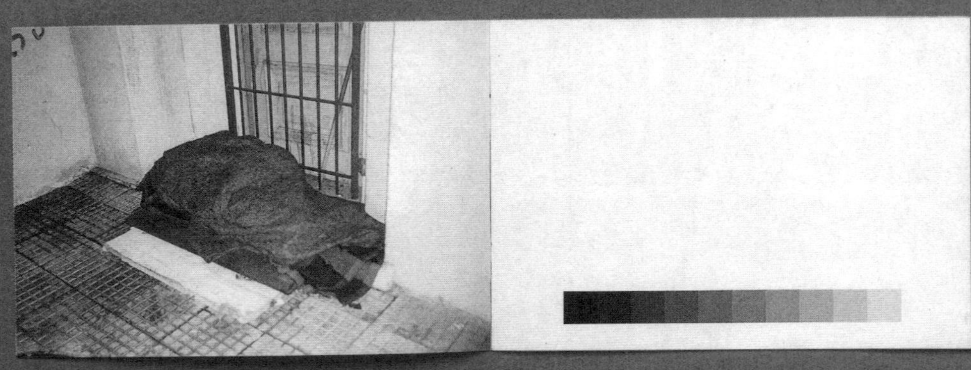
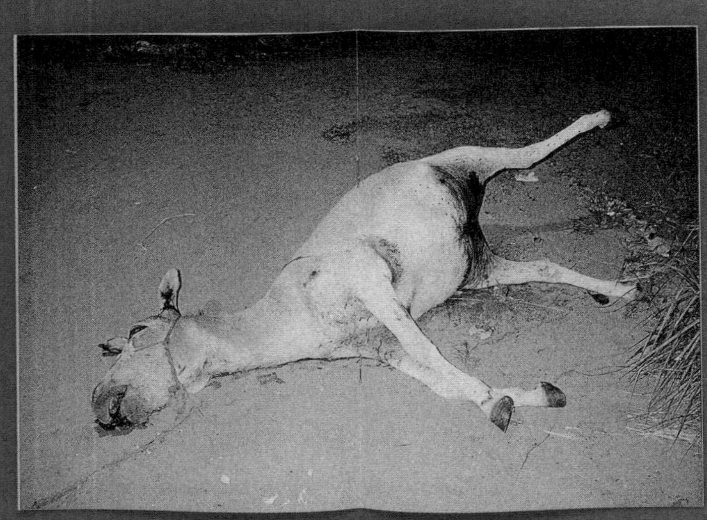
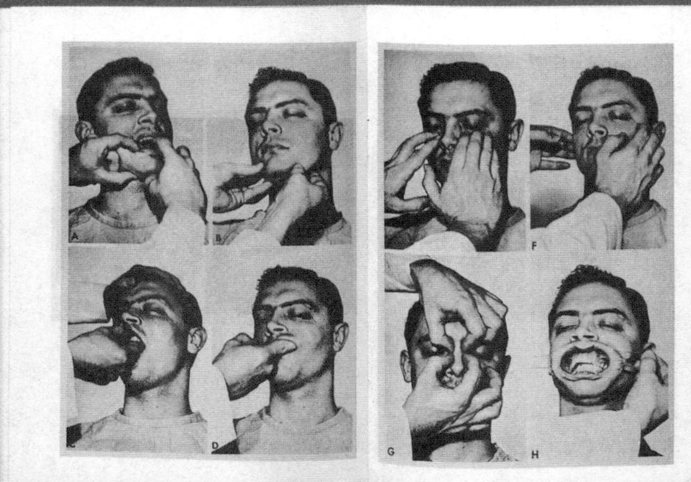

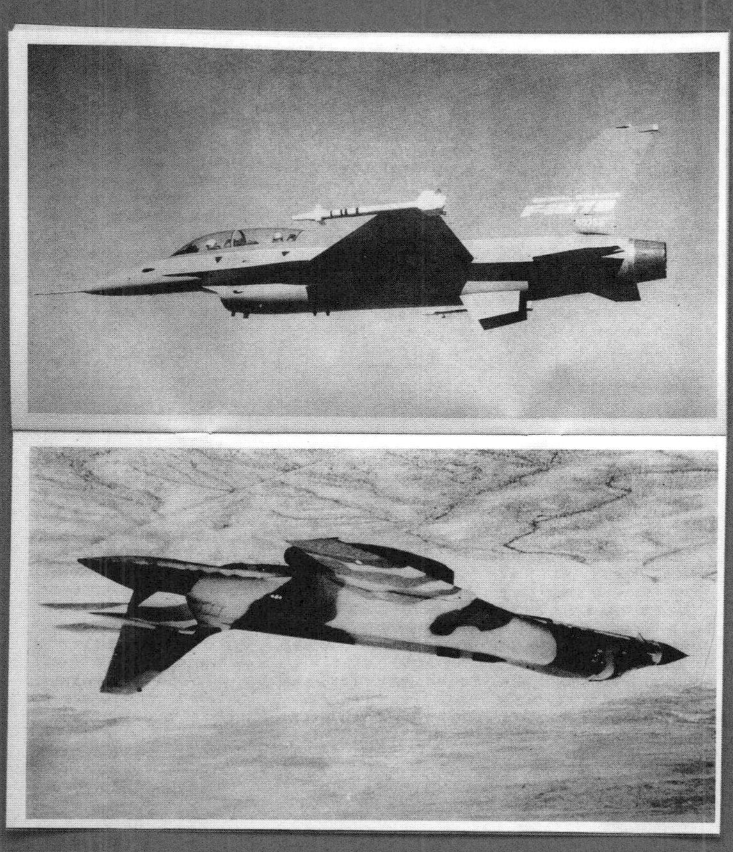

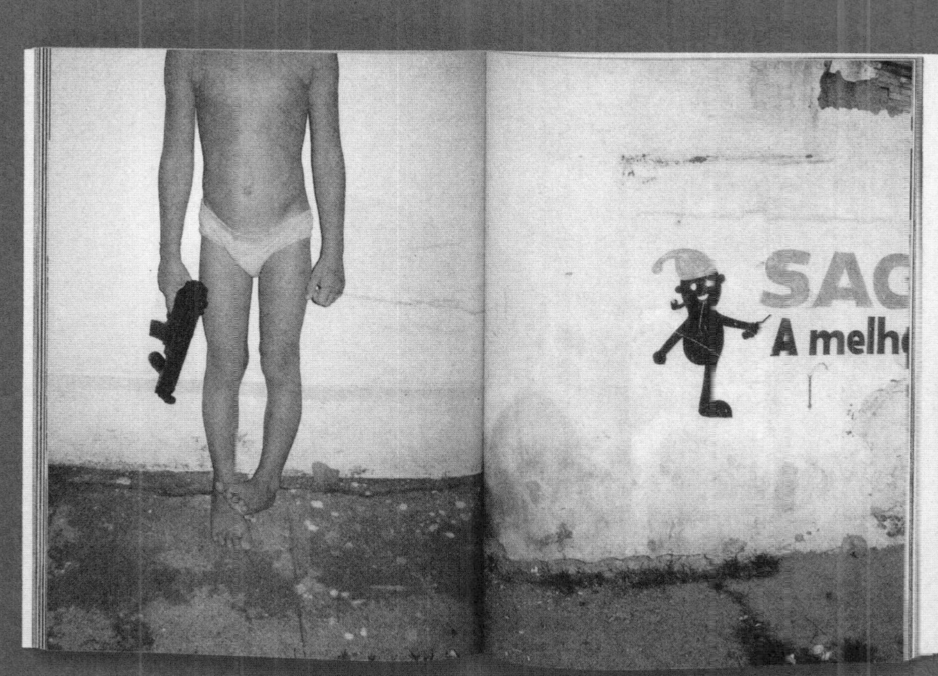

SAC
A melh

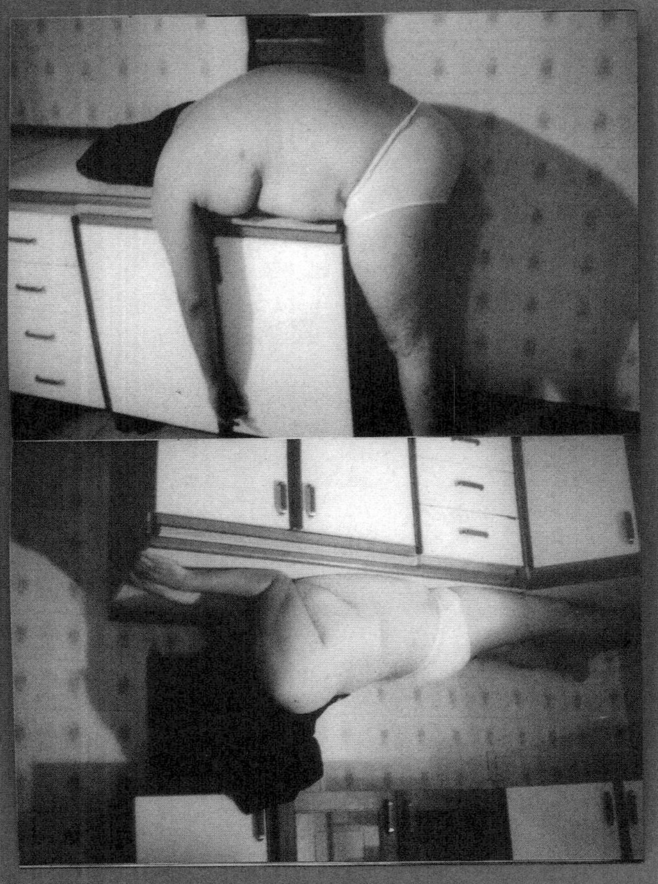
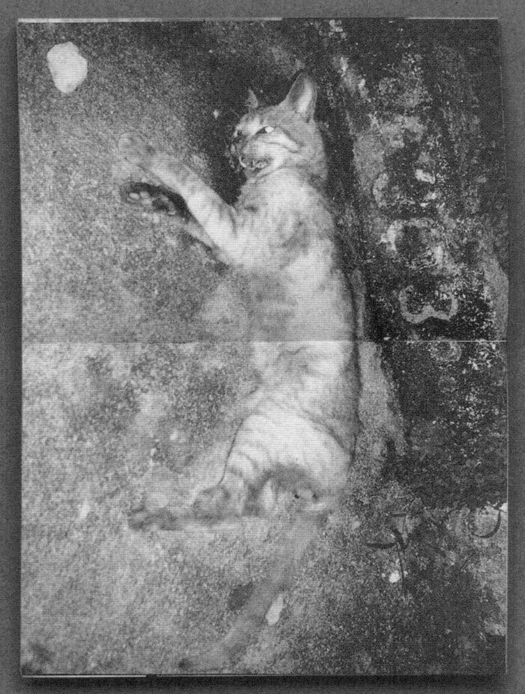
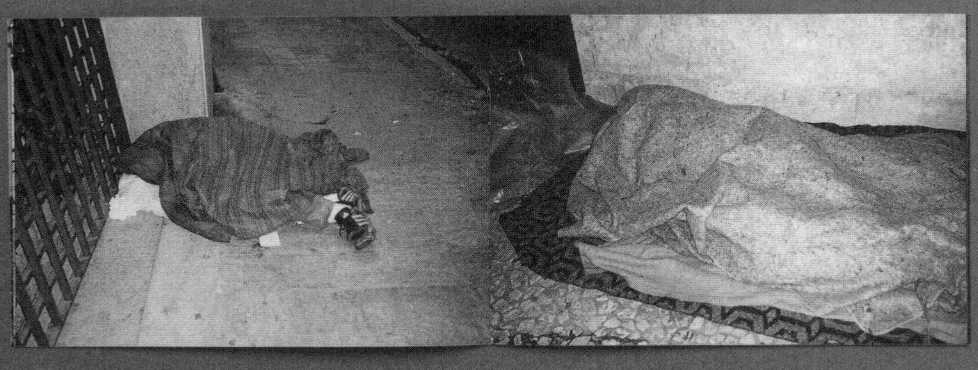
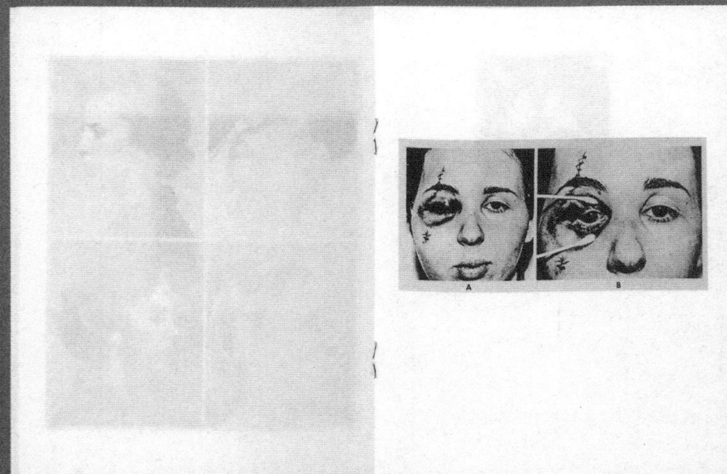
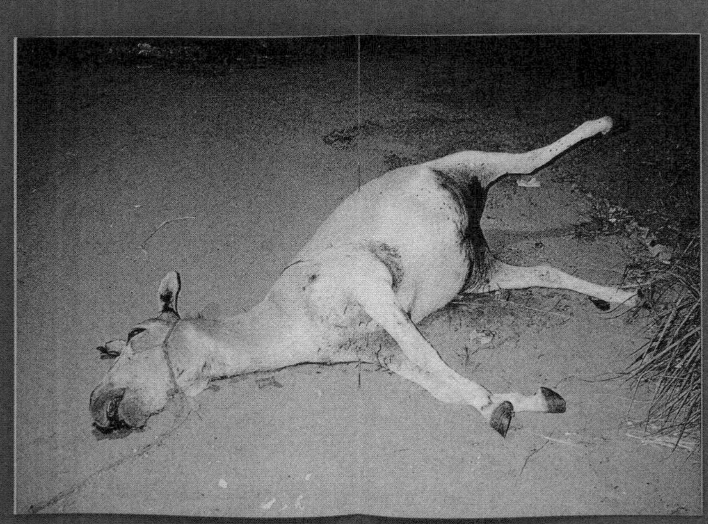

Germany

Ludwig II, Third Reich, Souvenir I,
Siedlung, foto.zine nr. 2 (Third Reich),
Der Baum, foto.zine nr. 2 (Caravans)

Brazil

O. Niemeyer, Superquadra,
Pomerode, Souvenir II, foto.zine nr. 1
(issue 5), Down the Rabbit Hole 2,
foto.zine nr. 2 (Caravans), foto.zine
nr. 5 (Motel)

Prostitution

foto.zine nr. 1 (issue 1), Praia,
Down the Rabbit Hole 2, Down the
Rabbit Hole, Souvenir III, Down
the Rabbit Hole 3

Cars

foto.zine nr. 3 (Accidents), foto.zine
nr. 5 (Fusca), Parking Lot, foto.zine nr. 3
(Stuttgart), Down the Rabbit Hole 3,
Der Baum

Wife

This Is Not My Wife, Home Is Where
The Dog Is, This Is Not My Son,
Set of 3 (Maria Lúcia), foto.zine nr. 4
(issue 4)

Son

foto.zine nr. 4 (issue 2), Privacy
Settings, This Is Not My Son,
This Is Not My Wife, foto.zine nr. 4
(issue 5), Home Is Where The Dog Is,
New Amsterdam / New Holland

Relatives

Home Is Where The Dog Is, This
Is Not My Son, Set of 3 (Maria Lúcia),
Courbe, foto.zine nr. 4 (issue 3)

Pets

This Is Not My Wife, This Is Not
My Son, Home Is Where The Dog Is,
Nina, Set of 3 (Mona Lisa)

Anonymity

Praia, Home Is Where The Dog Is,
foto.zine nr. 1 (issue 7), This Is
Not My Son, foto.zine nr. 1 (issue 1)

Trees

foto.zine nr. 2 (Niemeyer), Der Baum,
Ludwig II, Bonsai, foto.zine nr. 3
(Palm Trees), Superquadra

Animals

Nelore, Deer Park, Teddy Bear,
Rear Window, Home Is Where
The Dog Is, Down the Rabbit Hole 3,
foto.zine nr. 1 (issue 1)

Weapons

Paradiesvögel, Birds of Paradise,
Die Wolken, foto.zine nr. 3
(Hand Guns), This Is Not My Son

Violence

foto.zine nr. 1 (issue 4), foto.zine nr. 3
(Accidents), Facial Fractures,
Down the Rabbit Hole, foto.zine nr. 1
(issue 7), foto.zine nr. 1 (issue 1)

One plus One

Some notes about various types of double-page spreads
by Jan Wenzel

We need a photo book grammar! How else will we be able to describe its structure; all the rules of cohesion that are applied? Everyone who only sees books as containers, as receptacles for conveying pictures and texts, will be blind to this demand; but everyone who conceives books as a space-time sequence—as Ulises Carrión proposes—must confront this necessity. Because no single element is isolated within a space-time sequence—no individual picture, no individual text, no individual page—indeed, every one of these elements can only be grasped within its context, every one of these elements is part of a structure that creates meaning which we ultimately call *the book*.

But until now—we have to add—there has never been a photo book grammar, not even in part. There is no "formal school" as linguists are familiar with, and there is no Viktor Schklowski of the photo book, nobody who has done an in-depth study on the rules of cohesion and the subject of the photo book; there is no Roman Jakobson of the photo book, nobody who has probed more deeply into the mesh of contrast relationships and parallelisms; and no Boris Eichenbaum, nobody who has done a more in-depth study of the uniform and mirror-image repetitions in the arrangement of photographs. In that sense, the following can be no more than a rough draft; a first cautious groping effort to enter an uncharted territory; a step towards a "formal school" of the photo book. I am particularly interested in the smallest unit of the space-time sequence: the double-page spread. One single page is not a sequence—only when it is joined by a counterpart does the game of contrast and parallelism begin. The double-page spread is the most elementary form of montage; the hinge in the middle separates and connects the two partial surfaces of equal size. The double-page spread represents the smallest time unit within the book's space-time sequence. The double-page spread shows what the viewer should grasp in *a single* moment. If he goes on turning pages, he keeps the previous pages in the back of his head, present but, when opened, it is only a right and a left side. The rest of the book evades one's gaze.

Reading a photo book begins with gazing at double-page spreads; it starts with the attempt to grasp that mesh of contrast and similarity relationships that are created by the arrangement of the pictures. Erik van der Weijde's photo books are particularly suitable for describing various types of double-page spreads—mostly two equally large photographs face each other on opposite pages, the picture format rarely changes within the book itself.

The Contrast Relationship

Sergei Eisenstein wrote that montage means a clash: "the conflict between two subsequent images." But every montage can also be understood as a dialogue, as Michail Bachtin knows: a mutual illumination, a reciprocal influence and a divergence which lead to a much more distinct awareness, a more precise perception. The contrast relationship inspires the liveliest type of double-page spread. The pictures comment on each other and point out their differences. The viewer is asked to look at a picture in the light of another picture: The more similarities the pictures show, the more distinct their differences become—whether formal or contextual.

A white steel container with a black garbage bag. A black garbage can with a white garbage bag. The playful give-and-take with forms and colors begins, a differentiated feeling for the abundance of possibilities, a profound feeling for the change, the relativity of every form becomes possible.

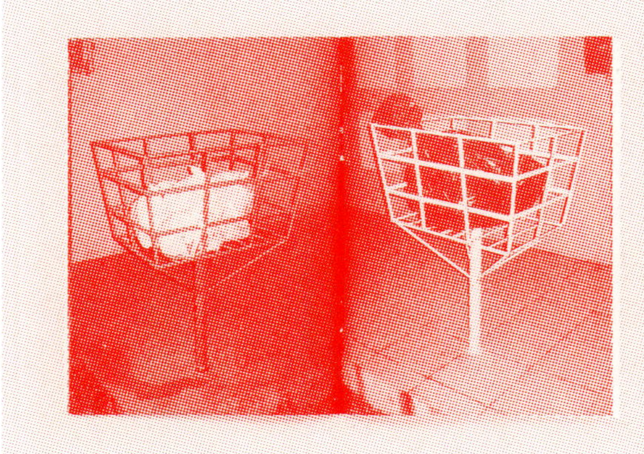

foto.zine nr. 5 (Fusca), 2013

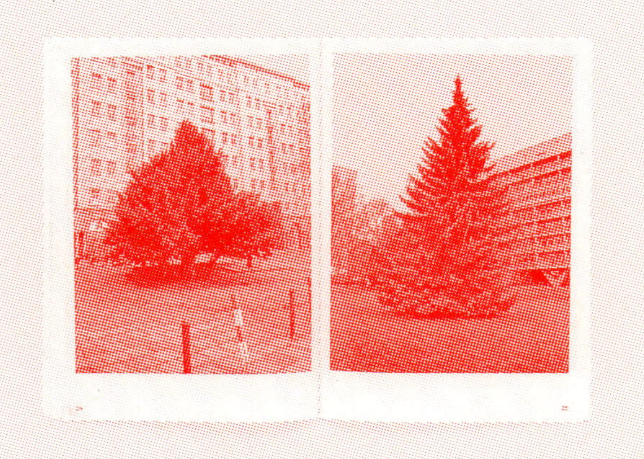

Der Baum, 2010

A tree in front of a Stalinist façade in the Karl-Marx-Allee in East Berlin; a tree in front of a highrise in West Berlin, designed by Oscar Niemeyer. A contrast relationship means an intensification, because it is the most condensed statement of a conflict. The opposites clash directly; every object, every concept, every standpoint is alienated by its counterpart. That means that we "see" and don't just "recognize" it. The contrast relationship works against the naïve nature of our gaze.

But the contrast relationship exhausts itself; it is impossible to put together a book based solely on this type of double-page spread. In order to unleash its full impact, it has to appear in contrast to the previous and following pages. Sections that emphasize the pictures' similarities must precede them. Or the point of conflict that forms the essence of the double-page spread has to change constantly—from formal aspects to spatial aspects, from historical aspects to aspects of perspective. In a staccato of that nature, an abundance of conflict lines would emerge. This is the underlying principle that maximizes the impact of *Der Baum*.

The Mirroring Image

The mirroring image is a form of similarity relationship. Both pages of a double-page spread relate to each other, creating a pull, an attraction.

This form of pictorial relationship on a double-page spread can be associated with very diverse effects. The simplest: The recurring elements that appear on both pages are reinforced, they seem to be dynamically duplicated. But these moments of mirrored imaging in the pictures paired on the double-page spread can also inspire the viewer with a dynamic perspective: the possibility that he himself can move around the depicted object to view the house, the couch or the person from different perspectives; or that the photographer—acting on behalf of the viewer—already did just that while taking the photograph, thus allowing the viewer's gaze to move from one position point to the next. In this way, a moment of motion is introduced to the double-page spread—the imagination of a body moving through the image space.

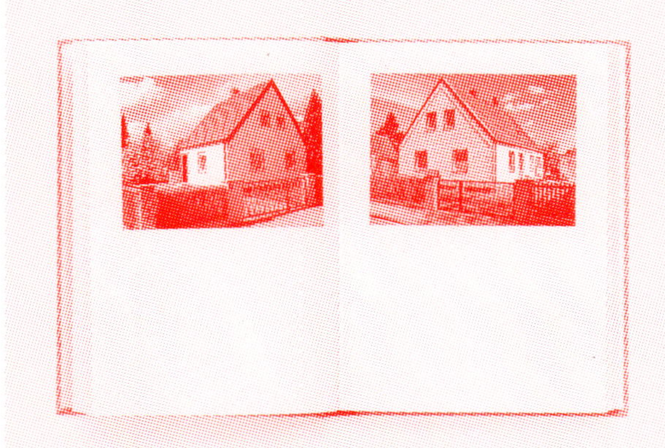

Siedlung, 2008

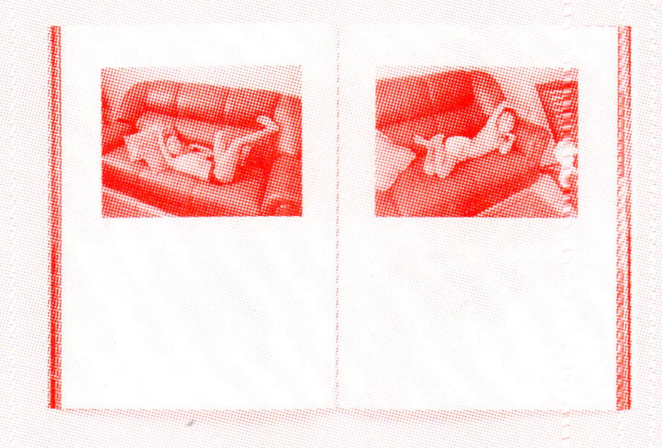

This Is Not My Son, 2009

In photo books of a truly serial nature where one and the same subject is depicted again and again, this type of double-page spread is also a form of minimal variation; the possibility of adding rhythm to the sequence of double-page spreads; an interruption of the sequence of pages. A circular motion, revolving around a central axis interrupts the linear sequence of pictures. The more Erik van der Weijde focuses on a single subject in a publication—whether it be a house, a cow, a pistol or a car—the more important this type of double-page spread becomes in order to keep the subject itself *in motion* and to prevent the viewer's interest from congealing. One just has to consider the way things are emphasized by the mirrored double-page spreads in *Siedlung* and the way the sequence is infused with its rhythm, its breath.

Of course, two photographs that seem to be mirrored on the double-page spread always refer back to the basic medial construction of the book; a left-hand page and a right-hand page and in the middle the axis of the hinge—the medium explains itself.

The Interrupted Picture

This type of double-page spread can only be found in one single book by Erik van der Weijde, in *Ludwig II*, the second part of the Bavaria trilogy. At first, it seems as if this form were pragmatically justified: By placing portrait and landscape formats on one page within the same print space, every landscape format is split into two portrait formats. The result is a uniform overall picture and equivalent image areas. Erik van der Weijde solved this problem in other books by turning landscape formats on their side, for example, in *This Is Not My Wife*; or by placing scaled down landscape formats on their side, a principle which was applied, for example, in *This Is Not My Son* or in *Nina*.

If all the landscape formats in *Ludwig II* are split—a decision that, after all, affects forty percent of the book's double-page spreads, because those pages always include panoramic views—and if the landscape images are

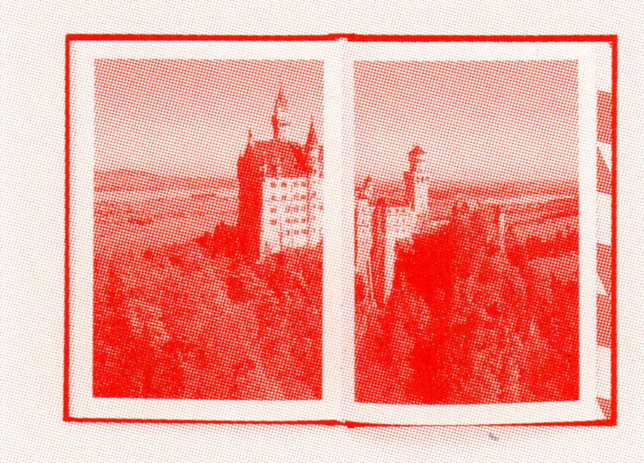

Ludwig II, 2015

Ludwig II, 2015

turned on their side or scaled down, they lose their effect; on the other hand, the moment of imagination is introduced to the images of a late Romantic Bavarian setting. The viewer has to piece together the given scenarios in his mind, he has to complete the panoramas by himself, because the idyll that is instilled in these landscapes is not depicted by a photograph, it is projected solely by the viewer's imagination to which these postcard motifs seem to obligate the viewer. Only the split picture, the picture in which the imagination is incorporated from the beginning as a constructive element, does justice to the motifs, whether it is Neuschwanstein Castle or the forest at Lake Starnberg. Interestingly enough, double-page spreads can be found in *Superquadra*, another book by Erik van der Weijde, that seem, at first sight, to be split in the middle. But not until they are more closely inspected is it possible to recognize two separate photographs that fit so well together that they apparently create a panorama. These double-page spreads are a variation of this type, they could apparently be called interrupted pictures.

This type of double-page spread which is most prominent in Erik van der Weijde's *This Is Not My Son* uses associative similarity relationships and the intuitive recognition of similarity, even in instances where it is not obvious. A single pictorial element which is included in a picture appears in an altered form in a picture on the opposite page. In this way, an incisive relationship is created; a similarity which the viewer must discover himself.

The son holds his teddy bear piggyback. You sense it's there more than you see it; on the opposite page you see a picture of the son wearing a bear mask. Here you have to sense the son's presence. The positions have changed, roles have been swopped.

The double-page spread becomes a point of intersection here, a place where allusions and implications intertwine. The pictures become permeable and diverse. On the left-hand side of the picture we can see a boy, his head

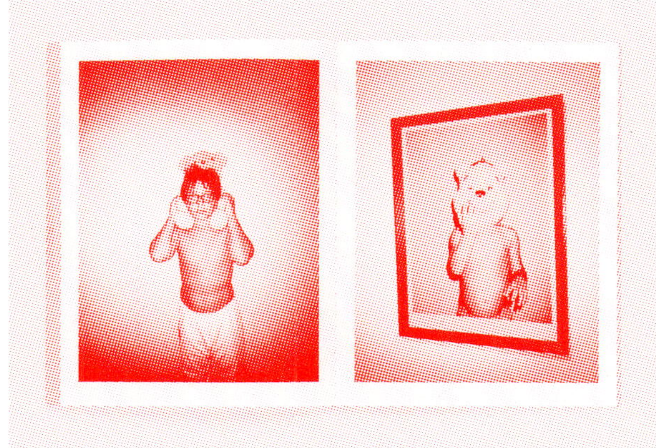

Home Is Where The Dog Is, 2014

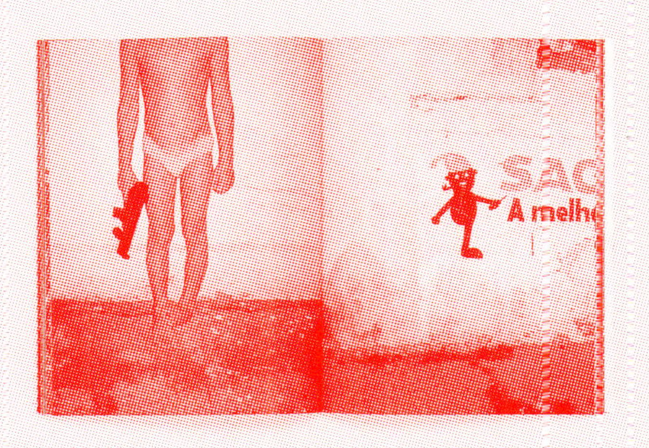

This Is Not My Son, 2009

is cut off at the edge of the page, he is holding a black toy gun in his right hand. On the right-hand side we see a wall where someone has painted a black figure whose right leg is missing. Whereas the figure on the left-hand side is larger than the picture permits, the one on the right-hand side is too small for the image space. If the toy gun on the left is a black line in the picture, the figure on the right lacks a black line—its leg.

The pictures on opposite pages mutually charge each other. Their encounter resembles the way language is used in a poem. The associations refer us to a third picture, to the semantic field of children's cruelty, to a desire to play with violence. This meaning is only generated through the entangle-ment of the pictures, an implication that only emerges in the associations on the double-page spread.

One single double-page spread where a concept is demonstrated by this kind of associative entanglement can become a leitmotif for a sequence. In the course of the following pages, while keeping this association in mind, you will find various elements where the appropriate motif is continued.

The Repetition

It was Pop Art in the sixties that discovered the visual power of serial art. An everyday object can attain an iconic aura as soon as it is shown multiple times. Cans, boxes of detergent, gas stations: Industrial manufacturing generated their aura; advertising reproduced things again and again and created their imaginary meaning. And also by using artistic methods of repetition, everyday objects can acquire a lasting virtue, no matter how trivial they are. Andy Warhol knew it, Ed Ruscha and Peter Roehr did, too.

All of Erik van der Weijde's books deal with the principles of serial art. A certain object, a certain person is shown again and again. That is why double-page spreads that "show the same thing" on both the left page and the right page are the type of double-page spread he uses most often in his books. By repeating the picture of an object over a series of pages, the image is reinforced. "... and once again and once again ..." is the basic beat

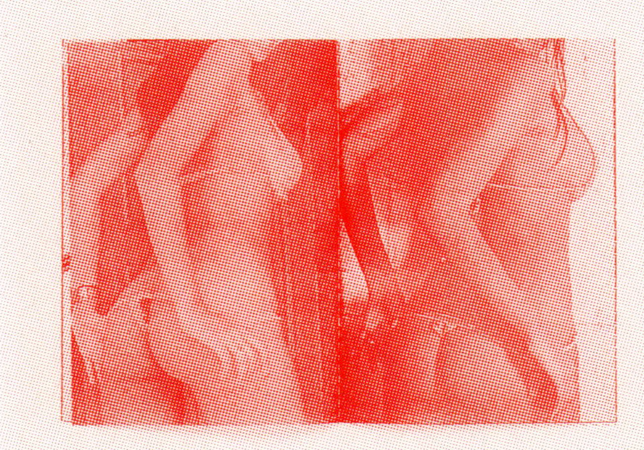

foto.zine nr. 3 (Untitled), 2009

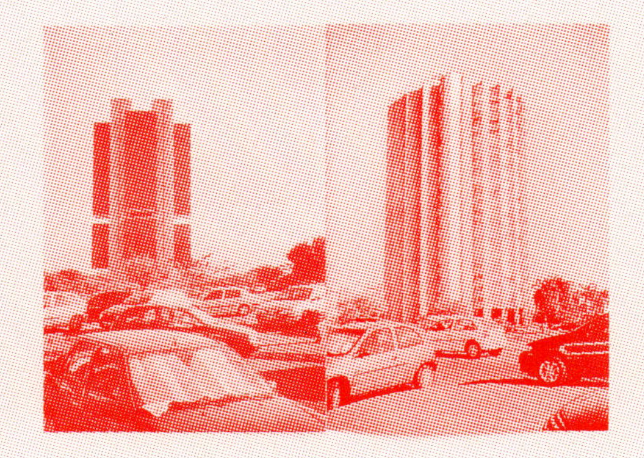

foto.zine nr. 2 (Caravans), 2007

of these books. The pictures may be similar, but they are never the same. And that is exactly what makes Erik van der Weijde's photo books so playful. Sounding out the space for similarities in order to show an object in an everyday manner, in its repetition, in its familiarity, in its banality.

But a photograph with that particular goal in mind cannot focus on the original image, the right moment or a surprising sequence of pages; a photograph of that nature has to allow for redundancy; the small, essentially meaningless differences; the weight of uneventuality. Only in that way is it possible to show the things that are *also* there. This type of photography always returns to double-page spreads that reproduce the objects. This type of double-page spread is the basis for being able to show things in their everyday aura.

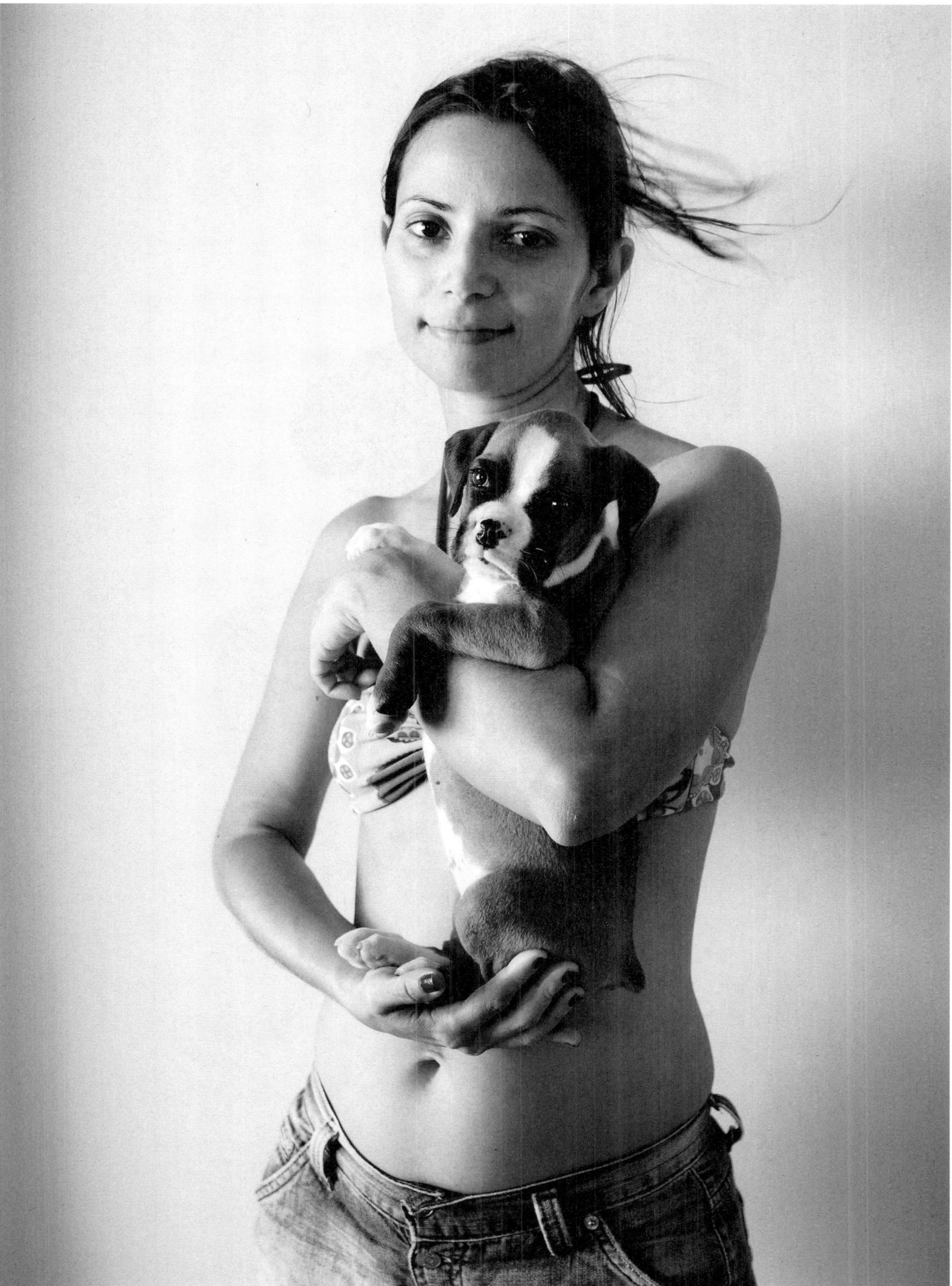

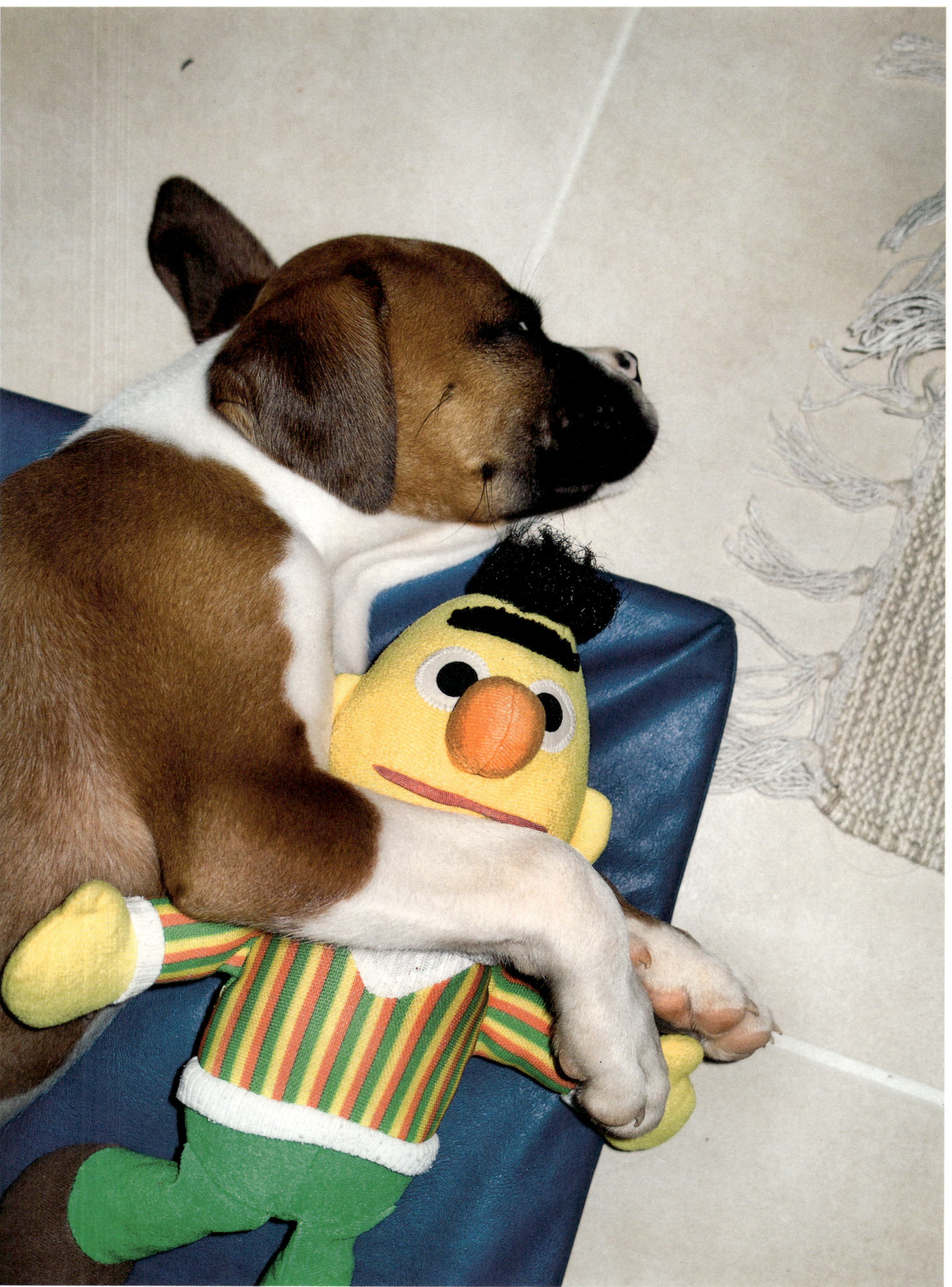

From the Page to the Sequence, from the Sequence to the Book

Erik van der Weijde in conversation with Jan Wenzel
First movement

Jan: You once called a book a contextualization machine. It is a medium that establishes its very own possibilities for organizing photographs: the page; the double page; the piece of paper that has both a front and back side; the sequence of pages—all those spatial relationships between the pictures. Let's start with the simplest and most elementary part: with the single page.

Erik: Actually the single page is never really on my mind. It is only a starting point to give an image an actual place. It's the transition from computer to this new context, as an actual hard copy. So maybe it's also the first step towards giving the image its meaning. By putting it onto a page, the image is not floating around on a hard disk anymore, but my choice to show it and say "have a look at this, this is important." The step of using the single page to assign a photograph to has now become such a natural step for me, that I haven't given it any real thought in years. Maybe even never.

Jan: The page is a threshold. First of all, the picture has to be placed on the marked white space of the InDesign document, so that it will later appear in the book. What sort of selection process occurs in advance?

Erik: After I finalize the shooting and all the images are in their folder with the project name, I scroll through that folder again and again, until certain similarities or just interesting parts in the images begin to pop up. What I decide to be the better pictures then, I save in another folder, which I name "to print." In this process I usually lose 50–70 percent of the images. From that new folder I start sketching in InDesign for possible spreads and 4–6 page sequences. Most of the time in this process I either lose another 10 percent or I change 10–20 percent with the other folder that will re-enter the selection.

Jan: In most cases you put one single picture on a page. There are rarely any photographs that cross over onto the next page, that spread across the binding, just as there is rarely a page with several pictures on it.

Erik: I find it far from ideal to have an image spread across the binding. There are solutions to show the entire image, only in a smaller way. I think the size of a photograph in a book doesn't need to be so big. If you want to show considerable size, probably an exhibition would be a better solution.

I used the single-image spread, for example, in *Eva / Maria / Heidi* (part of *Set of 3*), because the quality of the images was already so bad through the use of a cheap laser printer and colored paper that I felt the "loss" of this center part of the photos didn't even matter anymore. About the use of more images on one page, I don't do that often, because that kind of relationship between images, which appears within more than two photographs, I prefer to use in the sequence of pages. I find more than two images on a spread very confusing.

Jan: The principle of "one picture per page" leads to simplicity in the book's layout. The image and the single page are fused. One might even say: Your page layout is usually simple, just as simple as the picture's subject. It is the "doubly simple" medial operation that essentially makes a single picture, which in itself is trivial, become part of a contextual meaning which lends it an iconographic power, no matter how ordinary that picture may be—within an image sequence, a tree, a gas station, your own children can stand for all trees, gas stations and children.

Erik: Yes, I think there is a simplicity to that. There are more effective ways in the design of a book to work with less simplistic parts that demand more from the reader. I'm thinking of a sequence for example, where I can push into certain directions. I love the simplicity of the image and page, it's one of the reasons why photography and books go so well together.

Jan: Right page / side — left page / side, is there a difference for you? Are there pictures you would only place on the right side?

Erik: Yes, but that has only to do with images that are "leaning" too much in a certain direction. An image that clearly leans to the right would be difficult to put on a left page, so it would then lean towards the center of the spread. Also, in the spread, with two images, when these two images combined create a kind of new land-scape-orientated image, it's not possible to change the two.

This has a lot to do with how I design, because I am not trained as a designer. I feel more like a sculptor working with clay, adding some parts on one side or taking some away from the top or bottom. Here's where the right / left page also comes in. I will see if the image is on the right side or not, but mostly it's not a rational deci-sion. It's more about balance on the two pages open.

Jan: One plus one — a right page / side and a left page / side. Isn't that a very complex constel-lation?

Erik: Yes! For me that's where it all starts. It is one of the most fun things to work with, but it also sets the design for sequence in the book. I really love all possibilities the two opposite pages pro-vide. I can start a linear sequence on only these two pages, or start breaking images down, next to each other, or mirror images. I think there-fore the complexity is only in the amount of possibilities and thus to choose one: After that it's just following the chosen path.

Jan: Similar to a movie, two pictures come together. Immediately an entire network of con-sciously and subconsciously effective parallel-isms, uniform or mirror-imaged repetitions emerge; a network of contrasting and similar relations. I've opened to a double page of *Der Baum*: Can you describe this montage, this network that emerges between the two images?

Erik: Uh yes, the Karl-Marx-Allee and the Hansa-Viertel in Berlin. On one side, the Stalinist show-off housing project and the Western answer to that with the modernist Hansa-Viertel project. This is a spread I really remember putting together, be-cause it took me maybe five seconds to put these images next to each other and then I started doubting if this connection between the two imag-es and pages wasn't a bit too easy. But in the end I left it like it was, because there are many spreads in the book which apparently have nothing in common, so this "easy-to-read" spread would then give an opening in the reading of the book as a whole. This spread, I felt, takes a bit of the mystery out of the book in an otherwise mysterious work.

My first thoughts on these two images, before putting them together in this spread, were that they both were kind of cheesy, so one tree is surrounded by this architecture with stones all around and the other stands in the grass and has much more space around it. But on a certain level it definitely works ...

Jan: The contrast montage, the act of playing with opposites is a combination possibility; but not the only one. On pages 30 / 31 the motif is repeated on a nearly 1:1 basis — two locations but almost the same situation. On the opposite sides of a double page, the contrast is once again more powerful: on the left, two conifers behind a modern series of houses inspired by the Bauhaus style; on the right, three conifers in front of a conservative type of house. Both building styles probably stem from the same period but were influenced by contrasting architectural concepts. You photograph the trees, so they are in the middle of the picture. They lend the various con-texts a sense of stability and cohesion.

Erik: Yes, of course, but that is also what makes this book a bit double, or going in different directions. I have always photographed trees, already long before I had the idea of making this book. So, on the one hand, I have this con-stant factor, the tree, centered, on the other hand, a variety of subjects and places which I was pursuing at that time. So for some of the pictures, the tree was actually an innocent by-stander in the photograph of maybe an architectural shot and sometimes the other way around. But the continuity of the trees in this book is the only actual leading thread, it sometimes strings together two identical places or ideas and some-times completely different subjects. So be-cause of this variety of actual subjects — besides the tree — I use different spread designs like contrast, mirror and repetition. All these trees are byproducts.

Jan: The tree is a good example for discussing something I would like to call a "book picture." All the photographs in the book are part of a sequence. We see each of the pictures with the other pictures at the back of our mind. The pictures mutually charge each other. But the pictures present themselves in a different way than at a gallery, where a sequence is always present as a whole. The pictures in a book appear and disappear again, as soon as you turn the page.

In my opinion, the fact that the series *Der Baum* is so consistent and so complex has to do with it being a byproduct, as you say. If it had been planned, it would probably be more straightforward; but also less complex. In that way, the sequence has organized itself through the pictures with all the deviations and irregularities that were inscribed onto them.

Erik: I agree. There is this visual level with the tree as a motif that can lead you through the book, they almost pop up with the turning of each page, but the moment you start looking through the trees, through this visual motif, all the different stories start to appear. There are quite a lot of stories in this book, actually. Plus it took almost ten years to gather this amount of photographs with trees, so the complexity is probably hidden in different levels of the book and of the production of the book.

Jan: In your opinion, is it possible to "write" with pictures? Can we write a sentence or compose a melody with them? How would you describe what establishes a sequence? What creates meaning in a montage the moment a series of pictures is seen as a sequence?

Erik: Yes, I think so but I think it works exactly opposite to an actual sentence. When you write, the reader can visualize a scene or story and when you show a sequence of images, the reader can make up sentences or a story line. So my intention will probably never be translated 1:1, that said, if I intend to "tell" a specific story or sentences. For me, building a sequence is not so much to tell a closed story, but more to raise questions on a specific subject. In a sequence I can enter some (visual) keys that would hint towards questions or loose sentences that could make up a possible story or that just touch upon a subject. With the turning of the pages, like we said before, some images will linger on in the reader's mind, some stronger than others, and these will create points between which this melody is created. I have always used this idea

of a melody in sequencing my books, it is a very useful tool to guide this process. Also because it's not rational, just as my designing is not, but rather seeing what fits in my opinion. I sequence in the best way I can do—it's the only possible way I can do it, I mean, when a sequence is ready, there is no other way I could have done it and that's the sequence that should "work" also for the reader. This flow of the book is for me one of the most important parts, the turning of the pages, or any other active part that involves the reader, is what gives the book its soul. It's one of the main differences from showing works on a wall. Besides this rhythm that first appears in the sequence I can also define the flow and timing through a book. It might run towards a conclusion or it could draw lines between different points, like those drawings where children have to connect the dots.

Jan: How important are other elements of the book for your work: for example, the endpaper, or the style of binding? The question whether the book will be produced as a hardcover or as a softcover?

Erik: They are all important, but I don't think in equal amounts for each project. All these elements are part of the book, so there has to be a reason for each specific part to appear in that form, by keeping a balance between making sense and over-designing something. In some projects the back-end paper just doesn't have any function. The decision for hard- or softcover always has to do with the weight of the project, similar to building a house: If you have a wall that sustains the roof, it needs to be thicker than if the wall is just for dividing a space and doesn't need to sustain weight, so it can be thinner. The cover and its typography really function like an invitation. Does this book invite you to pick it up? The back-end papers can also play a role in functioning as one of those keys that give possible clues to what the project is about. For example in *Third Reich* and *Ludwig II*, which are part of the Bavaria trilogy, I used the Bavarian flag for this as a strong statement for the work's context. I prefer to use the back-end paper to do this, instead of on the cover, because on the outside this image would be screaming at you before you even pick up the book. The green back-end paper in *Pomerode*, for example, has a similar function. Where I use an almost washed-out version of the Brazilian flag colors for the cover, you get this color shock as soon as you open the book. And this shock then re-appears so to say in the subject matter, to have this totally German town, deep in the south of Brazil. So again it's a clue or key to the work.

Jan: And the binding?

Erik: The binding can also be a part of both the subject and the book as an object. For *Bonsai,* which I conceived in Japan and is in a way about the book as an object and the Japanese photo book, I wanted to reinforce that in the Japanese thread binding. For most of the zines I make, the cover materials are much less important. I see these zines more as single words or a sentence at the most, so the cover and other elements don't have to function as clues. In the zines the most important clue is always the title. For me, the zines are more like poetry, I even choose the titles in an almost poetic way, so they sound like poetry when you read one after another, in some cases. Where most hardcover books tell a story, the zines may tell one or two sentences.

Jan: The texture of the pictures, their surface, also plays a decisive role in your photographic work. Traditionally, the surface of the photograph was determined by the processing lab. Today this job is done at the computer with digital tools. In your photographic work, the lab is replaced by the print shop. Or more specifically, the surface of the picture is determined by the choice of a printing process and the paper, which conveys the picture, and, of course, by the quality of the printer. You used the risograph for printing with web offset and sheetfed offset. In Brazil, Estonia and Japan. With very good printers and with printers whose poor printing quality was used by you conceptually.

Erik: Even the printing technique sometimes becomes an element in the project. For *Contemporary Brazilian Politics*, which is based on newspaper articles about corruption in Brazil, I used a thin newspaper stock in combination with 100 percent black ink printing which is too much for this paper (the paper cannot absorb all the ink), so as a reader folding the pages, your fingers will get a little bit dirty as well. You become an active part of the subject.

The email conversation was held in November 2015.

Back and Forth

Erik van der Weijde in conversation with Anne König
Second movement

Anne: Hello Erik, my family is watching *The Simpsons*. So it gives me some time to start our conversation. Yesterday I went through *Siedlung* and *O. Niemeyer*. I don't know if you see any relation between these two books but I do. *Siedlung* is from 2008, one year later we met for the first time at Miss Read in Berlin. Probably you remember this tiny space under the roof of the Kunstwerke building. It was our first independent publishing book fair we attended and we were very excited. I didn't know ROMA Publications before and all the other publishers we met from then on continuously. In this crowded and tense atmosphere I found your book *Siedlung*. It intrigued me immediately, because I grew up in such a settlement, and to be honest: I hated it. I looked through your book, and I felt you were behind me watching me. Then you introduced yourself as the photographer of the book. I was surprised that you as a foreign photographer—I think we spoke English—chose this topic. How did you come up with it?

Erik: Ah yes, I remember Miss Read, it was a bit magical to be introduced to all these people I admired. I definitely see relations between *O. Niemeyer* and *Siedlung*, but I think I didn't see them at the time. Some parts, or some levels, of both books only became clear to me after I made them both. When I was doing the research for architecture from the Third Reich, not specifically for *Siedlung*, I was interested in architecture and the cultural landscape that was dictated by the idea of one person or group. Architecture has a lot of power, in the sense that it is meant to be used for long periods of time, for more than several generations. So if there's some specific idea from which a building was conceived, that idea also will be materialized and available for generations to come. So, while researching sites and addresses of buildings in Bavaria that were left over from the Nazi period I kept coming across these similar-looking houses in every city and village. The politics behind them, to in a way buy votes for the NSDAP by providing cheap housing and using that as a means to unite the people, intrigued me. This housing project was a more subtle example of the Third Reich architecture and its survival. The understated architecture in combination with my black and white images could give the subject matter some depth, I believed. I love your remark that you hated it. I never make books for people to just "like" them, or call them "nice."

The fact that my grandmother is German and never wanted to talk about the war when I was little was probably something of a starting point to become interested in German history, but the actual artistic fascination with the topic comes from a camping place in Bavaria I used to visit with my family. It's a camping site we visited dozens of times, and for me that place was like paradise. I loved going there and really missed it when back in Holland. One day, I must have been eight or nine, we were playing hide-and-seek with a bunch of kids in the TV room. I wanted to hide inside the green corduroy couch and then found a tin box inside it which was filled with collecting cards from the Third Reich. Back then I didn't know exactly what it was, but I knew that strange cross-like figure was something evil. When I showed it to my parents they told me it was a very evil collection of cards and we had to burn it. Only years later did I realize a bit more what I had found that day and that we had actually burned it up. So part of my photography has to do with recreating that evil collection within the context of my memories of paradise. You can say that my artistic approach is very personal, relying on childhood memories and trying to keep hold of them.

Anne: How strange that they burned up the cards, for a German it rings a bell. Why they could not just throw them away? In my childhood it was strictly forbidden to draw any of these Nazi symbols, but of course everybody did it secretly. I think the French-German sociologist Emile Durkheim said literally: A social law needs its exemption, the failure to keep it alive. But of course my grandparents did not speak about their involvement during the Third Reich. I've been trying to get something out of my grandfather but he has kept everything to himself. My grandmother burned up all the letters from him before she died. I'm sure that they were hiding horrible moments of their lives and they didn't want to share them with us.

During Christmas I talked to my father who is an expert on the settlement where my parents are still living. He told me that not all of these settlements were built for Nazis or members of the NSDAP. During the Nazi time, the Nazis also built social housing in this typical architectural style you photographed. The settlement where I grew up was built for alcoholics, unemployed people, families with a lot of children. My father told me that they forced the new owners to work for their new housings. They had to work a certain amount of hours for their new home but when they were doing it they did not know which one of the houses they would get. Really at the end when the settlement was finished they got their new house. Behind the houses were big gardens, in front of the house grew a cherry tree and behind the houses was the large garden with apple, plum and pear trees. All of them got exactly the same amount of trees. They should be enabled to make their living without external help. If they did not find a job they could at least feed the family with all the vegetables and fruit from the garden. Actually not such a bad idea. In 1977, when my parents moved to this settlement, you could still meet the first owners. I went there to school and I met the children and grand-children of them. One guy was called Captain for example. I don't know where he got this name from, because he was absolutely stupid. But he lived in the first house of the settlement and it might be connected to that position. But you should know that the standard of these houses was very simple and with no comfort. There were no indoor toilets, not all rooms had a stove, only cold water. When I moved there it was a cultural shock, I missed the comfort I was used to. Intuitively I felt that the atmosphere in this settle-ment was wrong. If I look at the first photos in your book I recognize the typical settlement owner. In English they say: My home is my castle. The settlement owners' version would be: My home is my fortress. How was the atmosphere during the shooting? Did you meet any of those owners? Did you speak to them?

Erik: A book I bought on eBay a few years ago, called *Heimat und Siedlung* has a quote by Adolf Hitler on the opening page which read: "Ich wünsche, dass jeder deutsche Arbeiter sein eigenes Heim besitze, und dass er sich in diesem Heim fühle wie in einer Burg." [see: www.erikvanderweijde.com/studio-research]

The atmosphere in all the settlements was very calm and quiet. In the photos there are no people and there were really very few people in the streets. Of all the hundreds of houses I photo-graphed I remember one person in a garden, seeing me taking pictures, who kind of shouted "Hey! What are you doing?" and I answered "Taking pictures!" in my best German—and that was all the interaction I had during the twelve days of shooting.

Anne: Erik, it has been a while since you sent me your answer. Now, we are in São Paulo together, in the same hotel and after breakfast we will go out together to see the Oscar Niemeyer buildings. But before we get to Niemeyer in our conversa-tion I would like to know how did you select the settlements you shot in your book? I could see on your site that you did a lot of research in advance.

Erik: I actually started with research for another project, *Third Reich* (2014), during my residency at the Rijksakademie in Amsterdam, in 2008. For this project I was looking up buildings built during National Socialism in Bavaria, Southern Germany and got a lot of my information from a book I had ordered online, *Bauen im National-sozialismus*. This book's lists varied extensively, over hundreds of pages, buildings and their loca-tions in Bavaria. Working my way through the book I found a lot of settlements that were listed, in almost every city. Learning more about the settlements and the politics involved in them, I decided they would make a good case study for Nazi architecture in general, especially because they were less recognizable as such. So by toning down the focus of the project, I gained some of the inherent mystery of the architecture.

In my studio I had a huge map of Bavaria, and every time I found an interesting site to visit and photograph I marked it on the map. In the end I connected most of the spots, so it would make one journey that would be photographable in about twelve days.

I ended up photographing both projects, for two books, during that trip in 2008 to Bavaria: *Siedlung* (2008) and *Third Reich* (2014).

Anne: Your reference book *Bauen im National-sozialismus, Bayern 1933–1945* was already focused on Bavaria. Did you choose Bavaria be-cause of your childhood memories or was it the best source you could find about the topic? I guess there are hundreds of books about the architecture of these settlements in Germany.

You mentioned that you shot the two book projects *Siedlung* and *Third Reich* in twelve days, basically on the same trip. The time span between the first book *Siedlung* and *Third Reich* is six years. It seems to be a long time compared to other book projects you did in between. I mean you are very quick with your other publishing projects. Did you know already when you took the photos for *Siedlung* that you would do *Third Reich* later, or did it come later to you that you could do something with the photo material you collected on the trip through Bavaria?

Erik: I chose Bavaria as a topic first, actually both the themes Bavaria and Third Reich architecture kind of came together at the same time. I knew I wanted to go back to Bavaria, in search of "something," and that I wanted to do a project on Third Reich architecture. Finding that particular book was one of those moments when the whole project really starts making sense and when different layers within one project come to manifest. Only a few weeks before I traveled I decided to separate the two projects, *Siedlung* and *Third Reich*, until then *Siedlung* would have just been a chapter in the *Third Reich* book. So after *Siedlung* I didn't want to become "that Nazi photographer" or anything, so it was my decision to wait a couple of years with the *Third Reich* book. But in most of my projects I am quite slow. It probably seems I am quite fast, because I put out many titles, but usually there are many years between the photographing of a project and the publishing of the book— *Privacy Settings* took me almost seven years! I worked on *O. Niemeyer* for six years and the same for *This Is Not My Wife*. The average I think is about two years, between gathering the material and publishing the book. I need this time to work on the edit and to feel which way the project has to go, I compare it to ripening fruit.

Anne: In general, how important are books for you in order to prepare a new photo book project?

Erik: They are very important for many projects. Sometimes I literally re-do a book that inspires me, but most of the time I have one or two books in mind that kind of guide me, already since *Praia*, my first book. That one is moderately based on Eric Kroll's *Sex Objects* and Paul Kooiker's *Showground*. *Bonsai*, for example, is a book with images I re-photographed from the pages of a book I bought at a Korean flea market, with Bonsai trees, so a very literal reference, just like *Teddy Bear*, for which I re-photographed a book on

how to collect (and take care of) teddy bears. Otherwise I use books as research, as is the case with *Siedlung*, but also *O. Niemeyer* and *Superquadra* are based heavily on books. Maybe *Der Baum* is the strongest example of the influence of one book on my work. [see: "Everyday Life, the Sequence, the Book, or Five Stacks of Books for Erik van der Weijde," pp. 41–46]

Anne: Time as an essential part of the photography work you do is obvious in the book *This Is Not My Wife*. The whole process of taking photos and publishing books seems to be that all publications are communicating with each other, they have their own language and they are influencing each other. But there is a difference between taking photos and choosing the right moment for bringing them out in book format. You are the only one who can decide what the right moment for printing a book is. So in your case I would say taking photos, finding the right moment and bringing a book out have some kind of similarities, though I know that you have the opposite of this old school photography attitude of "finding the right moment." But maybe there is a subconscious shift from shooting to printing? When you mentioned the time frame between *Siedlung* and *Third Reich* it seemed to be that you have a very clear schedule for your books. Once I saw the publication program from Moholy-Nagy after he arrived in the US where he went into exile. I was very impressed by his massive publishing list. At the end he had not a lot of time left, because he died quite young. But his ideas were already heading for the future. Do you also have your future publishing program?

Erik: Yes, it's important that different titles communicate with each other. They're all part of the same body of work, and works do influence each other.

About the "right moment" I can say the following: When I start a project, or I am in the middle, I collect images (shooting or collecting books, post cards and research material) in an obsessive way. Years ago, I thought I would keep photographing and collecting a certain subject forever, but eventually all projects came to an end. I have a very clear feeling when the moment is gone and the shooting (plus collecting) is finished. I sometimes try to shoot some more later but am never satisfied with those results. At that point it feels like I am not immersed enough in the subject anymore. So I know very well now, that I have to treat each subject obsessively, because it will come to an end and I need to get the most out of it before the moment ends. And the publishing of the work, ideally, is also within this time span. If I lose the moment, it can be that a project will not be published anymore, because the need is gone. Maybe it will re-appear in a new form years later, or it will stay on the shelf as unpublished.

I try to schedule my publishing program because not all the links and relations between books are very visible, so by programing I can make some things a bit more clear, for example, by mini series which use the same design. Also, from the start, I never wanted to become that certain photographer-publisher who only focused on this or that, so I deliberately try to surprise the viewers every time by apparently shifting directions. If you have a larger overview of more of my titles you can see that those shifts are not really shifts, but there are longer time intervals between similar subjects.

I always have between 5–10 projects in a state of 80/90 percent ready to publish and then I program for the future, yes, but these are small projections, like not to have two architectural titles close to one another, or too many family-related works in the same year.

I do have this fear of death and not being able to put out all the works I want to before I die and I think I would feel extremely unfulfilled if I can't make all the works I want to, in time…

Anne: I tried to compare the way you work with someone who is performing or improvising music. If you speak to musicians who are working in that field they tell you almost the same thing you said about the right moment. They always know when they have to play a certain paraphrase or motive as you know when you have to bring out a certain book or magazine. It is very intuitive what they do and the time span is much smaller than in your case. If we compare the way you work with an improvised piece of music your program seems to be a life-long project, a life-long improvised photo-publication project and the books and publications shape your artistic identity. You don't want to be the "Nazi photographer," didn't you say this? Which leads to this question: Who do I want to be? A very crucial question where the answer can change with every project?

Erik: The answer to Who do I want to be? does not really change with each project but instead gets shaped more with each project. I literally ask myself every time: What do I want to do? and What is my place within all this? So when I am

shaping my projects I am very specific and sharp in the choice of my subjects. Take, for example, *Pomerode*, which is said to be the most German town in Brazil, in which I only show a specific type of architecture and houses. Even though not explicitly, this work is about a certain period in German history, but also about Brazilian history, about vernacular architecture, about traditions, immigration, but within my body of work it is also about Nazi Germany, about collecting and photography, about tourism and, of course, my own life. So I choose to focus on one element that can still represent the whole scope of the project on different levels and this choice of subject matter and characteristics are in a way my answer to: What do I want to do? and Who do I want to be?

Anne: I would like to come back to the question of time and the need of a work. In some cases it can take years, but I guess you don't work 24/7 on one project like the Niemeyer one. You wrote, it took you six years. How did you start it?

Erik: The Niemeyer project is also the fruit of two different ideas that came together at some point. One of them was just simply being an admirer of modernist architecture and more specifically the tropical take of Oscar Niemeyer on it. Also I had come to realize what, in retrospect, had been the exact point in my life that made me decide to become an artist. I had been brought up as a Protestant child and even though I was a bit more artistic and curious than average, my plans for the future as a sixteen-year-old were still to go to law school and become a lawyer. But then I went to Brazil, for a one-year high school program. During this period I paid a visit to my friend from Belo Horizonte—she was the one who had lived in the Netherlands for a year and had become my good friend from a ballet class we went to together—and one morning we went for a walk around Lake Pampulha. I didn't even know who Niemeyer was back then at seventeen. I think I had been to a museum only once or twice and knew nothing about modernist architecture. So when I saw Niemeyer's Saint Francis Church by the water with its beautiful curves and detached tower I remember thinking "Wow, so this can be a church too!" Of course the whole experience for a teenager to live in a culture so different from the one he grew up in was mind changing, but still that morning by the lake with Niemeyer's works was the experience that pushed me into arts years later. Having realized this around 2006 and admiring the amount of works

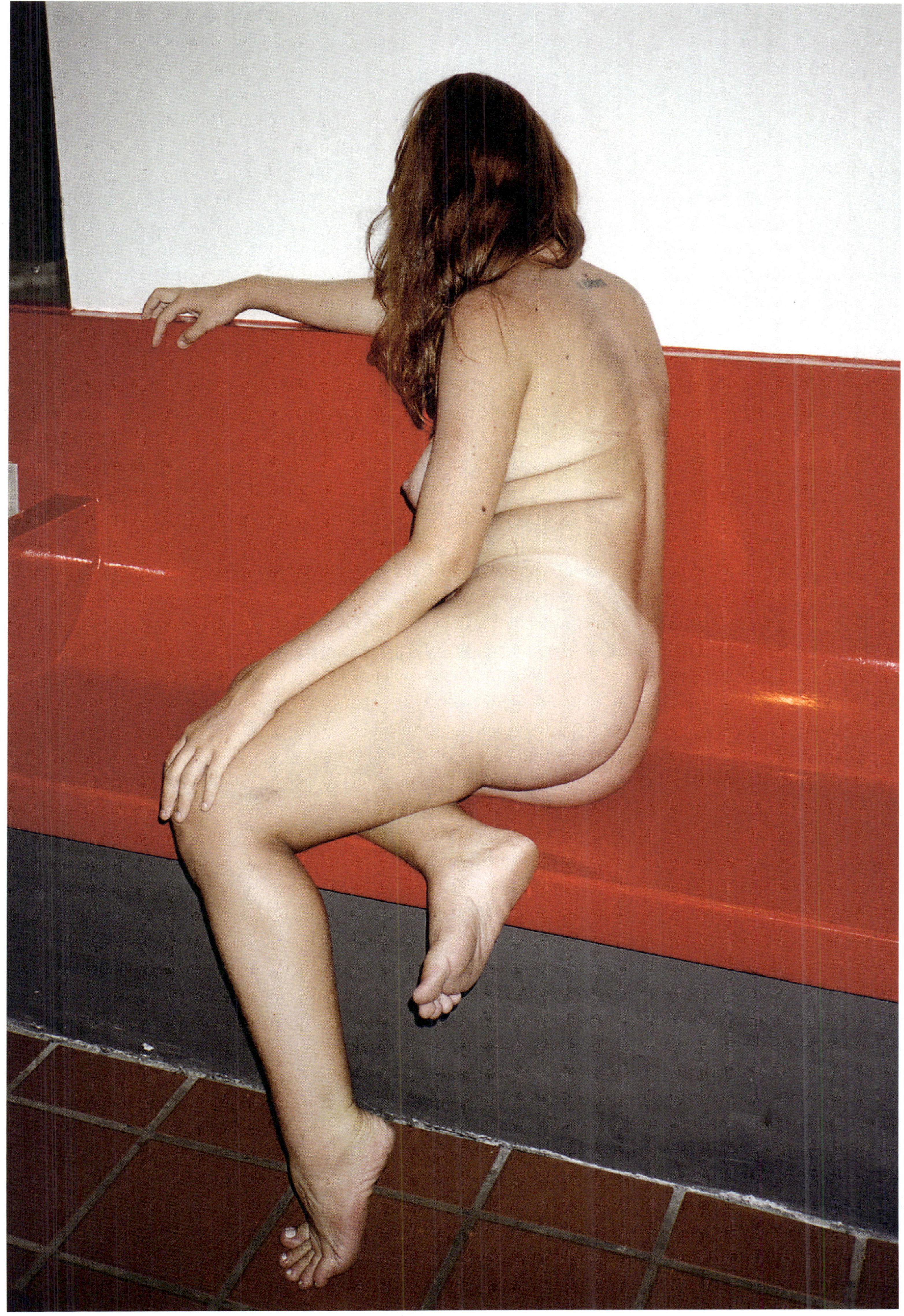

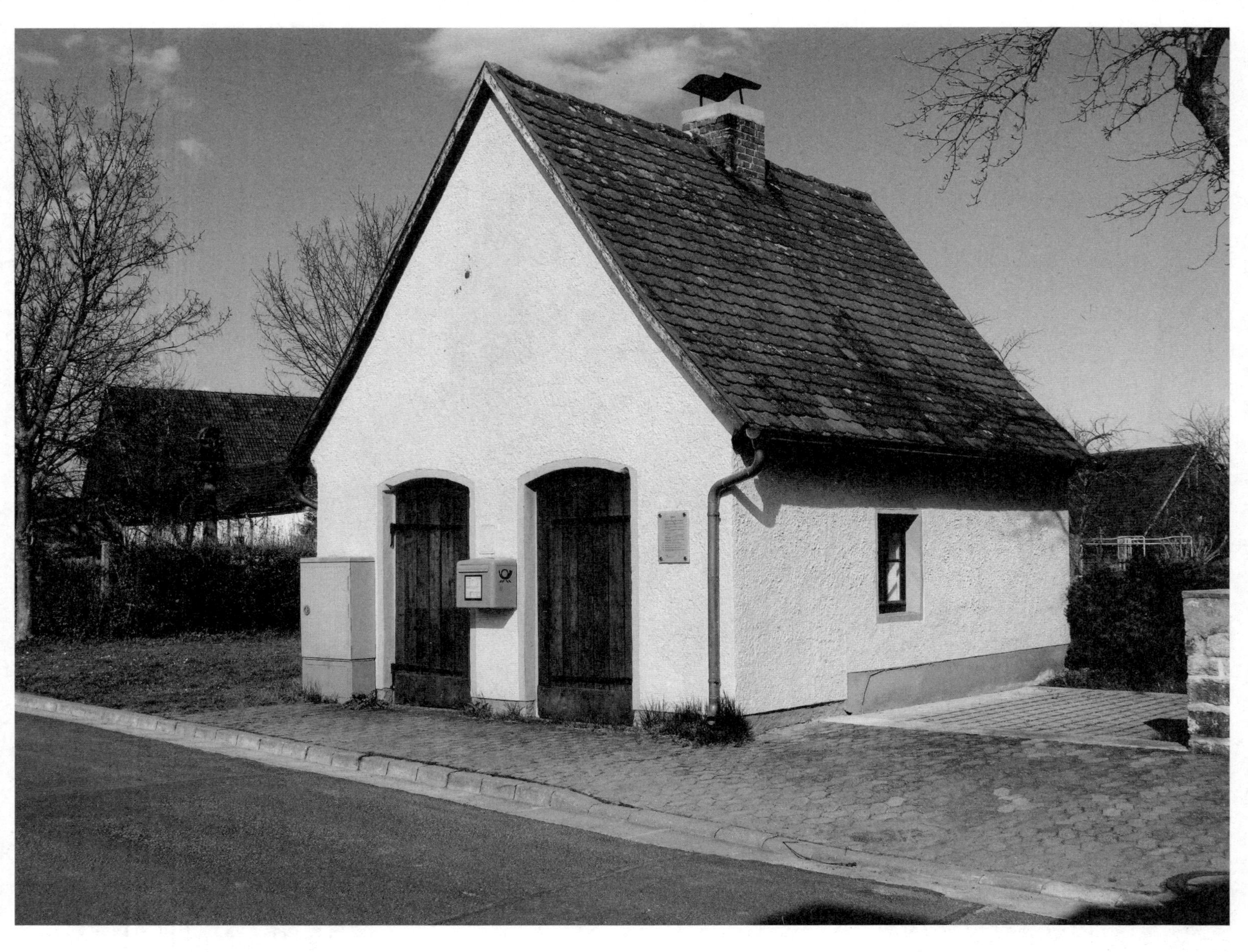

by Niemeyer, I wanted to follow in his footsteps in a way and photograph as many of his buildings as I could. For the next few years I tried to arrange my travels around Niemeyer's buildings. During this period of six years I also noticed that every time I came home from one of these trips on which I had photographed architecture I took more pictures of my wife at home. *This Is Not My Wife* was a project that grew simultaneously with *O. Niemeyer*, and in the end both books were published together in the same size and with the same design. In my 2012 exhibition *Niemeyer and My Wife* at Chert Gallery I worked out this idea of the two belonging together even more. You know that the female form is very present in Niemeyer's works and sketches which links the works in a more literal way, but also the opposite characteristics in both themes are recurring in my own work: the public and the private; the body and the architecture; the inside and the outside; the monumental and the daily.

Anne: This mutual influence between Niemeyer's architecture and the shape, the body of your wife which ended up in two of your main books, sounds perfect. Maybe too perfect. In the whole body of your work it makes total sense and I can understand it. But if I'm honest I have to say that it is hard for me to see the similarity between the architectural forms developed by Niemeyer and the female body. This is too simplistic for me or, in other words, I don't like this comparison. In the end it reduces the woman to her body in order to inspire the male artist / architect to shape his forms. You can find this pattern in art history — for example Auguste Rodin and Camille Claudel, she was his model, confidante and lover etc. It is very romantic from the viewpoint of a male artist but not from a female perspective.

I haven't seen so many Niemeyer buildings in reality, but from that what I've seen I had the impression that he was much more interested in presenting power through his architecture, also big curves do not change this impression. His buildings are about defining space. I remember what you said when we visited the Memorial Latin America in São Paulo. "Niemeyer seemed to be lazy when he built this memorial." The elements are spread over a huge territory. In between are long distances. You have to take a walk to experience and to see all the buildings he developed. The same I would say he did in Paris with the headquarters of the Communist Party. Once when I was in Paris and I had a long talk in front of this building with Sebastian Hau he told me how difficult it is to rent an apartment nowadays in the French capital. So we should not blame Niemeyer for the rental and real estate market in Paris, but if you see how tiny and how expensive space is in that city you are more than astonished about the waste of land around that building and the building itself. The white half bubble in front of the building looks like a UFO which landed in the middle of Paris. The fence which surrounds the whole area marks the territory. The building seems to be spooky. I never saw people behind the windows. What are the communists doing all day long there? Is there life? In your photos I couldn't see any people. Was it intentional to photograph the Niemeyer architecture without people or was no one there when you went?

Erik: You cannot underestimate the influence of the female body in the tropical, Brazilian culture. The ageless adoration, celebration and exposure of the body derives largely from the warm climate, especially in beach towns like Rio de Janeiro, where Niemeyer was from. In a famous quote he mentions the sensual curve and his contour drawings are filled with female bodies:
"I am not attracted to straight angles or to the straight line, hard and inflexible, created by man. I am attracted to free-flowing, sensual curves. The curves that I find in the mountains of my country, in the sinuousness of its rivers, in the waves of the ocean, and on the body of the beloved woman. Curves make up the entire Universe, the curved Universe of Einstein."
Personally I find nothing wrong with the simplistic translation of natural forms into art. I think it has been the basis for art ever since.
About the Communist Party Building in Paris, I think it would have been an amazing move if Niemeyer had built an enormous residential tower block, as he did, for example, in Belo Horizonte, instead of the weird under-sized semi-sphere in front.
When I photograph architecture and other objects, it's only the object that interests me. I find people very distracting in these photographs. So I always photograph at times when there shouldn't be many people around and I wait for everyone to leave the frame. My images are very simple, very straightforward, always with snapshot cameras and I believe that anyone should have been able to take that same photograph. At the same time I try to make my images iconic of that particular object, almost like a postcard, and seemingly easy, so that it could have been anyone who took the photo. The notion of postcards is important to me, as it's

an important part of tourism and traveling. It's very important that I, even though I hate photographing, go to specific places and take the photo myself. The act of going and being there is just as important as that anyone could have been there, or could have seen this or that. The quality of the photo is not that important to me and should never be "photographic."

Also, by not showing people in my photographs of this kind, I try to make a more universal comment, maybe on the object or the subject. By putting people in the images, they immediately gain a sense of time, which I think should be only in the mind of the viewer.

Anne: What you wrote about Niemeyer's inspiration and the tropical climate sounds convincing to me but the question is still: What are natural forms? This could be a long discussion now about the construction of gender. What are the natural forms of a female body? But I'd prefer to come back to other parts we started to discuss already.

I would like to know more about the Communist Party building in Paris. Did you do some research about it before you went there? I tried to find a bit more on the Internet, but I was not very successful. I found only what I knew already. Do you know why Niemeyer left the Communist Party in 1990?

Erik: I don't know anything about the Communist Party in Paris. I rarely do any background research on the sites I visit, apart from the information I might stumble upon, except for when the site is the actual subject. In the case of the Niemeyer book, there's no information on any location, or what each building is. There is this mystery in the amount of photographs of buildings, all designed by one man, over more than 80 years.

Niemeyer left the Communist Party of Brazil, because he was a close friend of the communist leader Luis Prestes, who didn't agree with the directions in which the Party was heading and when he left, Niemeyer left with him.

Anne: When I was in São Paulo I went to this Ibirapuera Park where a lot of buildings from Niemeyer are. The most interesting part was a kind of bridge where underneath skateboarders were practicing. I watched the moves and I was thinking that Niemeyer couldn't imagine the use of this space by these young people. The whole area is actually not made for skateboarding, but they're there because they're not allowed to do it in other parts of the city?

They seemed to enjoy it. There was no half pipe, no curves (!), nothing where they could do their jumps. That's what they do normally. I also saw young women on skateboards. In Europe it's hard to see that. Mainly you see boys and men. Under this bridge in the park I found the architecture of Niemeyer very alive.

Erik: The Marquise in Ibirapuera Park is part of Niemeyer's Museum of Modern Art and is used a lot by skaters, because it offers nice shade. Usually there's also a breakdance crew underneath and some parents teaching their kids to ride bikes. Because of the location of the park, most skaters in this park are upper-class kids.

Anne: In Ibirapuera Park there was another building by Niemeyer—the auditorium, I think. Visitors tried to get the best photo of it. I read *Edelweiss* and I know that you are very aware of the moment where these people appear or disappear. They seem to disturb your postcard picture which I can understand. But their absence is also part of your work, because you are anticipating them all the time, aren't you? I also see in your work the necessity of the contradiction between "hating photography and taking the pictures by yourself." It's a broken self-understanding of your attitude to photography, maybe post-modern, but at the same time it seems to be a fruitful friction which brings new images out. Postcard images which could have been taken by anyone else, as you said, but slightly different. And I think the difference comes out through the strong concept in the book format. When you took the pictures of the Niemeyer buildings how did you select them? How did you bring them into the book?

Erik: The buildings shown in my book are the fruit of my travel schedules and budget. As it never was an assignment or needed to be accurate in numbers, I mean I never meant to get *all* of Niemeyer's buildings in the book. I set out to photograph as many as possible. Some buildings I photographed just didn't have that postcard-look in the end, so they didn't make it to the final edit. In the first edition I published—the one with the soft cover—there were still a few images I didn't like a hundred percent, so in the second edition—with the hard cover—I decided to edit them out.

In 2007 I wanted to make a small zine with Niemeyer's European buildings, which became part of the *foto.zine nr. 2* set, and I had a small production budget to do new work at the Rijksakademie. So I bought an early morning plane ticket to Milan, where I rented a car and drove to the Mondadori building and on to Torino to photograph two more buildings and then back to Milan in the late afternoon to catch the plane back to Amsterdam. I used a similar schedule in 2012 when I was ready to publish the book but hadn't had the time and money to photograph Niemeyer's Pampulha project in Belo Horizonte. I lay in bed one night and felt obliged to myself to include Pampulha and got out of bed to buy a ticket for a few days later. Again, I flew out in the morning from Natal to Belo Horizonte, and working my way with taxis and long walks I was back at the airport in the evening. Besides the Pampulha buildings I managed to photograph five more Niemeyers in the city, but only two made it into the book. Ah, and both were only details, as I couldn't get the right "postcards" I wanted.

This style of getting the last few images in any project I consider as fill-in images. I am already so much aware the project is coming to an end that I photograph these final objects for an already defined place in the book. So I know, for example, that I need an image that leans a little bit to the left, to compose a perfect double page. Or I could use another frontal image to break up a certain sequence. It's part of closing most of my projects.

Anne: What you wrote about the fill-in images in the Niemeyer book. Is it common practice in all of your books or is it only in the case with Niemeyer? Or in other words: Do you already have a layout for the book before you start to take photos?

Erik: It is common practice in quite a lot of books. When I start photographing I never have a layout or format in mind, this only happens during the editing stage, in my studio. For the projects that take a longer period and for which I go out to photograph more frequently this means that after a while during the process and project, I have something of a layout in mind. In those cases I use this fill-in technique. This also means that some projects have started with more landscape-orientated pictures, but at a later stage I only photograph portrait, because the layout has been dictated by then. Something similar I can mention here is that, since I photograph digitally (2006) I always photograph in color and only later make the images black and white. But I keep the original files, so I can use them both, if I ever need to.

The email conversation was held between December 2015 and February 2016.

Reading Ed Ruscha and Talking with Erik

Erik van der Weijde in conversation with Jan Wenzel
Third movement

Jan: In my opinion, reading is one of the most elementary activities: sleeping, playing, eating, being out and about, loving, working, reading — as I see it, that is essentially what the catalogue of basic human activities consists of. Reading is a way of dealing with the world, books are a means of existence. They help people develop their ability to differentiate: Thanks to books, they know more and are thus able to experience their environment in a more precise and complex manner.

As a publisher I don't only see it as my duty to publish new books. It is just as important to work on new forms of reading; on ways of interacting and on the "metabolism" that has its origin in books. I would also like to make this intention the starting point of our conversation and involve you in what I am currently reading.

At the moment, I am reading a book with a collection of interviews by Ed Ruscha, *Leave Any Information at the Signal*. It is the first time that I have focused intensively on the work of Ed Ruscha. Perhaps I can show you some passages that I thought were especially interesting in the interviews with Ed Ruscha, in order to help you more clearly see the similarities and differences between Ed Ruscha's photo books and your understanding of the medium. In other words, a kind of crossmapping of your work — with the voice of Ed Ruscha in the back of your mind.

In an interview from 1965, Ed Ruscha described his basic understanding of photography and books in the following way: "Above all, the photographs I use are not 'arty' in any sense of the word. I think photography is dead as a fine art; its only place is in the commercial world, for technical or information purposes. I don't mean cinema photography, but still photography; that is, limited editions, individual, hand-processed photos. Mine are simply reproductions of photos. Thus, it is not a book to house a collection of art photographs — they are technical data like industrial photography. To me, they are nothing more than snapshots."

Erik: My photographs are registrations, or snapshots, of moments and places I v sit. So I feel quite close to what photography means for Ruscha. I always use snapshot cameras to quickly register the moment in which I find myself. Or to register a certain place or building I am looking at. I think I could compare my earlier photo zines to the technical data of which Ruscha speaks, but once I got more familiar with the power of collections of photographs, especially combined with the possibilities of the book format, I started using my work more to raise questions. I wasn't trying to tell a story, but more working w th questions like "What does this or that mean?" Also, in my work, titles or very short sentences became more and more important to the work without losing the snapshot aesthetics. Considering any single picture of mine, I've always said "It's just a photograph." I believe the power of photo-based work, for me, lies in the combination of the collection and title — or small phrase accompanying the work. And in what combination do these three elements — the single snapshot, the collection and the title — flourish better than in a book?

Jan: The interaction between the words and the picture can take on diverse forms. Because, traditionally, books are the medium used to convey the written word. For Ed Ruscha, the words on the cover (the titles) are the most important element of his publications. Essentially you can say that his preference for photo books had its origin in his fascination for language and the written word:

"The first book came out of a play on words. The title came before I even thought about the pictures. I like the word 'gasoline' and I like the specific quality of 'twenty-six.' If you look at the book you will see how well the typography works — I worked on all that before I took the photographs." And in an interview from 1972 he says, "The titles are not always first, but the title is very important." Ed Ruscha favors numbers as the first "word" of a title, because they suggest something factual. And if it isn't a number, then it should be a word that expresses quantity, such as *various*, *some* or *a few*. But the words' design is just as important to him as the words themselves, the typography. "Type always gives it a manual look. It has that factual kind of army-data look to it that I like."

We shouldn't forget that the sixties in Europe and America were the era of concrete poetry. The visual quality of the language, the image of the words, played an important role. The frequent use of text and words can also be found in Pop Art. Letters strongly appealed to that generation of artists. But I don't believe it was so much the literary quality of the texts that made words so interesting for that generation as a tool of the imagination. It had more to do with the advertising they constantly encountered in urban and medial contexts. "It's like a Western town in a way. A store-front plane of a Western town is just paper, and everything behind it is just nothing."

The simplicity of Ed Ruscha's thin books —the secret to their success—is always based on a tautology, mind you, a dynamic tautology, that is created by confronting the word with the picture, by making a double statement, two elements that recharge each other.

Erik: Although I seldom come up with the title first, I always set the title in the very beginning of a project. I love how this title/image tautology may work, but also how titles link different book projects to each other. My favorite trilogy is a trilogy rather in title, than in subject, it's the *Deer Park / Parking Lot / Politics*, which I conceived as such. Besides the titles' poetic resemblance, all three have the same format. But I doubt anybody has ever noticed these three titles as a trilogy...

I really feel that titles in works that look so simple are the most important element. In most of my books I even like the title more than the images. I think it's where the most happens, you know? An image is just an image, but a word has so much more meaning...

My feelings towards typography are not that strong. For me typography is much more a playful part in the work. I was never trained in graphic design or typography and I am sure that for every cover of my works, at least five other versions would work in the same way, probably not more than these five though.

Jan: In an interview that Ed Ruscha had with David Bourdon in 1972, I just discovered a sentence that shouldn't be underestimated when discussing the design principles of his books: "Sometimes the ugliest things have the most potential." This statement is made in connection with the publication *Real Estate Opportunities*, but it also applies to many other publications.

Erik: I do agree with the notion that sometimes the ugliest things have the most potential. Personally I think I have always been looking for ugly things, or what is considered as ugly by society-set standards, to look for what I consider beautiful. Not what TV or commercials dictate as beauty. And in that search there is usually the greatest potential. Not only in work, but in a way of looking at the world. I compare it to looking under the rock, lifting it to see what's underneath.

Jan: There are pictorial worlds beyond the spectacular image, everyday pictorial worlds that hardly play a significant role in the media: gas stations, trees, single-family houses, street lights ... In an interview with Henri Man Barendse that was published in the magazine *Afterimage* in 1981, the interviewer asks Ed Ruscha straight off why he takes pictures of gas stations, and Ed Ruscha answers, "Because they were there." —They are not a symbol of something, they are simply there. That could be the key statement for a radical, democratic vision of esthetics that takes our everyday world seriously—and believes that everything is of pictorial value, because it is there, or more precisely: Because it is *also* there. "I don't know why I picked gas stations, except that they had been unreported." Was your series of trees derived from a similar intention?

Erik: Actually *Der Baum* is one of the very few series that was conceived when it was already halfway finished. I had bought a little booklet on eBay, from the publisher Der Eiserne Hammer, called *Der Baum*. I realized how much I like pictures of trees. Photographs of trees are much more interesting to me than real life trees. When I got the book in the mail and I went through my own archives, I suddenly found many trees I had photographed for previous projects and never used. I had been unconsciously photographing all these trees in historical and otherwise significant places. Maybe "because they were there," as Ruscha puts it, but there's a big difference in photographing things because they are there, on the one hand, and then deciding to make a publication out of that on the other hand. I always thought that Ruscha must have really liked how the gas stations looked as photographs, in their two dimensional form. Just as I felt with the trees. And maybe the decision of what to photograph is much less important than the decision of what to publish, especially after 2006 for me when I switched to digital photography. I started photographing much more and much faster, but the decision of which series to use became more important and apparent in my work.

Jan: In the same interview there is a passage I feel like repeating when I read it, much like an actor I simply feel like reciting the text I wasn't familiar with beforehand: "I don't mean to beat a dead horse, but I wanted to ask if you feel your books are all autobiographical, because they do have a peculiar existentialist thread running through them." And Ed Ruscha replies, "There's a dryness which I went for, actually. I liked that, having it dry and simple and, in a way, unartistic." How would you answer a question like that?

Erik: All my books are very much autobiographical. I have always felt that my subjects came out of this highly disorganized place deep inside of me and that by publishing a work I could file it under a certain topic and put it back into a more organized bookcase—myself. And I think we covered most of these topics in the way we present my work in this book, with the different background colors. Every project has been a subject I wanted to understand better, like why, for example, I find certain things interesting. That dry, unartistic way of showing things I also use. I use it to not put too much emphasis on each single subject and I hope that this book will be able to explain a bit of the underlying common theme, linking it all together.

Jan: My impression of both Ed Ruscha and you is that these publications are autobiographical, because they reveal a distinct individual sensitivity, a distinct taste, a distinct sense of irony. Even though only gas stations or trees are depicted, it isn't objective, it isn't documentary. It is extremely personal, charged with a particular attitude. And only by presenting these things in this way do they become interesting. Ed Ruscha describes the process in an interview he had with Willoughby Sharp in 1973: "That's going to be hard to get at because what it amounts to is a style of living and the taste of things…filtering the taste with the style of living and then coming up with statements.—Like *Colored People*. That's a product of everything I buy, and every way I live. All that stuff goes into the funnel and comes out as *Colored People*."

Erik: I have always liked the metaphor of a funnel and have used it in many of my talks. It seems such a simple idea, but I believe it's the core of being an artist. That sentence, "filtering the taste with the style of of living and then coming up with statements," is what I realized I was doing just when I finished the *foto.zine* series. Before that I always thought I had to do more: Make things bigger, or shout harder, but this realization of being that funnel that produces statements was very liberating. And now it makes me very satisfied to read these words from Ruscha as well.

Jan: The seventeen books from the years 1963 to 1978 which are listed in Ed Ruscha's *Catalogue Raisonné* were published with an amazingly large number of copies. For example, a total of 6000 copies of Every Building on the Sunset Strip were printed, regarding most of the other publications a total of 3000 to 4000 copies were printed.
There is an interview from 1972 entitled "My Books End up in the Trash" where Ed Ruscha tells a tale about the distribution of his books. Let me read this passage: "After the book leaves here, it's for whatever anyone wants to use it for. I'd love to have the facts on where my books are… I had a daydream once not long ago about an imaginary person known as the Information Man, and I wrote it down. Let me read it to you:
"The Information Man is someone who comes up to you and begins telling you stories and related facts about a particular subject in your life. He came up to me and said, 'Of all the books of yours that are out in the public, only 171 are placed face up with nothing covering them; 2026 are in vertical positions in libraries, and 2715 are under books in stacks. The most weight on a single book is sixty-eight pounds, and that is in the city of Cologne, Germany, in a bookstore. Fifty-eight have been lost; fourteen have been totally destroyed by water or fire; two-hundred sixteen books could be considered badly worn. Three hundred and nineteen books are in positions between forty and fifty degrees. Eighteen of the books have been deliberately thrown away or destroyed. Fifty-three books have never been opened, most of these being newly purchased and put aside momentarily.
Of the approximately 5000 books of Ruscha that have been purchased, only thirty-two have been used in a directly functional manner. Thirteen of these have been used as weights for paper or other small things, seven have been used as swatters to kill small insects such as flies and mosquitoes, two were used as a device to nudge open a door, six have been used to transport

foods like peanuts to a coffee table, and four have been used to nudge wall pictures to their correct levels. Two hundred and twenty-one people have smelled pages of the books. Three of the books have been in continual motion since their purchase; all three of these are on a boat near Seattle, Washington."

What does the Information Man tell you when he stops by?

Erik: Fifty percent of my books ended up in Germany, in bookcases of men aged between 22–75. Ten percent ended up in France, where most of them went to young Parisian women aged between 18–25. Ten percent went to Japan, more specifically to male graphic designers who like to smell and feel paper. Ten percent went to Belgian book collectors who dress really well and spend more than the average European on good food and good books. Fifteen percent went to the US. Again, mostly male collectors from the creative sphere or old hippies (sixty percent New York and forty percent California). Two percent is in stores as we speak — waiting to be sold. One percent went to rich Brazilian kids who don't realize they spend more on books than entire families can on food. One percent I gave away or traded for books I wanted. Something I very, very rarely do. One percent went to my father, who thinks he's making a good investment. One percent I still have, thinking it's a good investment. I am ninetynine percent sure these numbers are correct.

The email conversation was held in November 2016.

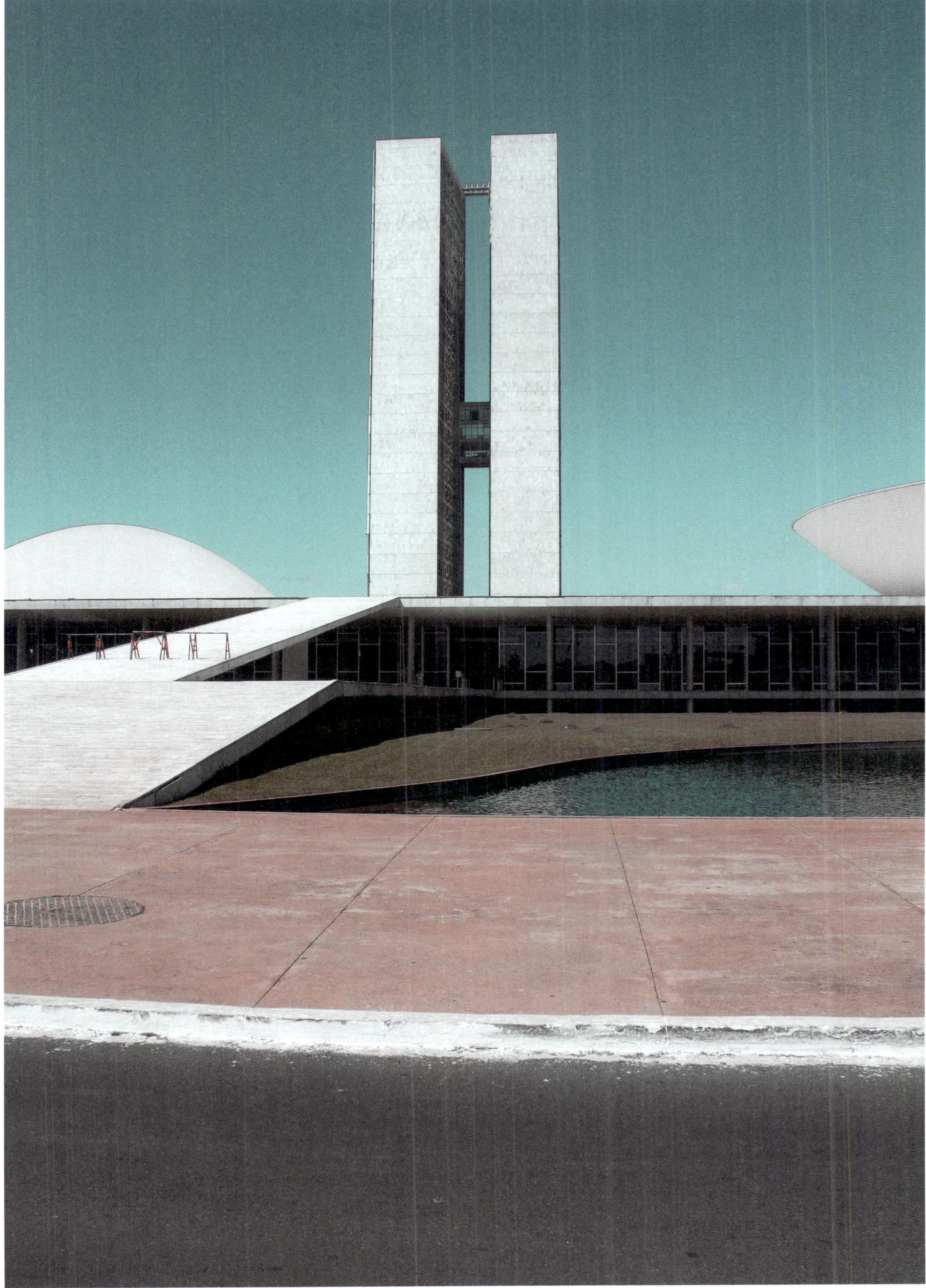

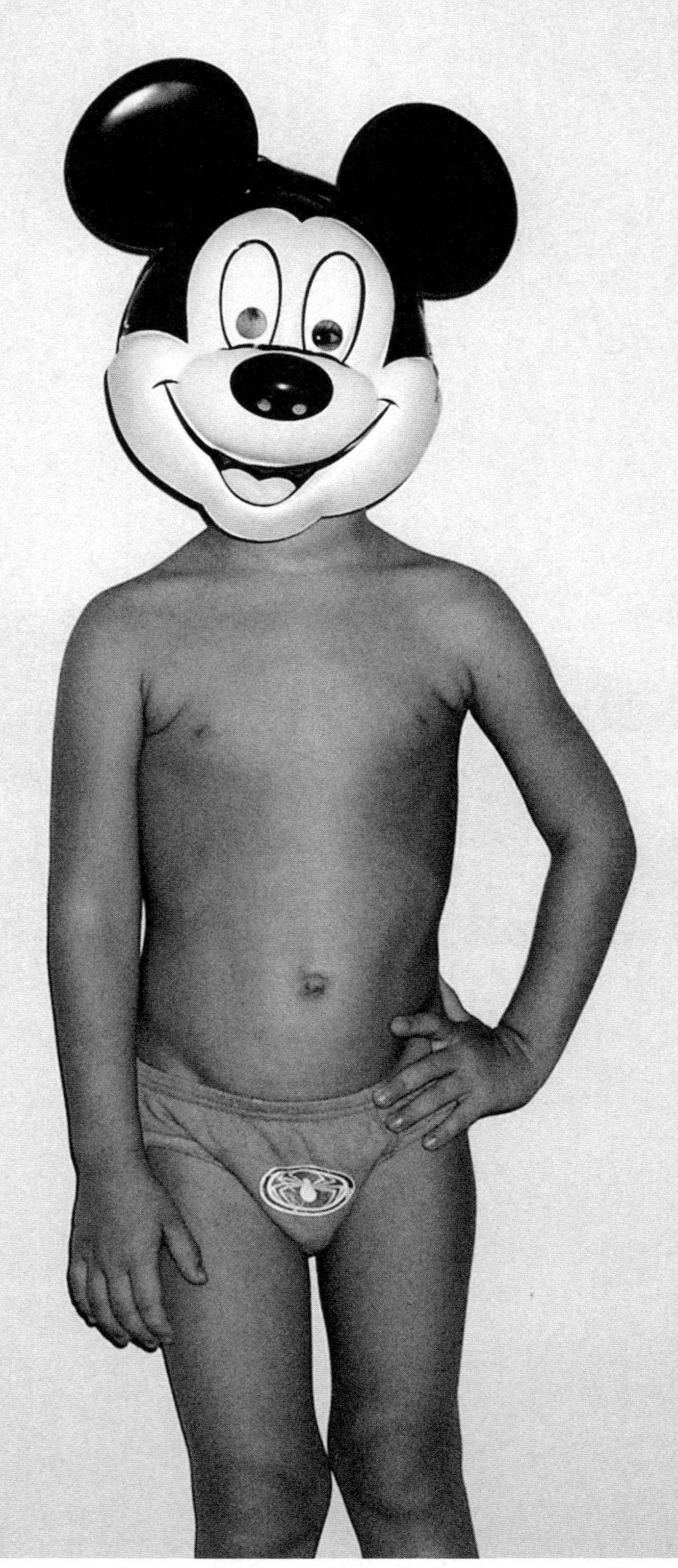

The Unfinished Projects

Erik van der Weijde in conversation with Anne König
Fourth movement

Anne: In our conversation about *Siedlung* and *O. Niemeyer* you wrote that you can work for a long time on a specific project, but you never work on only one project. Usually there are maybe four or five different projects you are working on, plus *Subway*. You mentioned that you have a "work in progress" folder with about ten unfinished publications. What kind of projects end up in that specific folder?

Erik: Some projects take just a few months, from conception to publishing, others can take years. And then there are the projects which in the end you decide not to publish. If a publication will not add any significance to what I have already done before, I might decide not to print it. Or sometimes the momentum for a title is just gone.

Anne: Would you like to tell me on what you are working, or is it a secret which I could understand totally? I personally don't like to speak about works which are not finished yet. I always think that they need a kind of protected space.

Erik: I agree with you about the protection for unfinished and unpublished works. I am completely open about my sales and figures, those numbers are exactly what they are. I mean, why be mysterious about that? But for unfinished works it's a bit different. All the choices I make in the process, all the times I decide not to do something, is part of the end product. That's the thing I am 100 percent sure about: It is right the way it is. By showing too much from an unfinished work, including versions of a project of what it also could be, there's a chance to weaken the final thing. I never like to see photo books with contact sheets. They show too many failures, or images that in the end weren't chosen and take a lot of the mystery out of the actual work. But for the sake of this conversation I can name one example of a project I am working on, for which, probably, the ship has sailed: I don't feel the need to finish it anymore. A series of photographs taken in Hiroshima in 2011, at the Motomachi housing project, has been waiting on my hard disk for a while now. When I photographed this

modernist project — last part of the rebuilding in Hiroshima — I kind of had it in mind as a follow-up after *Superquadra*. Both touch upon a similar theme and it could have been a logical step. But in the end it wasn't "at least as good as" *Superquadra*, so why then publish it? With all my works I try to push forward a bit. Both myself and the work. So if the work doesn't meet my own expectations, I won't publish. A few images from Hiroshima were published in *The White Review* magazine and some were included in my exhibition at Camera Austria. So yes, there were some good images, but as an entire work, it was just not good enough to publish.

Anne: I've never been to Japan and all I know about Hiroshima comes from the film *Hiroshima mon amour* by Alain Resnais with the screenplay by Marguerite Duras. But the film actually is not so much about the new city. It is this conversation between the French woman and the Japanese architect who fall in love with each other. But this love is overshadowed by the bad experience of the woman during the Second World War in France. It is a very strong text by Marguerite Duras where she uses the writing method of repetition to tell the traumatic experience of that woman. Basically, the love is with no hope which stands as a metaphor for Hiroshima as well.

I read that in 1956 the Japanese government planned to rebuild the area along the Otagawa river on the site of a former military camp which was used as a large overcrowded refugee camp for homeless people after the destruction caused by the atomic bomb. When the film was shot at the end of the fifties probably the Motomachi housing project you photographed in 2011 did not exist yet. Did you consider all this prehistory of the rebuilt area when you started to work there? Or is it exactly the historical meaning of the buildings which makes it much more difficult to deal with compared to *Superquadra*?

Erik: I haven't seen the Resnais movie. I have it on my hard disk, but never got to actually watching it. For my research on the Motomachi project I tried to read as much as possible on the topic, but in the end only one or two key details in the subject mattered. I mean, if the Motomachi project had not been built on that refugee camp site, I would still have photographed it. What counted for me was that it was the final part of the whole rebuilding project for Hiroshima, with its modernist solutions for something like a ground zero—both in space and time. The rest of the pre-history of the area is inherent to the area and thus in my series of images as well, but not something I would highlight. Many times people ask me if I interviewed or photographed the people who live in the housing estate—which I never did. The people are inherent to those houses, together with their stories, but that's not something I would be looking for or want to show. I think the question raised, if I photographed or interviewed these people, is already enough within the whole project. For the Hiroshima project that was similar. The hearing or reading of the title *Hiroshima* already says it all. I mean, people from one part of the world dropped an atomic bomb on people in another part of the world, killing over a hundred thousand. Adding too many details to that fact would just be unnecessary.

Anne: So how do I have to imagine the photos you took in Hiroshima at the Motomachi housing project? With or without people? Pure architecture—similar to *Superquadra*?

Erik: Pure architecture, yes. Black and white again, although I shot them in color. No people in them, just like the other architecture titles, but this time most of them in a portrait orientation, as opposed to the landscape in *Siedlung* and square format in *Superquadra*. What I liked in the images were the harsh shadows, which really went along with the modernist architecture. I was there on a sunny day so I wasn't even nervous about the rain getting in the way. I have good memories about that whole trip. This project would have been published with ROMA Publications and we had even decided on the color of the font on the cover, which should have been yellow. But, as I mentioned before, I just couldn't get the series a little bit better than *Superquadra* and that's why Roger (ROMA Publications) and I decided we'd better not publish it. I think that if I had published *Siedlung* and *Superquadra* by myself, I might have published this one also. Sometimes it's good to have an outside party stimulate you—or to put the brakes on.

Anne: At the recent NYABF incidentally I met the editor of *The White Review* where he mentioned the collaboration with you. We exchanged some issues but, unfortunately, I didn't receive issue number 6 where you published some photos of the *Hiroshima* series. Actually I think that Ben Eastham didn't bring the first issues from London to New York. He had issue number 10 onwards with him.

So, do I understand it right: If you don't publish a certain project as a publication it doesn't mean that the material can be used in other contexts? What images did you select for the literature magazine *The White Review* and did you also publish some other photos of the "unfinished projects" in other magazines already? And do you change your mind about an unfinished project if something has been published in a magazine?

Erik: Actually quite a few unpublished projects end up with bits and parts being published in other outlets, mostly in magazines and sometimes on websites. Never the whole series, but I think magazines are well suited for teasers and smaller pieces. I compare some of these printed series with songs: Whereas the whole album would be the book, I take just a "song" and get it published in a magazine. The thing is that publishing a part in a magazine or on a website does not feel at all like making a work, or making similar decisions as in making an artwork. There is no creation involved. The creation was in making the book (which by then "exists" on my hard drive), but showing a part is more like playing the song.

So I also do not change my mind after publishing in a magazine because actually the work is already finished by then.

What I selected for *The White Review* I really don't know anymore but probably something "graphic." In magazines I tend to show more of the better pictures, as there is no room for playing with time and space, as would be in a book. In the books the bad pictures can also be of use to give rhythm to a series, but in magazines I go for the more "catchy pop song."

Anne: So, what else of the unfinished projects ended up in a magazine? And what other projects do you consider as unfinished? Give me one or two more examples, because I'm feeling a bit like wandering in the dark. I can't guess what you have been working on. The last paragraph in your Publishing Manifesto says:

"15. All books that are not made are, at least, just as important" as the published ones?

Erik: As an artist's contribution for *Cura Magazine* a couple of years ago, I showed images from *Toyota*, the book I published this year. It had been sitting on my hard drive for years already. Waiting for an opportunity. So that's a sample of a project that did become a book a few years after the magazine contribution. But I have other finished projects, such as my father-in-law watching TV, portraits of Brazilian journalists—who usually look like models, I have 36 views of Mount Fuji ready—but then as a phone card collection I bought on eBay. A few different architecture projects, one of which with barns in the area of Garmisch-Partenkirchen, a project I shot in the hospital when my son was on IC for a week titled *UTI* (*IC* in Portuguese), and of course *First Blood*, volume 3 in my Bavaria trilogy…

So, what I mean with that point in the manifest is more about choice making: The viewer normally doesn't get to see the *no* choices I make, to *not* do something. But all the times I decide not to do something, that should also strengthen the decisions of things I *do*. Let me try to explain that with an example. I didn't publish the Mount Fuji series, because I thought I was doing too much of found-footage-based work. So by the end, deciding not to publish that, I give more credit to my own photography.

For me all the times I say no to something are really important, because it is not easy to say no. You need to have a clear vision of where you want to go to be able to say "no."

Anne: Didn't you show us the father-in-law series when you were in Leipzig last November? Isn't it that funny series of images where he is lying in front of the TV. I remember that you went through these images very fast like an animation movie and the man changed his position slightly from one image to the next one. Actually I liked that animated photographs, though they were not meant to be shown like that I guess.

Erik: Yes, it's that series, somewhat funny… You could consider them as animation, but it's not what I wanted with them. Simple animations like that resemble the flip-book too much and I hate flip-books. I think that's a bit too banal in form. I like banality but not in form. Many of my zines are on that border of formal banality as well, but for me the flip-book animation is a bit too much.

Anne: When we met at the New York Art Book Fair recently we talked about the future. It was your last book fair as you said and you decided to change your career due to a lot of different reasons. Last year in November we experienced the attacks in Paris where almost all photographers and publishers were in the city because of Paris Photo. Terror hit us. Some of us became depressive afterwards, others could forget more easily. You missed your family in Brazil, and traveling, which was a dream at the beginning of your artist career, changed into something which you wanted to stop. You said, you wanted to be closer to your family. Traveling to art book fairs is over.

During our stay in New York you went to a coffee fair to prepare your new business as a coffee shop owner in Natal. Is this fundamental shift also something which is linked to the point of saying "no"?

Erik: Maybe the career shift is a way of saying "no," I hadn't thought of it like that before, though. But it sure has to do with choice: The deliberate choice not to continue doing something. Even if it's something I'm good at. Again I compare this choice with making music. I think many bands would have a much better catalogue of their own music, if they just call it quits at some point. From the point of view of 4478zine, the "no" part was rather important, but from a more private point of view, the decision to do something else, which I also like, was to see if I could pull it off. I am very curious to see if I could set up and run a much more local business, employ people and grow financially and personally…

The email conversation was held between May and September 2016.

Catalogue Raisonné

Index of published projects, 2003–2016

Amsterdam
Omoplata / Super Labo, 2013
16.2 × 24.2 cm, 32 pp.
edition of 500 copies, offset
printed in Japan, softcover with
thread-sewn spine

Archivo
Van Zoetendaal, 2008
28 × 43 cm, 16 pp.
edition of 5000 copies, rotation
offset printed in the Netherlands, unbound tabloid sheets

Av. Paulista
4478zine, 2006
15 × 22 cm, 4 pp.
edition of 500 copies,
offset printed in the Netherlands,
unbound pamphlet

Birds of Paradise
4478zine / Brooklyn Shelf Life, 2012
29 × 38 cm, 16 pp.
edition of 1000 copies,
rotation offset printed in the US,
unbound tabloid sheets

Bonsai
4478zine, 2011
17 × 24 cm, 32 pp.
edition of 500 copies, offset
printed in the Netherlands,
thread-sewn softcover with dust
jacket

Contemporary Brazilian Politics
f.f.s.e., 2011
13 × 20 cm, 20 pp.
edition of 500 copies, offset
printed in Brazil, staple bound
softcover

Courbe
Temple Paris, 2015
15 × 21 cm, 24 pp.
edition of 50 copies, risograph
printed in France, staple
bound softcover, including
interview booklet

Deer Park
Edition Taube, 2011
13 × 20 cm, 24 pp.
edition of 200 copies, risograph
printed in Germany, silkscreened
saddle-stitched softcover

Der Baum
4478zine, 2010
17 × 24 cm, 48 pp.
edition of 500 copies, offset
printed in the Netherlands,
thread-sewn softcover with dust
jacket

Der Baum (special edition)
4478zine, 2010
17 × 24 cm, 48 pp.
limited edition of 25 copies,
offset printed in the Netherlands,
thread-sewn softcover with
dust jacket, including a photograph, signed and numbered

Die Wolken
4478zine, 2012
17 × 30 cm, 24 pp.
edition of 600 copies (200 red /
200 blue / 200 black), offset
printed in Brazil, staple bound
softcover

Down the Rabbit Hole
Kaugummi Books, 2008
14 × 20 cm, 20 pp.
edition of 100 copies, laser
printed in France, staple bound
softcover

Down the Rabbit Hole 2
Kaugummi Books, 2009
15 × 21 cm, 20 pp.
edition of 100 copies, laser
printed in France, staple bound
softcover

Down the Rabbit Hole 3
Kaugummi Books, 2009
13 × 19 cm, 20 pp.
edition of 100 copies, laser
printed in France, staple bound
softcover

Exit
Erik van der Weijde for
The Word Magazine, 2015
13 × 19 cm, 16 pp.
edition of 500 copies, offset
printed in Belgium, staple bound
softcover

Facial Fractures
Blondi, 2015
15 × 21 cm, 24 pp.
edition of 200 copies, offset
printed in Brazil, staple bound
softcover

foto.zine nr. 1
(composed of 8 untitled issues)
4478zine, 2005
various formats, 108 pp. in total
edition of 300 copies, offset
printed in Brazil, various media,
sealed in a plastic bag

foto.zine nr. 2
(composed of 5 issues:
*Third Reich, Patinoire, Caravans,
Church Houses, Niemeyer*)

4478zine, 2007
15 × 22 cm each, 12 pp. each
edition of 400 copies, offset
printed in Brazil, unbound
softcovers, held together with
a banderole

foto.zine nr. 2 (special edition)
(composed of 5 issues:
*Third Reich, Patinoire, Caravans,
Church Houses, Niemeyer*)
4478zine, 2007
15 × 22 cm each, 12 pp. each
limited edition of 30 copies,
offset printed in Brazil, unbound
softcovers, held together with
a banderole, including a signed
photograph

foto.zine nr. 3
(composed of 5 issues:
*Palm Trees, Hand Guns, Untitled,
Accidents, The Stuttgart Issue*)
4478zine, 2009
15 × 21 cm each, 22 pp. each
edition of 300 copies, offset
printed in Brazil, staple bound
softcovers

foto.zine nr. 4
(composed of 5 untitled issues)
4478zine, 2011
14 × 19.5 cm each, 24 pp. each
edition of 500 copies, offset
printed in the Netherlands, staple
bound softcovers, in collaboration
with Linus Bill, Takashi Homma,
Erik Kessels, Paul Kooiker and
Eric Tabuchi

foto.zine nr. 5
(composed of 5 issues: *Buzios,
Fusca, Motel, Jardins, Lixo*)
4478zine, 2013
15 × 21 cm each, 116 pp. in total
edition of 400 copies, offset
printed in Brazil, staple bound
softcovers

Gebilde
Edition Camera Austria, 2014
11.3 × 17 cm, 96 pp.
edition of 500 copies, offset
printed in Austria, perfect bound
softcover, edited by Maren
Lübbke-Tidow, texts by Pierre
Dourthe, Frits Gierstberg,
Maren Lübbke-Tidow, Dan Rule,
Erik van der Weijde and
Jan Wenzel

Groene Hilledijk
Erik van der Weijde, 2003
19 × 13 cm, 102 pp.
edition of 45 copies, photocopied
in the Netherlands, staple bound
softcover with Japanese binding

Gulasch Suppe
Blondi, 2013
15 × 21 cm, 20 pp.
edition of 100 copies, offset
printed in Brazil, staple bound
softcover

Havaianas
4478zine, 2013
16 × 26 cm, 16 pp.
edition of 400 copies, offset
printed in Brazil, staple bound
softcover

Home Is Where The Dog Is
4478zine, 2014
19 × 25 cm, 160 pp.
edition of 600 copies,
offset printed in the Netherlands,
thread-sewn softcover

Home Is Where The Dog Is
(special edition)
4478zine, 2014
19 × 25 cm, 160 pp.
limited edition of 30 copies,
offset printed in the Netherlands,
thread-sewn softcover,
including a silkscreen print,
signed and numbered

Lamp Posts, Albert Speer
4478zine, 2009
46 × 63 cm, 12 pp.
edition of 100 copies,
silkscreened in the Netherlands,
unbound broad sheet

Ludwig II
4478zine, 2015
14 × 20 cm, 80 pp.
edition of 300 copies, offset
printed in Lithuania, clothbound thread-sewn hardcover

Most Wanted
by Takayuki Yamamoto
4478zine, 2014
22 × 30 cm, 80 pp.
edition of 400, offset printed
in Estonia, half-Canadian wire
bound softcover

Nelore
4478zine, 2012
16 × 24 cm, 24 pp.
edition of 400 copies, offset
printed in Brazil, staple bound
softcover

Nelore (special edition)
4478zine, 2012
16 × 24 cm, 24 pp.
limited edition of 15 copies,
offset printed in Brazil,

staple bound softcover, including
a felt handmade Nelore doll

New Holland / New Amsterdam
4478zine, 2013
14.8 × 21 cm, 24 pp.
edition of 200 copies, offset
printed in Brazil, staple
bound softcover, in collaboration
with Pierre Le Hors

Nina
4478zine, 2016
17 × 24 cm, 32 pp.
edition of 300 copies, offset
printed in Lithuania, thread-sewn
softcover with dust jacket

O. Niemeyer (first edition)
Rollo Press / 4478zine, 2012
25 × 18.5 cm, 104 pp.
edition of 700 copies, offset
printed in Estonia, thread-sewn
softcover with dust jacket

O. Niemeyer (second edition)
Rollo Press / 4478zine, 2013
25 × 18,5 cm, 96 pp.
edition of 500 copies, offset
printed in Estonia, thread-sewn
hardcover with three-color
foil stamp

*Paradiesvögel
(Birds of Paradise 2)*
4478zine, 2015
20 × 28 cm, 48 pp.
edition of 400 copies, offset
printed in Estonia, staple bound
softcover

*Paradiesvögel (Birds of
Paradise 2)* (special edition)
4478zine, 2015
20 × 28 cm, 48 pp.
limited edition of 40 copies,
offset printed in Estonia,
staple bound softcover, comes
with one of three ammunition
sizes (75 mm / 95 mm / 140 mm
rounds) for the tanks, in
different editions, all handmade sewn vinyl, signed and
numbered

Parking Lot
4478zine, 2011
13 × 20 cm, 20 pp.
edition of 200 copies, letterpress
printed in Japan, thread-sewn
softcover

Parking Lot (special edition)
4478zine, 2011
13 × 20 cm, 20 pp.
limited edition of 20 copies,
letterpress printed in Japan,
thread-sewn softcover, including
a silkscreen print, signed and
numbered

Pomerode
4478zine, 2015
24.5 × 16 cm, 60 pp.

edition of 400 copies, offset
printed in Estonia, clothbound thread-sewn hardcover

Praia
Erik van der Weijde, 2004
15 × 21 cm, 104 pp.
edition of 500 copies, offset
printed in Brazil, perfect bound
softcover

Privacy Settings
4478zine, 2013
22.5 × 17 cm, 60 pp.
edition of 500 copies, offset
printed in Estonia, clothbound thread-sewn hardcover

*Quick Magazine #3: Erik
van der Weijde: Theory of Ruins*
Quick Magazine /
Ourpress Publishing, 2011
14.5 × 21 cm, 20 pp.
edition of 250 copies,
risograph printed in Germany,
staple bound softcover,
edited by Arno Auer

Rear Window (first edition)
Café Royal Books, 2010
15 × 21 cm, 20 pp.
edition of 100 copies, laser
printed in the UK, staple bound
softcover

Rear Window (second edition)
Café Royal Books, 2010
15 × 21 cm, 20 pp.
edition of 100 copies, laser
printed in the UK, staple bound
softcover

Set of 3
(composed of 3 issues: *Mona Lisa,
Eva / Maria / Heidi, Maria Lúcia*)
4478zine, 2012
14.8 × 21 cm each, 28 pp. each
edition of 50 copies, laser
printed, mimeographed
and rubber stamped in Brazil,
staple bound softcovers,
sealed in silkscreened envelope

Siedlung
ROMA Publications, 2008
16 × 24 cm, 256 pp.
edition of 500 copies,
offset printed in the Netherlands,
fabric bound thread-sewn
hardcover

Siedlung (special edition)
ROMA Publications, 2008
16 × 24 cm, 256 + 10 pp.
limited edition of 40 copies,
offset printed in the Netherlands,
fabric bound thread-sewn
hardcover, including a signed
and numbered silkscreened
sewn-in quire.

Souvenir I & II
4478zine, 2012
6 × 9 cm, 20 pp. in total

edition of 100 copies, offset
printed in Brazil, 2 sets of cards,
each encased in a silkscreened
plastic pocket

Souvenir III
4478zine, 2013
24 × 32 cm, 10 pp.
edition of 100 copies, silkscreened
four-ring binder produced in
the Netherlands, 32 A6 cards,
2 A5 cards and 1 A4 card offset
printed in Brazil

Subway Magazine
4478zine, 2014 – ongoing
17 × 24 cm each, 32 pp. each
edition of 900 copies, offset
printed in the EU, staple bound
softcovers

Superquadra
ROMA Publishing, 2010
16 × 24 cm, 176 pp.
edition of 700 copies, offset
printed in the Netherlands, fabric
bound thread-sewn hardcover

Tables to Meet
Erik Erik Erik, 2014
14.8 × 21 cm, 320 pp.
edition of 800 copies, offset
printed in Estonia, clothbound thread-sewn hardcover,
in collaboration with Erik
Kessels and Erik Steinbrecher

Teddy Bear
4478zine, 2014
20 × 28 cm, 48 pp.
edition of 400 copies, offset
printed in Estonia, saddle-stitched
softcover

Third Reich
4478zine, 2014
14 × 20 cm, 96 pp.
edition of 700 copies, offset
printed in Estonia, clothbound thread-sewn hardcover

Third Reich (special edition)
4478zine, 2014
14 × 20 cm, 96 pp.
limited edition 40 copies, offset
printed in Estonia, clothbound
thread-sewn hardcover, including
a numbered cardboard box
with 6 two-color silkscreen prints

This Is Not My Son
Rollo Press / 4478zine, 2009
18.5 × 25 cm, 108 pp.
edition of 100 copies, risograph
printed in Switzerland, perfect
bound softcover with dust
jacket printed with Print Gocco

This Is Not My Wife
Rollo Press / 4478zine, 2012
18.5 × 25 cm, 104 pp.
edition of 700 copies, offset
printed in Estonia, thread-
sewn softcover with dust jacket

Toyota
4478zine, 2016
17 × 24 cm, 32 pp.
edition of 300 copies, offset
printed in Lithuania, saddle-
stitched softcover with dust jacket

Type 1
4478zine, 2013
10 × 15 cm, 16 pp.
limited edition of 60 copies,
risograph printed in Switzerland,
staple bound softcover

Wassertürme
4478zine, 2006
15 × 22 cm, 12 pp.
edition of 500 copies,
offset printed in the Netherlands,
unbound softcover

Projects in chronological order

Published 2016: *Toyota*, *Nina*

Published 2015: *Ludwig II,
Pomerode, Paradiesvögel,
Facial Fractures, Courbe, Exit*

Published 2014: *Gebilde, Home
Is Where The Dog Is, Tables to
Meet, Teddy Bear, Most Wanted,
Third Reich*

Published 2013: *O. Niemeyer*
(second edition), *foto.zine nr. 5,
New Holland / New Amsterdam,
Souvenir III, Havaianas, Type 1,
Privacy Settings, Amsterdam,
Gulasch Suppe*

Published 2012: *Souvenir I & II,
Set of 3, Birds of Paradise,
Die Wolken, O. Niemeyer* (first
edition), *This Is Not My Wife,
Nelore*

Published 2011: *Bonsai,
Contemporary Brazilian Politics,
Deer Park, Quick Magazine #3,
foto.zine nr. 4, Parking Lot*

Published 2010
Der Baum, Rear Window
(second edition), *Rear Window*
(first edition), *Superquadra*

Published 2009: *Lamp Posts,
Albert Speer, foto.zine nr. 3, This Is
Not My Son, Down the Rabbit
Hole 3, Down the Rabbit Hole 2*

Published 2008: *Archivo,
Siedlung, Down the Rabbit Hole*

Published 2007:
foto.zine nr. 2

Published 2006:
Wassertürme, Av. Paulista

Published 2005:
foto.zine nr. 1

Published 2004:
Praia

Published 2003:
Groene Hilledijk

Applied Publishing Studies no.1:

Erik van der Weijde
This Is Not My Book

Concept:
Erik van der Weijde with
Fabian Bremer, Pascal Storz
and Jan Wenzel

Editing:
Anne König and Jan Wenzel

Editorial assistance:
Ames Gerould

Design and typesetting:
Fabian Bremer and Pascal Storz,
Spector Bureau

Copyediting:
John Middleton

Translation:
John Middleton and Amy Klement

Reproduction photography:
Andreas Langfeld

Lithography:
Carsten Humme

Printing:
Pöge Druck, Leipzig
Thomas Siemon, Leipzig

Binding:
Buchbinderei Mönch, Leipzig

Paper:
Bavaria Glänzend 90 gsm
Munken Print White 1.5 90 gsm

Text credits:

"Everyday Life, the Sequence,
the Book, or Five Stacks
of Books for Erik van der Weijde"
by Jan Wenzel, first published
in Erik van der Weijde,
Gebilde, Graz: Edition Camera
Austria, 2014

"Prostitution, Art Books and
Marketing" and "Costs and
Profits" by Erik van der Weijde,
both first published online
in 2015: www.4478zine.com

© 2017 Erik van der Weijde,
Spector Books, Leipzig

The cover of this book is inspired
by Urs Lehni's designs for
This Is Not My Wife and *This Is
Not My Son*.

This publication was made
possible by the generous support
of the Mondriaan Fund.

A special edition of *This Is Not My
Book*, a box with 16 fine art prints,
will be issued in a limited run
of 9 + 2 AP, signed and numbered.

Published by:
Spector Books
Harkortstraße 10
04107 Leipzig

Distribution:

Germany and Austria:
GVA, Gemeinsame Verlags-
auslieferung Göttingen
GmbH & Co. KG
www.gva-verlage.de

Switzerland:
AVA Verlagsauslieferung AG
www.ava.ch

France and Belgium:
Interart Paris
www.interart.fr

UK:
Central Books Ltd
www.centralbooks.com

US and Canada:
RAM Publications +
Distribution Inc.
www.rampub.com

Australia and New Zealand:
Perimeter Distribution
www.perimeterdistribution.com

South Korea:
The Book Society
www.thebooksociety.org

Other countries:
Motto Distribution
www.mottodistribution.com

First edition
Printed in Germany
ISBN 978-3-95905-117-0

Erik van der Weijde
would like to thank

the wife, the son, the parents,
the brother, the friends,
the gallerists, the colleagues,
and the publishers

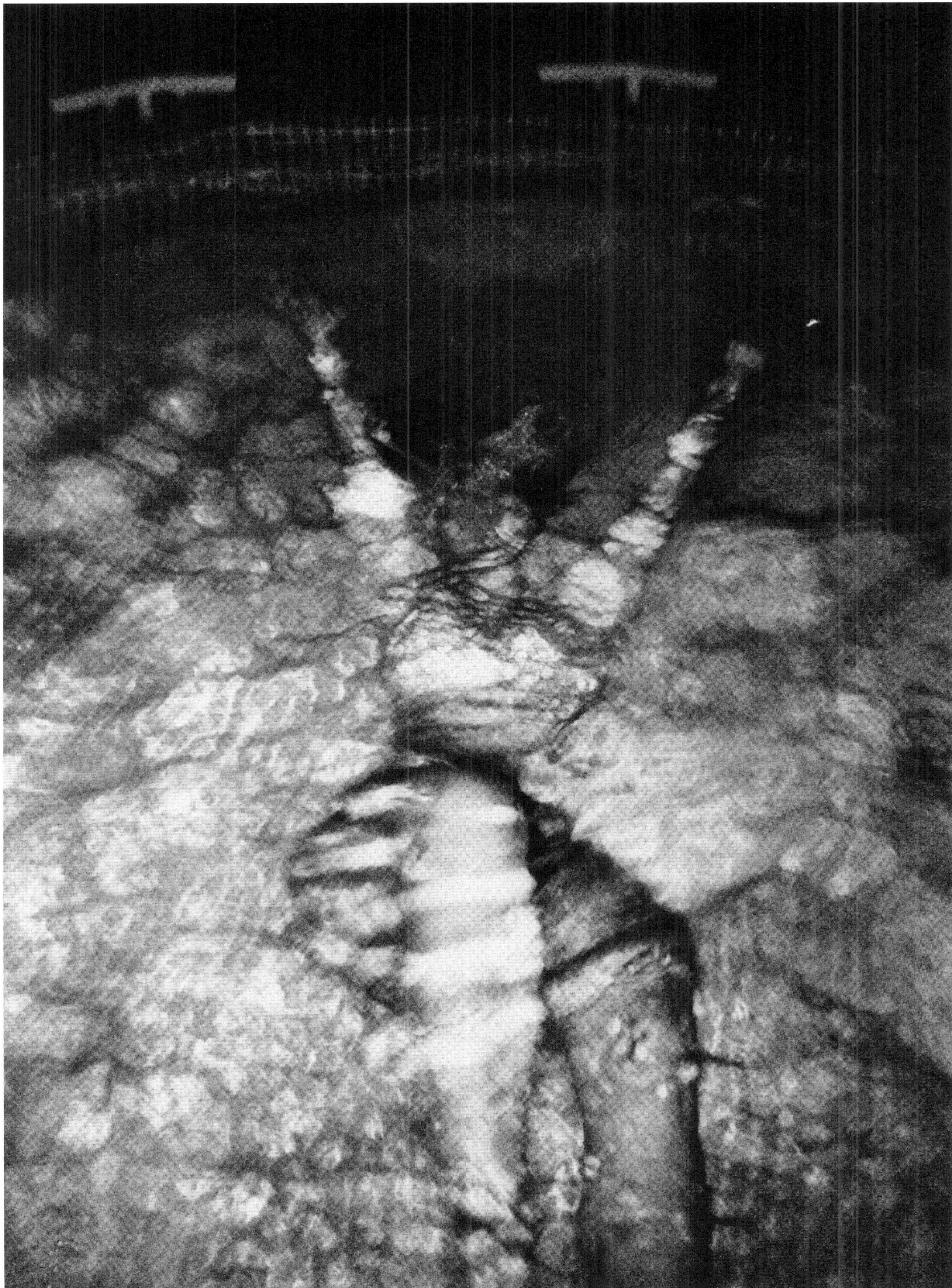

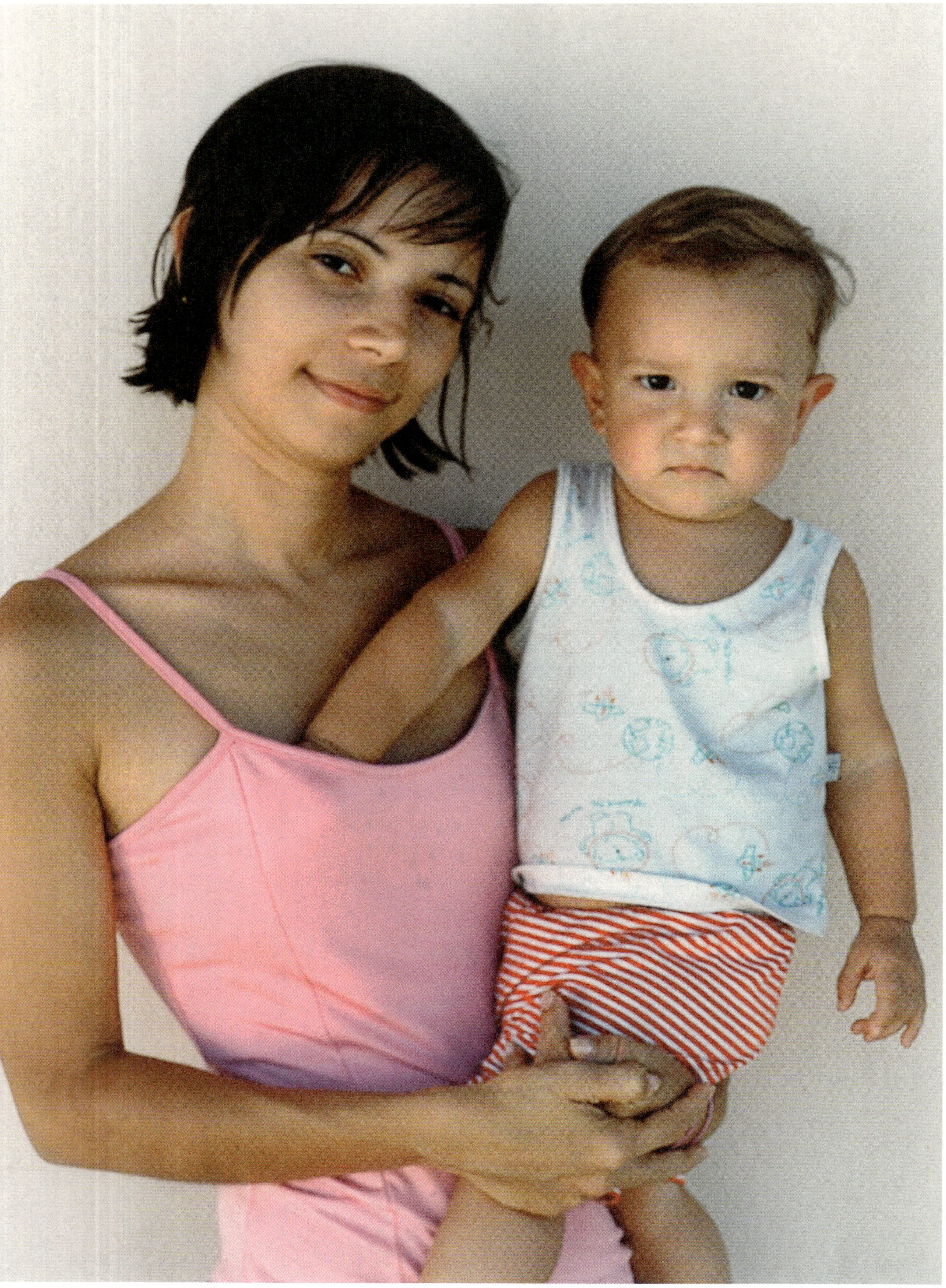